TOO GREAT A TEMPTATION

Too Great A Temptation

the seductive

power of

America's

super church

Dr. Joel Gregory

THE SUMMIT GROUP ☙ FORT WORTH, TEXAS

THE SUMMIT GROUP

1227 West Magnolia, Suite 500 • Fort Worth, Texas 76102

Printed in the United States of America.

94 95 96 97 98   5 4 3 2 1

Library of Congress Cataloging-in-Publication Data

Gregory, Joel C., 1948-
    Too great a temptation: the seductive power of America's super church / Joel Gregory.
        p. cm.
    Includes index.
    ISBN 1-56530-141-2 (alk. paper): $24.95
    1. First Baptist Church of Dallas—History—20th century. 2. Gregory, Joel C., 1948- . 3. Criswell, W. A. (Wallie A.), 1909- . 4. Baptists—Texas—Dallas—Clergy—Biography. 5. Dallas (Tex.)—Church history—20th century. 6. Texas—Church history—20th century. 7. Big churches—Texas—Dallas—History—20th century. I. Title.
BX6480.D26G74 1994
286'.1'092—dc20

                                                                94-34124
                                                                    CIP

Jacket and book design by David Sims

To Grant and Garrett; they saw it all and took it like men.

Table of Contents

71

Chapter Three

THE SEARCH FOR A "SUCCESSOR"

109

Chapter Four

THE CLASH BETWEEN DIVINE WILL AND HUMAN AMBITION

149

Chapter Five

BIG-TIME RELIGION

Acknowledgments

My thanks belong to Dr. Terry Denton for the suggestion that this book be written. He is a long-time friend and another author for The Summit Group. I wish to thank those at The Summit Group who asked me for the book sight unseen and those who worked with the editorial and promotional preparation of the book. Mark Hulme, Len Oszustowicz, Mike Towle, John Hawkins, Liz Bell, Brent Lockhart, and others of The Summit Group were of help and also became new friends in the process.

My supervisor and friend at Greenwood/Mt. Olivet Advanced Planning, Arlie Davenport, was kind to encourage me and understand my absences during the preparation of the manuscript. I want to thank the secretaries and staff of the Advanced Planning office for their kindness to me throughout this period of transition.

A few friends in the denomination have continued to encourage me, not to say that they approved of this book or the contents of the book. Freddie Gage, Jimmy Draper, and Jack Graham have been loyal friends during an entire time of sweeping transitions in my life. Also, Richard Blair has been a true confidant and encourager.

My two sons have maintained an active interest in this book and encouraged me in the writing. They experienced the times of the book in an intensely personal way and have made constructive comments on the manuscript.

I further express affectionate appreciation for the tolerance and patience of my wife and friend, Sherry. During some significant times for us, she stood by as I finished the manuscript.

Introduction

꒰

After several years in the public eye as a religious leader, I suddenly disappeared in September 1992. I resigned as pastor of what some would consider the most powerful Protestant church in America, the First Baptist Church in downtown Dallas. This sudden departure was intriguing to Baptists and nonBaptists alike. It seemed to capture the attention of unbelievers as well as believers. The stated and actual reason for my departure was the dysfunctional transition with the previous pastor of forty-eight years, the legendary Dr. W. A. Criswell. I had been promised a transition of "a few months." After two years, he had announced his intention to remain for two more. I quit.

The immediate cause for this book was a casual comment made by a friend over lunch in late spring 1994. Dr. Terry Denton had just co-authored a humor book on travel, *Never Say "Hi, Jack!" in an Airport*, with The Summit Group in Fort Worth, Texas. He suggested over lunch that I should write a book about my experiences in Dallas at First Baptist. He asked my permission to suggest that to the publisher. I acquiesced in his request. In turn, The Summit Group asked me to write this book. I had given serious consideration to such a book shortly after leaving, but did not care at the time to relive the experience by writing of it. The delay was fortunate. Time has given me more perspective.

First Baptist is an institution of awesome religious and secular power. With its own newspaper, college, radio station, and television outlets, it influences public opinion in a way unparalleled by similar institutions. By the nature of its membership, it infiltrates the power structure of a city and a region. The members of the church have had access to both public and private venues to explain what they think happened in my resignation. When I left the church, I lost access to such platforms.

I have written this book because of the genuine concern expressed to me by hundreds of people. They inquired what happened to me. But I have also written it because of the rumors invented by folks both inside and outside the church. Some folks could not imagine anyone walking away from it all and thus could not accept my stated reason as the actual reason. In the aftermath of the resignation, I was the object of constant, fantastic fictions, ranging from "a girlfriend at a truck stop in East Texas" to having settled with the church for "a million dollars for every six months I had been pastor." Most recently, I am told on good authority, there is a "conspiracy theory" that I came to the church with the intention to leave from the very beginning. The longer these stories have circulated, the wilder and more humorous they have become. At first I tried to track them down, but then I found that nobody would own up to them. It was like chasing dandelions. Had the highest and most senior circles in the church not waged such an insidious, anonymous campaign of defamation against me, I would never have felt free to write this book.

But those reasons alone would not justify the writing or the reading of this book. The super-church movement is a phenomenon of late twentieth-century Christianity. These huge ecclesiastical institutions not only shape the lives of their own members but also influence American culture and politics. In many respects First Baptist, Dallas, is the mother church of all the super churches. They have aped its organization and cloned its pastor,

W. A. Criswell. What happens at First, Dallas, is both a model for and a prediction of what will happen in other religious behemoths. To the extent this influences other churches, it is a religious concern. In the face of super-church impact on American politics and culture, it is a larger secular concern.

I neither desire nor expect to do damage to First Baptist, Dallas, or W. A. Criswell in the writing of this book. The church was organized in 1868. It has flourished through Reconstruction in Texas, the Great Depression, two world wars, and the upheaval of more recent American society. The church is there, like Gibraltor. In the larger scheme of things, this book will not dent the armor of the church; it is not intended to do so. It might give its thoughtful members pause to reconsider their stewardship of the institution and it may serve as a warning to the lay custodians of other large churches. I have sought to let Dr. and Mrs. Criswell tell their own story in this book by their actions and their silences. Criswell is a larger-than-life character who has already passed beyond legend to myth in his own lifetime. His reputation in church history is secure. No one can gainsay the Herculean achievements of his life. It is trite to say he has done many good things. But like many such figures, there is another side of the story as well. When a minister becomes a virtual apotheosis, an icon standing above confrontation, it can do strange things to a church. I found out. Among other things, this book is a study of the peculiar synergism between a religious body and a leader who has reached a virtual quasi-divine status. In such an ethos the whole becomes more than the sum of its parts. Criswell has done a lot of good, but he has done more than that.

Since this book belongs to a rather ill-defined genre of literature, there should be some disclaimers. This book is not an account of every day I spent at First Baptist, Dallas, from

January 1991 until September 30, 1992. Such a wooden chronology would be repetitive. Nor is this a record of all the good things done by First Baptist. It is part of a common set of assumptions that most churches do good things in a community. I take it for granted that the reader understands that the church visits the sick, cares for the widows, feeds the poor, and counsels the confused. First Baptist does all those things well and many others. Of necessity this volume focuses on some things that were not so good.

This book is not a personal memoir of the Gregory family. In the aftermath of the resignation, my former wife and I decided mutually and reciprocally to go our separate ways. We both publicly accepted responsibility for this decision and attributed it to long-term differences in our understanding of marital roles. It is no surprise that life in the parsonage has its own stresses; the taller the steeple the greater those can become. To make this book an exhaustive personal memoir would invade the privacy of others who desire no such invasion. They have suffered enough because of the events reflected in the narrative to follow.

In the same way that this book is not a record of everything good done by First Baptist, it is not an exhaustive record of everything evil. Some readers will opine that I have been too hard on the church or Criswell. As a matter of fact, I have omitted the most insidious things that could have been reported. If the reader objects to what I have recorded, the reader would have objected even more to what I did not record. For one thing, a full record of everything that happened to me might have landed the book on the fiction shelf; some of it is beyond belief. Those offended by this book might take cold comfort in one fact: it could have been worse.

Work on the book itself contained some peculiar, if not laughable, moments. For example, in the activities preparatory to the release of this volume, I was told to meet a photographer at the church location for outdoor pictures with the church as the backdrop. When a security man recognized me, we were asked to leave the public sidewalk. Falling back to a more distant position, the distinguished photographer tried to make a picture with the towering neon sign blaring "First Baptist" in the background. They turned off the sign, probably one of the few times its radiant light has not diffused Ervay Street at night. To me this was a poignant and pathetic attempt to hide the identity of the institution. They can turn off the sign, but there is nowhere to hide First Baptist, Dallas.

Will this book hurt the Christian church? The reader can be the jury to decide that. If one thinks that the church is about power games, position, politics, and the maintenance of personal influence, this book will hurt. If one thinks that the church is about servanthood to humanity, a redemptive ministry, and a self-forgetfulness on the part of the church itself in which the church is not an end unto itself, this book might help. It is my deepest conviction that the kingdom of God will prevail; what happens to local congregations is of less consequence.

Chapter One

❧

Escape from First Baptist

*F*irst Baptist Church of Dallas sits at the intersection where the Way of the Cross intersects the American Dream— Via Dolorosa at Wall Street. Such an intersection has no stop lights, not even a yield sign. Where the road to the cross and the road to success meet there can be a head-on collision between a man's ambition and his desire to serve God. I know.

My collision took place September 30, 1992, on a Wednesday night at 7:00 P.M., when I resigned as the pastor of the largest Southern Baptist church in the world, arguably the most powerful Protestant church in America. The resignation shocked the congregation and the evangelical world. Later the *Dallas Morning News* on its front page reported that the resignation "sent tremors through the twenty-nine-thousand-member congregation, the fifteen-million-member Southern Baptist Convention, and evangelical Protestantism."[1]

Earlier that Wednesday, at 6:45 P.M., I sat in my lavish $80,000 pastoral office, the gift of an anonymous benefactor. Before me was the leather-topped mahogany desk littered with

---

[1] The *Dallas Morning News*, November 2, 1992, page 1A.

memos, unanswered letters, unreturned phone calls, and the detritus of an executive office. On the exceedingly long credenza in front of the bullet-proof picture window of my second-story office sat my Greek New Testament and assorted biblical commentaries. Outside, my secretary Marcia Will waited to close and lock the office after I exited to the sanctuary.

I took a last look around the office as pastor of the nation's largest Baptist church. It was really the command and control center of a religious empire with worldwide influence: five square blocks of downtown Dallas real estate, a nine-hundred-student K-12 academy with two campuses, a three-hundred-student college, a five-hundred-bed shelter, thirty mission congregations, and a radio station.

In the glass-fronted hutch to my right sat the Boehm bird plates given me by Patsy Wallace, a deacon's wife who had decorated the office. Outside the door to my right was the office of my full-time personal assistant. Beyond that was the pastor's elaborately furnished personal conference room. On the walls hung oil paintings I had selected from various Dallas galleries. The conference table had been donated by the CEO of Texas's largest utility company. To my left was a door disguised as a panel in the wall, an escape route in case some demented person meant me harm. The hallway from the door led to a hidden staircase that enabled me to leave the inner office without encountering any unwanted visitors in the reception area. My sons had enjoyed playing with the door when they visited the office. On the wall I eyed my doctor of philosophy diploma earned at Baylor University. There also hung the oil painting of Charles H. Spurgeon, the nineteenth-century London Baptist pastor and hero of most Baptist pastors. It had been presented to me at Spurgeon's College in London, where I had spoken at graduation.

In my trembling hand was a 289-word statement of resignation. No one except my wife and sons knew that I was going to read it. I felt furtive as I walked past my unsuspecting secretary's door to carry out the deed that would change my life forever and cause no small disturbance to a huge institution.

I walked down the second-floor hallway of the Criswell Building. Just down the hall from my office was that of W. A. Criswell, senior pastor of the church. He had already taken the steps down to Old San Jacinto Street. A private street in the heart of downtown Dallas, closed by the city and dedicated to the church, the street itself stood as testimony to the church's power.

After walking down the steps, I met Tim Hedquist, the church administrator who had joined the staff a year earlier at my invitation. Both analytical and intuitive, he later said he knew I was about to resign. In fact, out of the pressure of the moment, I literally bolted ahead of him across the street and into the building. From that point on the events are a montage of emotion, fear, relief, confusion, and ambivalence.

From the north entrance I walked through the wooden door of the century-old sanctuary. From the south door Criswell entered. It was the same rite of entrance we had followed since I came as pastor twenty-one months before. Criswell sat where he had sat for forty-eight years, on the right of the pulpit as the congregation saw it. The normal Wednesday night crowd of several hundred waited in the antique pews of the historic landmark.

As the musician led the informal Wednesday evening choruses, my heart raced and my hands perspired. I looked at the famous pulpit not three feet in front of me. Across the century figures as diverse as Woodrow Wilson and Billy Graham had stood behind that diminutive carved desk. Only weeks before I had stood there preaching to President George Bush while my family sat with him and the first lady. The same pulpit had supported Dr. George W. Truett, the greatest Baptist pastor in American history, from 1897 until he died in 1944, when Criswell came.

In minutes, I would stand behind that pulpit to end a lifetime of ministry and to walk away from a legacy of history. The aftershock would change things forever for my family, the three hundred employees of the church, and its "twenty-nine thousand" members. The church claimed that many members, although that many members could not actually be identified. Still, there was, and is, no doubt about the massive size of First Baptist Church in Dallas.

I had accepted the call thinking that I would be the pastor of the church. In reality, I was there to extend the tenure of W. A. Criswell. I had been told there would be a transition within "a few months"; there was no transition at all. In retrospect and in stark reality, my situation and the particular circumstances surrounding my short tenure at First Baptist anticipates a critical situation soon to be duplicated in hundreds of super churches that aped First Baptist, Dallas as their model.

There are moments which define us in everyone else's mind for the rest of our lives. They mark us indelibly, imprint us with a tattoo that will never be erased. Clair Booth Luce once told Richard Nixon that the significance of any person in history, no matter how complex, can be captured in one sentence.[2] Doug Brady, the young lawyer who was secretary of the deacons, would later tell me: "You will always be remembered as the man

---

[2] *Time*, May 2, 1994, p. 28.

who resigned from First Baptist, Dallas." This is the story of the strange odyssey that led me to First Baptist, and the disillusionment that caused me to resign.

❧

THE RESIGNATION

SO I STOOD to the pulpit as the unsuspecting congregation waited for me to begin the normal Wednesday evening exposition. Instead, I read the single sheet of paper on which I had typed the statement of resignation earlier in the day:

In November 1990, this congregation called me to become pastor. I assumed that responsibility January 1, 1991. This was presented to the congregation as a transition between Dr. Criswell's pastorate and my leadership. Both the committee and the senior pastor presented an understanding concerning the apparent good will on the part of all parties. I have and do express love and veneration for Dr. Criswell. He has publicly expressed his affection for me.

Recently the senior pastor has announced in several contexts his desire to continue in that role until his fiftieth anniversary. He is the respected patriarch of this congregation. He has the sole right to determine God's will for his life, as do I. In recent conversations with me, the congregational leadership has expressed both their concern that the transition continue and that Dr. Criswell achieve this landmark of leadership. They preferred but did not require the solution that I work this out with the senior pastor in private conversation.

This places unilaterally on my shoulders the burden of solving what the congregation and its leadership might have solved. For me to force the issue and make demands for myself neither honors God nor conforms to my personality. The entire process has left our family in an intolerable situation. Any conceivable future circumstance presents the specter of a divided congregation, a distracted pastor, and a diminishing return. It is apparent that there is a double agenda. The ultimate agenda, however, is the prolonging of the incumbent's ministry rather than the enabling of the new pastor's.

None of these things can be a surprise to the informed members of this congregation. In light of these circumstances I immediately and irrevocably submit my resignation.

It took one minute to read it. I had thought that there might be an immediate vocal response, a cry of, "No, no," a chorus of congregational cacophony. What met me was uncomprehending shock. The people's collective face appeared as if I had without reason slapped them silly. The sanctuary was shrouded in that silence that exceeds silence, that seems to suck up and absorb sound. Standing in the pulpit, I was shocked myself that I had actually done it.

Earlier in the day I had prepared brief notes for Tim Hedquist, the administrator, and for Marcia Will, my secretary. They were notes of apology that I could not in good conscience tell them in advance of my intention; that would have placed them under enormous pressure to intervene directly or indirectly. Now I turned to the right side of the pulpit and handed those notes to Hedquist. He took them without a word.

On the left of the pulpit was W. A. Criswell. I did not look at him or speak to him. In the two years that have followed my resignation we have not exchanged a word. I felt that I owed him no apologies. For his part he had often told me, "I never review anything. Never review it, lad." He truly meant that. The only direction was forward. For him there was no reason to dissipate energy second-guessing the past. I presume that is how someone maintains the psychic energy to last fifty years as pastor of a huge Baptist church. Weighing every encounter and conflict of five decades would drain the soul. I had no question that I would never hear from him again, and no regrets. I literally have nothing to say to him.

Looking back, I can see a touch of comedy within this moment of personal tragedy. For some reason I thought someone might physically stop me from leaving the auditorium.

Looking back, I can see a touch of comedy within this moment of personal tragedy. For some reason I thought someone might physically stop me from leaving the auditorium, so I had hired a private detective to escort me to the outside and see me to my car. Oddly enough, he turned out to be Baptist. He had watched me on television. In the paranoid haze of the day's events, I must have seen this as a stroke of divine providence. So my Baptist detective and a beefy assistant seated themselves near the Old San Jacinto Street door on the north side of the sanctuary front. As I left the platform they fell into step with me.

Once outside, we broke into a run until we reached Ross Avenue where he had parked. We jammed ourselves into his car as if a Green Beret detachment were pursuing us. I had parked my own vehicle, the 1992 Honda given me by First Baptist Church, east of the First Methodist Church of Dallas on a cross street. When we arrived there, I bailed out of the detective's car, jumped into the driver's seat and took off through downtown Dallas toward Stemmons Expressway. I turned off my cellular phone lest anyone from the church call me and ask where I was going. In hindsight, this Keystone Cops routine seems silly, but in the stress of the day I did not want to be hindered from a hasty exit.

When one dares to do what no one believed would or could be done, there is a moment of heady relief, a sense of empowerment at choosing a destiny. It is a strange emotion to feel. I had just divested myself of a religious empire. There are forty thousand Southern Baptist churches and twice that many preachers. Many of them would have paid any price, undergone any struggle, and faced any contempt to keep what I just surrendered. Most of them would think I had lost my mind. But as I threaded my way through the traffic, I felt an intermingled sense of relief and personal power.

ᐁ

DALLAS IN THE REARVIEW MIRROR

ON STEMMONS EXPRESSWAY I headed toward the Eagle Mountain Lake Boat Club, an hour away from downtown Dallas. It was north of Fort Worth, my hometown, and felt familiar and safe. To spare the family, I had sent them ahead to a cabana at the club. We would stay there four days hiding from the media and the members, listening to the halyards tinkle against the masts of the sailboats docked in their slips.

The route out of Dallas to the boat club skirted the north central part of the Dallas-Fort Worth metroplex. While I drove north on Stemmons, my mind flashed back to comfortable dinners in the homes of affluent church members living in Highland Park. The people as individual families had been more than kind to us. They had welcomed us, fed us, underwritten world-wide travel for us, deluged us with gifts, affirmed us with compliments, and given us a regal way of life. It was not because of them that I had done what I had just done, but the whole of First Baptist, Dallas, was somehow different from the sum of its parts. Individual members were fine people and dedicated Christians. Collectively they could not deal with W. A. Criswell. I felt like Karl Wallenda before his final, fateful balancing act. I had balanced for a long time. Now it seemed surrealistic that I had jumped off the wire.

Even in my state of near-shock, I knew I had to get the word out. The Wednesday night crowd was only a fraction of the Sunday attendance, and I wanted all the members to read the actual statement of resignation that I had made. I rightly assumed that the church would never print my statement. (They did not even print it in the weekly *Reminder*, the house organ of the church.) By indicting Criswell for not keeping his promise to me, I had dared to say that the emperor had no clothes. I had said the unsayable, and they had no intention of printing the unprintable. I also wanted the larger public to see the statement. For that reason, I stopped at the Kinko's on Airport Freeway (an east-west highway connecting Dallas and Fort Worth) and faxed my resignation statement to the *Dallas Morning News* and the *Fort Worth Star-Telegram.* I left the boat club cabana number where their reporters could reach me.

Driving past Dallas/Fort Worth International Airport, I tuned the car radio to the church's radio station, KCBI-FM

"Sonshine 89" as they called it with evangelical flair. Every word spoken from the pulpit of First Baptist was broadcast on the station. KCBI is licensed as an educational station belonging to the Criswell College, but for all practical purposes it is a 100,000-watt public relations outlet for First Baptist Church (FBC), Dallas, Inc.

Every other Wednesday evening, while I drove to my Lakewood home, I could listen to the one-hour-delayed broadcast of my Wednesday evening message. Those weekly ten-minute drives down Gaston Avenue east toward the pastor's home had a curious, schizoid quality. Inside my car I listened to my Wednesday evening Bible study while driving toward our $465,000 home. Outside were the desperate residents of the multi-ethnic east Dallas neighborhood. Pimps, prostitutes, and pushers hustled one another in a constant parade of humanity needing redemption.

The irony of that juxtaposition was not lost on me during that weekly drive. I represented one of the Big Outposts of God's Kingdom, but how insular it all seemed, driving through inner-city squalor while listening to the stereo FM transmission of my own words spoken an hour before.

On Wednesday evening, September 30, 1992, however, there was no pastor's message broadcast. There was no mention of anything controversial or unpleasant. During the normal slot for my message the station played bland, elevator-music-style evangelical ditties. With an inward smile, I imagined the scene at KCBI an hour earlier. My messages on Wednesday were taped at the studio for delayed broadcast. One might imagine the desperate instructions relayed to the surprised technician, not to mention the on-air DJ, that The Statement be squelched. So driving toward the boat club I heard not a mention that the pastor and CEO of FBC, Inc. had jumped ship.

∞

REACTION

THAT IS, there was no mention on the church-owned station. Before I arrived at the boat club, the local TV stations had flashed the news on their mid-evening teasers, promising "details at ten." A variety of radio stations peppered the airwaves with reports of the resignation and reactions. Within twenty minutes of the resignation Baptist leaders on the East Coast had been called. The communication system that could rival the CIA network—the Baptist grapevine—would assure that thousands around the country heard the word before bedtime that Wednesday.

To nonBaptists such interest might seem strange; why would anyone care that the preacher of a big church quit? In the byzantine Baptist bailiwick, however, it was the equivalent of a pope's resignation. Even the *Brazilian Baptist* national newspaper would carry the story with a blaring Portuguese headline and a picture. The *Los Angeles Times* gave the story big play in a corner of the country where Southern Baptists are considered hardly a notch above snake handlers. The next morning it dominated the headlines of Texas papers and received play in denominational periodicals across the nation. But there was not a word on KCBI as I drove to the boat club.

Of course, I wondered what was happening in the sanctuary as the high-rises of "Big D" receded in my rearview mirror. I would later learn that everyone just sat there in silence for a while.

Tim Hedquist, who was the center of sanity in the church for weeks to come, finally stood to the pulpit and called the church to prayer. W. A. Criswell seemed as if in a trance. His parchment skin paled more than usual across his broad-boned face. After prayer and appropriate comments, the shocked congregation was dismissed.

Ronald L. Harris, a personal friend and the high-powered media minister I had brought in from a former pastorate, told the *Morning News* that "for a few seconds afterward, when the pastor left, people just sort of sat there. It's about like the grief process you'd have after some sudden, catastrophic event. First there's shock, then disbelief."

Hedquist assisted Criswell from his platform chair. The old patriarch seemed unable to comprehend the situation, but I knew better. Criswell has the brain of a main-frame computer. I used to laugh at allegations from Baptist antagonists outside the church that W. A. was "senile." Dr. Richard Land, a former dean of the Criswell College and a D.Phil. from Oxford University, once commented to me that Criswell can play chess on three levels. His reference was to a sci-fi chess set constructed around a spiral center-pole where moves were not only on a horizontal plane but also a spiraling vertical plane. Criswell's thought processes were always operating on several levels. He is an amazing combination of analysis and intuition.

The next morning Criswell's only comment in the *Morning News* was to say that Dr. Gregory "is one of the best preachers ever heard in this generation. He is a sweet friend and prayer partner." The old Artful Dodger had done it again. Criswell and his wife Betty had been undermining me since I set foot in the place twenty-one months earlier. He knew that I knew; I knew he knew that I knew it. We all knew it. We had gone through this public arabesque posturing as if we enjoyed total oneness in the best of all possible worlds. To paraphrase Robert Browning: "God's in his heaven and all is right at dear old FBC." While Criswell cried crocodile tears, he was planning his public response for the next Sunday, a semi-resignation that left everyone confused and was, as time has proved, no resignation at all.

In the dream-like confusion that followed, sobered and crying members milled around the 2,020-seat sanctuary. The huge church choir and orchestra were practicing in the adjoining Mary-C building, erected by the late Mary Crowley to accommodate the music program. A messenger was dispatched to tell the several hundred musicians what had just happened in the sanctuary. Fred McNabb, the walrus-like, mustachioed minister of music and one of the more competent staff members, called the stunned musicians to prayer. They fell to their knees in the multi-tiered choir room, prayed, and then wandered out like zombies.

The first semi-official response to my resignation came from the deacons. FBC, Inc. had more deacons—three hundred of them—than most Baptist churches have active members. Bo Sexton, a genuinely able and committed man who was chairman of the deacons, was out of town when I quit, and I regretted what the resignation would cause him to endure. A star athlete first in high school and later at the University of Texas, Bo is a man of impeccable character who had resigned the vice-presidency of Campbell-Taggert (of Campbell Soup fame) when they took on a beer line. Subsequently, he opened his own company, Bakery Associates. His wife Ethel was a vivacious lady who was also an on-air star of our radio station, famous for her advice on finding

13

rare objects at garage sales. Together they looked like Mr. and
Mrs. America. Bo was the epitome of what every executive in
Dallas hoped to be—handsome man, beautiful wife, fine family,
great career, and respected church leader.

Even in Bo's absence, however, there were dozens of deacons
on the premises. They hastily assembled themselves like soldiers
falling into formation at reveille or sailors manning their battle
stations. Criswell staggered into the meeting still looking dazed.
No one knew what to say. There was anger, frustration, and disbelief over my resignation.

Finally, one senior deacon who was already disgruntled with
Criswell made a motion that W. A. be fired on the spot. No one
ever imagined that such a thing would be privately thought,
much less publicly spoken, at dear old FBC. Never mind that the
church had been brought to the greatest crisis in its 125-year
history because Criswell wouldn't quit. You just could not say
that. No one else had the fortitude to endorse that radical idea,
so the patriarch survived the salvo.

It was decided that it would be better for all three hundred
deacons to meet the following Sunday at 4:00 P.M. The
Wednesday night meeting dissolved in a sort of prayerful haze as
the deacons ebbed out of the room and gathered in knots of
concern in various corners of the old building. By that time the
thousand folks in various meetings, committees, task forces,
nurseries, and enterprises of the church were finding their way
through the dusk to one of the three parking garages owned by
the church. They would drive mostly to north Dallas where they
would sit in muffled family discussion awaiting the ten o'clock
news to see what had happened. They would make thousands of
phone calls to others of the "twenty-nine thousand" members

and to relatives around the world. And they would wait for Sunday to see what was next.

∾

THE LONGEST THIRTY MILES

ALL OF THIS was taking place as I drove to the boat club in northern Tarrant County. The skyline of Fort Worth before me replaced that of Dallas behind me. The two cities are just thirty miles apart, but it is the longest thirty miles in the nation.

Fort Worth is a large West Texas town with a relaxed lifestyle and a cozy, down-home, country-western line-dance mentality. Fort Worth is more like Abilene and Dallas is more like New York City than they are like one another. Fort Worth is blue jeans and Dallas is Brioni suits. Criswell never tired of Fort Worth jokes: "What does Fort Worth have that Dallas does not? A great city nearby." A number of times he asked me in front of the congregation on television, "And you're from Fort Worth? That's just amazing. God can do anything." There was always a nervous, tittering laugh at this half-concealed, contemptuous humor. I always felt that Criswell considered me half-hick because I came from Fort Worth. Now I was back home, and as I drove I reflected on how it had all started.

At age sixteen I had "surrendered to preach" at the Connell Baptist Church, a middle-class neighborhood church on the west side of Fort Worth. From the time I was a sophomore at Arlington Heights High School my direction was firmly set. I preached in rest homes, jails, and wherever they let teen-aged Baptist preacher boys say a word. After that, it was off to Baylor University, where I majored in religion and Greek with a minor in history. I graduated summa cum laude in 1970, although I had also married and pastored, living on a church field my junior and senior years. That is, we lived in a parsonage next to the church where we served. Obviously, this was not a case of absentee-pastor commuting. I had been president of the Ministerial Alliance at the "world's largest Baptist university" and was expected to do well in the ministry. It was then off to gigantic Southwestern Seminary where I earned a master of divinity degree while living on a church field thirty miles away and commuting to the school. It was an arduous and tiring grind to earn a professional degree, while caring for a congregation that more than doubled during the three years of seminary.

Our first son, Grant, was born my last month of seminary. We moved him to the drafty country parsonage of the Cottonwood Baptist Church in Falls County, Texas, where we fought off the field rats inside the farm house as I wrote papers for Ph.D. seminars at Baylor twenty miles away. Mercifully, in 1977, the Emanuel Baptist Church in Waco called me to be pastor. It was ten blocks west of Baylor. The attendance doubled from two hundred fifty to five hundred, while I fought to finish Ph.D. work and pastor an exploding inner-city church at the same time.

My next call to pastor came from the historic Gambrell Street Baptist Church across the street from "the world's largest seminary" (Baptists are addicted to "big") in Fort Worth. That put my ministerial career into orbit. "Seminary Hill," as the area was called, served as a crossroads of Baptist life. The church zoomed from four hundred to twelve hundred in attendance and gave my ministry a new visibility in the Baptist world. It was at that time the first soothsayers among Baptists predicted that I would follow W. A. Criswell to the pulpit of First Baptist Church, Dallas.

In 1978, the new president of Southwestern Seminary, Russell H. Dilday, joined Gambrell Street. He became a one-man promotional firm for Joel Gregory. Along the way he asked me to join the faculty of Southwestern. In 1982, I resigned the church, moved across the street, and began a three-year stint as a preaching professor. This enabled me to fly around the country preaching every weekend and surveying the larger perimeters of the Baptist Zion. A dozen churches tried to engage me as pastor: First Baptist churches of San Antonio, El Paso, Plainview, Texarkana, Abilene, and similar Baptist bulwarks across the South. I felt obligated to teach for a decent amount of time in light of Dilday's friendship. By the third year of faculty life, however, I was ready to spring back into the pastorate. The huge (there it is again, Baptist bigness) Travis Avenue Baptist Church in Fort Worth had been looking for a preacher for two of the three years I had been at the seminary.

It seemed too close for comfort and was, after all, in my hometown (a prophet is without honor, and all that). But Travis called me and off I went. By that time Dilday had jumped into the national denominational battle. The faculty meetings were votes of confidence that we all stood behind him. Not quite sure where I stood or where he was going, I became increasingly nervous at these blanket endorsements of wherever he might choose to take the institution. So I went to Travis Avenue. The church exploded in attendance, launched a national television and radio ministry, and catapulted me into the front ranks of national Baptist leadership. Starting in 1985, I served a two-year term as president of the five-thousand-church Baptist General Convention of Texas.

In 1988, I preached the "annual sermon" at the Southern Baptist Convention in San Antonio, the most distinguished preaching venue possible. My message at the annual donny-brook was a dazzling success. I flew out of Fort Worth every week to preach somewhere in the nation, living on airplanes and writing sermons for the next Sunday at Travis. I had made the Baptist Big Time. There was only one thing bigger, and it was the biggest of all—FBC, Dallas. FBC was, and is, the golden fleece, the holy Grail of all Baptists, and the Vatican of the conservative Baptist movement.

As I pulled into the boat club that September evening in 1992, I reflected how far it was from Fort Worth to Dallas, how far a sixteen-year-old preacher boy had traveled to be the pastor of First Baptist. I remembered the years of labor, study, obscurity, fatigue, and work that had brought me from nowhere to such a place. It was all gone with the wind in one night. And that was all right with me.

ℂ𝓋

SECLUSION

INSIDE THE CABANA at the boat club, my family was fastened to the television. One station trotted out its file footage of the night I was called to be pastor. There were the four of us nearly two years earlier, thunderously received by the congregation after we were escorted in by the pulpit committee leadership. The occasion was fraught with history. It seemed to be a marriage made in heaven. Watching it from the wry perspective of what had actually happened lent a curious unreality to the moment. It must have been a similar feeling to that experienced by a losing incumbent presidential candidate watching the tape of his first and only inauguration. Not long after the news I went to bed. I was bone tired.

The next morning I awoke early to drive to the nearby conve-
nience store for a copy of the two major metropolitan dailies.
The *Morning News* screamed out the announcement in the headline. As I had hoped, they printed the complete text of my resignation in a shaded box. Also as I had expected, Criswell made no
direct comment on the resignation. The paper quoted me saying
that I had resigned rather than give the impression that there was
a power struggle between me and Dr. Criswell. "I got out of the
picture before there was a power struggle," I had told the reporter.
Had there been any clash between the two, "the membership
would have been the big loser." The paper gave the initial
response of one member, one Craig Rogers that I did not know.
Mr. Rogers's immediate analysis was, "Maybe he wasn't the right
man for the job, and this was God's way of letting us know."

I felt that I had gone through a rather rigorous twenty-one
months thus to accommodate divine providence.

The paper had called Dr. Morris Chapman, the newly elected
executive director of the Southern Baptist Convention. A few
years before I had literally put my career in the ministry on the
line to endorse Morris for the presidency of the convention. My
endorsement knocked a herd of Baptists off the fence and
helped sweep him to victory against his moderate foe. It also had
cost me dearly among the left-wing members of Travis Avenue,
where I was pastor, as well as in the seminary community where
respect for the "inerrantists" was a notch beneath the admiration held by the professors for common cockroaches. Morris
expressed his "shock" and understood that it was "tough" to follow Criswell. In good Baptist fashion, he was praying for everybody involved.

The paper went on to report that the search committee had
spent twenty-seven months looking at seventy candidates from

sixteen states. It quoted a few poignant lines from my trial sermon almost two years before.

I spent Thursday at the boat club speaking with a few close friends in the ministry who had attempted to reach me. They were to a person sympathetic, encouraging, and understanding of the move I was forced to make. Ed Young, the president of the Southern Baptist Convention whom I had nominated the preceding June, gave me carte blanche to come to Houston and stay at his guest place. He would later suggest a job. Former presidents of the denomination, such as Jimmy Draper and Adrian Rogers, commiserated with me and offered their support. The day was spent in returning phone calls and getting news reports from various Texas dailies that carried the stories. There was an anesthetizing sense of detachment as I sat on the patio of the cabana and watched the sailboats on Eagle Mountain Lake.

The most difficult calls were to the men I had brought to First Baptist as staff members. With a staff of three hundred, I had needed a few of "my own people." Tim Hedquist left a splendid position at the huge Bellvue Baptist in Memphis to become second-in-command at First. A gifted, intelligent, and fearless leader, there was not another man in the nation who could fill the post as Tim did. He caught hell from the Criswell forces from day one. He was the first subordinate staff member in forty-seven years to act utterly without fear of consequence from either of the Criswells. Even I had more fear of them than he did. Of all things, he looked W. A. in the eye and told him the truth, a very rare commodity at First.

In staff meetings Tim would disabuse W. A. of the fantasy world which the church had built around him. He told Criswell the truth about the attendance (it was literally thousands less than W. A. thought), the money (millions less), and the situation itself (a different world from the one occupied by Criswell). He was despised by the circles around the Criswells just because of that boldness. But he had me behind him, and not even they were ready to take that on (although they constantly tested the waters).

My conversation with Tim was quiet and subdued. No one knew better than he my reasons for the decision. Unknown to me, he had told leaders a few days before the resignation that they had better act or they would lose me. When I was off the scene, the Criswell retinue would turn their full wrath on Tim. He deserved better. Fortunately, Bo Sexton and the sane leadership of the church protected him from what I would best describe—being as diplomatic as I can here—as a fanatical element within the church.

Harder still were conversations with Ron Harris and Michael Gabbert. Ron had helped me build a national media ministry at Travis Avenue. A man with nationally respected skills, he had invented the position of "media minister." I had brought him to the church from our radio station, where he was an on-air personality. He had immediately transformed the media area from pathetic confusion to elegant professionalism. We were planning a national expansion of radio and television ministry. All that ended on the spot with my resignation. As with the demise of the pharaoh, the servants were buried along with their leader. Ron became the public spokesman for the church during the days following the resignation. His eyes red with tears, he interpreted to the watching metroplex what had happened.

Dr. Michael Gabbert had been my star student during professorial days at Southwestern Seminary. He served as my grader and as a part-time research assistant at Travis Avenue. When I went to First, I began to cultivate him to come as my assistant pastor. His wife had grown up in the church. He moved from a tiny town in West Texas to downtown Dallas. His office was adjacent to mine; he worked with me in research and in answering the endless correspondence that came to the office as the result of a national ministry. In some ways, the talk with Michael was the most difficult of all. He had hitched his young wagon to my star, and then the star fell.

Others had come to the church staff from previous friendships and churches. Dr. Gary Waller, a rising star on the faculty of Southwestern Seminary, had agreed to be a part-time troubleshooter helping me untangle some of the administrative nightmares that popped up on a daily basis. Pat Gilbert, an able children's minister, had come from Travis. Each of these and their families would be profoundly disrupted because of the resignation. As I reflected on this, however, I foresaw a worse consequence for them had I remained. The battle lines were already being drawn before I left. If there had been a public battle for leadership of the church, they would have been embroiled in a no-win situation.

I apologized to each of these men for bringing them into the church under the circumstances. They knew my situation; they knew that Criswell was not supposed to stay for four years after I had started; they knew that it created an intolerable burden of dysfunctional leadership. Ron, more than the others, looked for some ray of hope that I would reconsider and stay. He wanted to tell the press that. I could not give him that hope.

The full fury of FBC hatred would be vented on these good men in the months to come. A vocal minority in the church would vilify them, insult them and their families, and seek to destroy their careers for no other reason than they had been there with me. The blind and raging Criswell partisans wanted blood because I had embarrassed the Great One; since my arteries were no longer available for puncture, they turned to my associates. It is to the credit of Bo Sexton, deacon chairman, and his associates that they survived at all. It is to the credit of those, and others such as Pat Gilbert, that they had the stamina to survive the firestorm of the coming months.

～

AT THE CHURCH

UNBEKNOWNST TO ME, on Thursday—the day after the resignation—the executive committee met in emergency session. Bo had flown all night to be there. The executive committee consisted of all living, former deacon chairmen, who comprised a distinguished group of Dallas executive, legal, and business leaders. Most of the men had become good friends to me during the two years. Some of them were currently inactive in the church because of animosities between them and Criswell, or them and others.

In their Thursday meeting they voted unanimously not to accept my resignation. They requested that the current deacon officers meet with me to ask for a reconsideration. That meeting would not happen until the next week, when we returned home from hiding at the boat club.

The same article that informed me of that intent also quoted four members and "one former member" who criticized the resignation and called my motives into question. None of them were church leaders and I didn't recognize their names. The press, as always, liked a Baptist spat. In the days to come they would quote a cohort of marginal members who suddenly materialized to protect the Criswell image and persona. In the months of conflict that followed one of them wrote a Sunday opinion piece in the *Dallas Morning News*. The column could have been penned by William Buckley, so chaste was the prose, so sophisticated the usage, and so elegant the syntax. Some who knew him observed that the man in question could not have written such an opinion piece in ten lifetimes, which led others to surmise that it was penned by a higher power—not meaning the divinity. Such pseudonymous contributions to the paper would appear at regular intervals for months to come. I cannot swear that the names used were definitely pseudonyms, but I can't conceive of any other possibility.

While this lunatic fringe raged on—and at FBC this fringe included more than a few tassels—the respected and elected leadership of the church said nothing. Many of them were in the bind of a lifetime. They had been under W. A.'s pastorate since they were children. To turn on him would be like evicting grandfather from the family reunion. On the other hand, they knew very well that he was supposed to quit within months of my arrival. That was the deal. They could neither criticize him nor call me to task for quitting under the circumstances.

So they did nothing but wait for Sunday. So did I, but not because I planned to go back. I was intrigued to see just how W. A. would land on his feet. No Criswell watcher doubted that he would. The only question was how.

Sunday morning, October 4, 1992, provided one of the more unusual settings since the Baptists of First started meeting in 1868. The church decided to cancel all live radio and television coverage. The congregation would meet for private purposes. There would be singing and prayer. When Criswell was briefly recognized, he gave a masterful demonstration of the double-speak that served him so well. Half the people left thinking that he had resigned and the other half was certain that he had not. Criswell never specifically said that he was resigning. He promised to devote himself to the church's Criswell College and serve "as a fellow member of this church." In true Criswellian self-deprecation he intoned, "It all depends on what the church wants me to do. I am a fellow member of the church, and if they want me to sweep the floor or raise the window—anything. I want the church to be blessed by God."

He insinuated that he would leave his office at the church and move to the Criswell College. Of course, none of this ever happened. It was all so much holy smoke. In the evening service poor Bo Sexton had to stand before the same people who heard the same thing that morning and explain to them that Dr. C. had not resigned. He attributed this misunderstanding to one church member interviewed by one reporter after the service. That was as artful a construction as he could place on this prima donna performance by a master of double entendre.

By Monday morning the *Morning News* interpreted the original Greek of Criswell's statement to mean that he was moving his office from the church to the college. Since he already maintained an office at home, an ornate office in the Lincoln Properties high-rise across from the church, his historic office at the church, plus an elaborate office at the college, no one would know where he had moved. Criswell knew that the heat was on to lower his profile at the church in order to save his own skin. In the immediate aftermath of the resignation the vast majority of members were angry at him, not me. It was only after the defamatory machinery was set in motion by his circles that a significant shift in opinion took place. At the moment Criswell knew that he had to make some gesture to appease the angry congregation. He blew enough holy smoke to buy time for his PR machine to organize against me. When in motion, that would be more effective than the Wermacht.

ॐ

BACK TO THE SCENE

BY MONDAY I was ready to return to Dallas. We dreaded the onslaught of distraught members who would try to intervene. Nevertheless, we crept back to our lavish new home on Club Lake Court looking out on the ninth fairway of Lakewood Country Club. It was eerie to step back into the house where a few days before we had hosted a "fellowship" for new members. What I saw now was a half-million-dollar mortgage. Although the church was bound to make the payments for a while under my severance agreement, I had reason to believe they might welch on the deal. We would stay in the house for a couple of months before it sold to the first person who saw it, a lawyer/state legislator who fell in love with my $35,000 study, added to the house after we arrived.

Not long after we arrived a news crew from Channel 4 (Dallas/Fort Worth's CBS affiliate) knocked on the door. A comely lady reporter and her camera-carrying comrade thrust a minicam into the house and nailed me. Expecting something like that, I gave a brief pre-rehearsed speech that was intended to make me look as patient as Paul and benign as St. Francis.

By this time my emotions were wearing thin. I wanted to get out of the church, out of the house and as soon as possible get out of Dallas. I really did not expect that my resignation would be as big a deal in the media as it turned out to be.

The main event of our return was about to happen. The chairman and vice-chairman of the First Baptist Church Dallas fellowship of deacons were to call upon us at home. Bo Sexton and I had talked to set up the meeting. Along with Bo came David Wicker, the vice-chairman and, as custom has it, the chairman-elect. David had made a fortune with Sysco in the food supply business and was, like Bo, a level-headed and faithful member. His wife had been on the committee that called me, and together her family and David's had been in the church for generations.

I really had no idea what to expect in the Tuesday meeting with the two lay leaders from First Baptist. Both men were personal friends, men I trusted, and men whose word to me had always proved true. Yet both men were caught up in the strange mystique that surrounded W. A. Criswell. Although they knew that his continued role at the church undermined any chance for me having even a moderately successful ministry, they appeared reluctant to confront him personally.

For weeks before the resignation I had conferred with them and other powerful lay leaders in the church. One Saturday morning in late summer, a cadre of FBC elite sat around a breakfast table in the mixed grill room of the Lakewood Country Club. As the foursomes putted out on the eighteenth green just beyond the grill, we discussed the dilemma that had developed over the twenty months of my pastorate. There sat the men who had invited me into the pastorate. They were the power brokers in the nation's largest church. Dick Clements, an east Dallas real estate broker who chaired the pastor search committee, had demonstrated love and loyalty to our family. He had been a constant encourager and attentive to every detail of our personal needs in moving and establishing a home. Ralph Pulley, a graduate of Baylor Law School and a practicing attorney in Dallas for forty years, was the vice-chairman of the pastor search committee. Ralph and his son Tom took my son Grant and me to the Master's golf tournament in Augusta, Georgia, accommodated us, fed us, and treated us like a king and a prince. On the table in our family room stood a beautiful pair of Waterford crystal bookends, a gift from the Pulley family. When the teenage chapel choir tour to the Barcelona Olympics was in financial trouble, the Pulleys joined with me in putting up personal security for a loan to keep the chartered plane.

The men sitting around that country club grill room table were friends. Ralph Pulley was second to none as a loyalist to W. A. Criswell. To Pulley, every word of Criswell was ex cathedra. Yet even Ralph observed, "This transition has gone into reverse."

The group had debated the options. A formal, official group of deacon leaders could go to Criswell and tell him to move on. An informal, non-official group of Criswell's own supporters might casually visit him and suggest that his presence was obstructing my ministry. The group agreed that there was danger if any such groups approached Criswell. The potential for inflammatory misunderstanding in the church was enormous and real.

For one reason, Mrs. Criswell taught a Sunday school class with three hundred in attendance. The class was broadcast on KCBI-FM radio to thousands more who listened each Sunday morning. The class formed the bedrock of the Criswells' continued power in the church. Those three hundred gave a million dollars to the work of the church annually. The first hint of a challenge to W. A. could provoke a revolt of this "church within a church."

If there was anyone that everyone feared more than they reverenced W. A., it was "Mrs. C." No one around the breakfast table relished the thought of an on-air diatribe against them during her Sunday school lesson. So awesome was the fear of her power that she was often spoken of in terms of her residence. In the same way that Washington reporters will metonymously note that "the White House" said this or that, the people of FBC would speak of "Swiss Avenue," the historic street east of downtown Dallas where the Criswells occupied their million-dollar home. People would tell me that certain criticisms about me, "came from Swiss Avenue." One source close to Swiss Avenue told me in solemn tones that Mrs. Criswell "would totally destroy First Baptist Dallas rather than lose her power." Such sentiments did not nerve any of us to take on W. A. directly.

If there was anyone that everyone feared more than they reverenced W. A. it was "Mrs. C."

So it was that the preferred solution from that Saturday breakfast meeting was for me "to work things out with Dr. Criswell." In other words, with my vast tenure of twenty-one months, I was supposed to evict a living legend who had been around for forty-eight years. Just how I was to go about that was left up to my own creativity. The lay leaders did say that if my attempt to oust the old man did not work, they would think of something else.

This course of action seemed bound for disaster. The moment it was perceived that I had given W. A. the heave-ho, the

Criswell fanatics would tar me with such a wide brush that any other effort would have been beside the point. To win that battle would have been to lose the whole war. For me to play the matador and wave that red flag before Dr. C. would only have gotten me gored. My friends would probably have preceded me back into the ring, but by that time I would have hemorrhaged so much there would have been no way to win. Half the stands would have jumped into the arena with the bull.

∾

CATCH-22

IN THE DAYS FOLLOWING that power breakfast, I began to see the Catch-22 for what it was. The only way for the whole thing to work would be a voluntary resignation by Criswell. By that time I knew that he would not give up anything not taken from him. The lay leaders would not fire him and I was not about to sacrifice myself in a no-win confrontation that would brutalize me, enrage Mrs. Criswell, make W. A. a martyr, raise hell in the church, make headlines in the papers, and polarize the entire conservative wing of a sixteen-million-member denomination. The power and the glory of pastoring the big kahuna was not worth it to me.

In a curious way, it was Criswell's closest friend and ally that made up my mind. Jack Pogue, a bachelor in his fifties and Dr. Criswell's business partner, met with him literally every day. After the 8:15 A.M. worship service, Jack was always sitting outside Criswell's office. He would go in for a conference with the senior pastor in between the two worship services. No one was closer to Criswell. To my surprise and in spite of warnings from many, Jack Pogue was very good to me. When I was stuck with a Fort Worth fourplex that I could not unload, Jack intervened with a personal guarantee of my credit. It was a generous act that he had no obligation to do. Jack was the alter ego for Criswell, a son Criswell never had, a younger buddy, and a brilliant business associate who made millions for the Criswell Foundation.

When the discussions of "the problem" reached a critical mass, Jack was called in as an emissary to Dr. Criswell. In the same way that the chief of staff for the White House can bounce things off the president without committing an act of *lese majeste*, so also Jack Pogue could relate to Criswell. Jack had a kind of radar that could read the reactions of W. A. and Betty Criswell with astonishing accuracy. When Pogue told the Criswells about the discussions of the Saturday Lakewood power breakfast, he was deputized to give me a response.

Jack and I met for breakfast at an IHOP in North Dallas, a distinctly pedestrian venue for a conversation that would lead to a decision ending my life as I had known it. Jack genuinely commiserated with my position. He said, "You are in a no-win situation. I would hate to be in your shoes." Jack had often warned me of reports about Mrs. Criswell's relentless criticism. As we dallied over our breakfast, Jack and I looked at the alternatives, which were the same as those outlined by the deacons: A formal group could go to Dr. C., an informal group could go to Dr. C., or I could force the issue.

Jack gave a business-like assessment of each alternative. Whatever happened, if anything were done to Dr. C., Jack had a forecast: "There will be a line behind Dr. Criswell, a line behind you, and a line leaving the church. I will be in that line." Jack is a rather slight, leprechaun-like man with burning black eyes. He fixed those eyes on me and told me what would have been the case for many members: "I respect the office of pastor; I would not fight you. But I love W. A. Criswell. I could not stay if he were embarrassed. I would simply leave."

I sensed genuine empathy that day from Jack Pogue. He might have known better than anyone the impossible situation in which I found myself. I was supposed to lead a 125-year-old downtown megachurch into the future. Yet I could not lead it because of the presence and undermining activities of my predecessor. How could you be the president and CEO of Chrysler if Lee Iaccoca were still in his office down the hall as senior CEO, contradicting your orders?

I then suggested to Jack what by this time was obvious to me—I could simply quit. To my surprise he nearly came out of his chair: "That would be a disaster for you, for Dr. Criswell, and for the church. Don't even say that." That is, we had a problem with no solution but the status quo. I was already being lamed and would soon be condemned for limping. I was basically told "just hang in there" and somehow, some way, someday something would work out.

Unknown to Jack, however, his analysis of the situation crystallized my thoughts like nothing else. I am sure that he met with me in genuine sympathy and certain that he did not want me to resign. I left the IHOP that morning, however, knowing that the way was clear. I saw those three lines he mentioned, and foresaw a bloody battle in a historic church. I knew what must be done.

∾

THE DEACONS VISIT

BO SEXTON AND DAVID WICKER came to visit their former pastor in the posh great room of his half-million-dollar parsonage. Outside the vaulted, arched windows that stood two stories high, the sun of the waning north Texas summer pierced the room. The manicured lawn planted by the church radiated its greenish hue into the room. The Bradford pear ornamental trees planted twenty-one months before had marked those months by their symmetrical growth.

The two men entered our home in a subdued but friendly manner. What I had done necessarily altered our relationship for all time, somewhat like the revelation of an infidelity. I had no idea what their demeanor would be before the fact. My precipitous reaction had triggered the most intense crisis in the history of the century-and-one-quarter-old institution, the very heart of Dallas and the Southern Baptist Convention. Thousands of families had been thrown into very real grief. A thousand-student academy and a three-hundred-student college had been placed in a state of confusion. Understandably, the men might not have been in the most affable frame of mind.

Gracious men that they were, they began with an inquiry about our family and welfare. We exchanged assurances of love, prayer, and general good will. After enough of that, the men turned to their general exasperation that I had resigned. They felt they had done what they could. David Wicker stated, "We were almost ready to hand you the whole thing." I did not inquire about the meaning of that statement. I have subsequently wondered what further behind-the-scenes maneuvering had taken place since the Lakewood breakfast that Saturday weeks before when I revealed my discontent to the leaders.

The two leaders reported that the executive committee of the church had refused my resignation. There followed a delicate tap dance around the issue of whether or not my resignation was actually "irrevocable" as I had stated in its text. I assured them that it was. Contrary to what some members would say, I had no intention of "forcing Criswell out" and returning to the church in a Roman triumph, hoisted on the shoulders of deacons and leading a retinue of conquered Criswellites. It was obvious that the two deacons did not want to offer me a return and be refused. As gently as I could, I repeated that I had no intention of returning to the church.

There was nothing altruistic about my sentiment by this time. To go back now would be like leaping into Krakatoa at full eruption. I had humiliated Dr. C., enraged Mrs. C., and generally created a firestorm of support around Swiss Avenue. The Sunday after my resignation the television news showed scores of members from Mrs. C.'s class gathered in the front lawn of the Criswell mansion singing, praying, clapping, and generally urging the old man to go on forever. The months ahead would reveal that no defamation was too repugnant for the Criswell forces to level at me. I had no desire to die on that cross. As mean as they were to me after I left, God knows what they would have done to me had I stayed.

Having determined that I would not come back, the discussion turned to matters of severance. On my arrival as pastor the corporate officers of the church had signed a severance document. That simple document promised six months' salary if "any untoward circumstances" developed. We all knew that meant "if W. A. refuses to get out of the saddle"—a fifty-fifty bet—but no one wanted to wreck the deal by actually saying it in so many words. The severance document further promised to pay my $5,000-per-month mortgage until the house sold.

Suddenly unemployed, I had a heightened interest in their willingness to keep their word. A week before the resignation I had asked the deacon secretary, Doug Brady, a young attorney, to revise the severance document. He presented me with a fuller version that more explicitly stated the church's absolute commitment to my support if I left for any reason whatsoever. The tone of the document seemed to suggest that anyone stupid enough to resign First Baptist, Dallas, should be paid for six months just to keep them off the streets; such a demented person ought to be supported for the good of the general commonwealth.

All of these severance agreements had been signed by the corporate officers of the church, making them legally binding under Texas law. However, they had not been approved by the three-hundred-member deacon board. In the aftermath of my resignation, this inflamed the deacons. Never mind that my life was ruined, my career over, and my family shattered—a number of the good men were outraged that they should pay me a thin dime. As men of honor, the officers insisted that they keep the agreement. As I would find out, however, that did not mean what it sounded like. They would subsequently attempt to alter every codicil in the agreement and dare me to take action.

However, at the moment in the ebbing discussion with the two deacons, a sense of bonhomie descended over my living room, and all seemed to be well. I was gone, wished well, and promised their support. We prayed, they left, and I retreated to my study behind the house. At forty-four years of age I had reached the absolute pinnacle of my profession. I had earned a Ph.D., inherited the strongest church in the country, preached to the president, and then quit. How does anyone find himself in such a position?

Chapter Two

❧

In Retrospect: Seduced by a Super Church

For a nonBaptist, the seductive appeal of First Baptist, Dallas, might rest beyond rational comprehension. For a Baptist preacher, however, its allure exceeds facile description. What Rome is to the Catholic, Salt Lake City to the Mormon, or Canterbury to the Anglican, so is FBC Dallas to the Baptist. But that does not express it. There is also the appeal that Maxim's has to the gourmet, the Burgundy region of France to the connoisseur of wine, with a dash of the attraction Las Vegas has for the gambler. Since preachers are supposed to be spiritual, they are not supposed to lust for a position. Yet for generations of Baptist preachers, the magnetism of FBC Dallas evokes something in the spiritual realm akin to sexual lust in the fleshly realm.

First, the physical setting of the church is Dallas, Big D, the capital of materialism in that corner of the western hemisphere. Dallas understands two things: money and power. You are valued according to how much you possess of one or both. If the gods of materialism blessed you with both, you are virtually worshipped. Lest you think this overblown, go live there for awhile.

Physical appearance counts not for everything, but almost. As a seminary professor in the early eighties making the grand sum of $26,000 per year at Southwestern Seminary in Fort Worth, I would be summoned to the City to the east to speak in tony Baptist venues. The Park Cities Baptist Church invited me regularly in the early eighties. That church sits astride Northwest Highway, the exclusive avenue that runs through one of the prestigious municipalities of the world, Highland Park. Like its sister city University Park, Highland Park is surrounded by Dallas. Both towns were founded as tax retreats, and more recently, as lily-white inurbs to protect the wealthier residents of Dallas from the depredations of the minorities. (When house shopping in the transition to First Baptist, we were assured that no black students would invade Highland Park High because it was an unwritten rule that no family on Highland Park would dare have a live-in maid with any children, God forbid.) When I drove up to Park Cities Baptist Church for the first time, I thought I had died and been resurrected at a mink ranch or been reincarnated in a Cadillac showroom.

Whenever I made my pilgrimage to the east for an occasional preaching engagement, I learned to prepare myself for the "Dallas look-you-over." In Fort Worth no one much gives a hoot what you look like. I'm sure that in some of the downtown law firms a few genteel Cowtown yuppies care, but not like Dallas. When I entered a Dallas church as guest preacher, the greeters and other members did not even try to hide a head-to-toe scan of coiffure, shave, tie, shirt, suit, and shoes. I do not mean your usual, casual glance. They x-ray you. All of this is done in two seconds, but a very obvious two seconds. This happened to me everywhere downtown and north of downtown Dallas. I was not alone in noticing this rather rude, local habit.

If you don't have money in Dallas, the next best thing is power. At every level—from the black ghettoes of Oak Cliff to the boardrooms overlooking the north Texas empire—the city does understand power, power plays, loss of power, and new power. I sometimes had the feeling that there must be a scoreboard in some clandestine urban chamber where all this power was inscribed and the winners/losers were noted. This power mystique involves everyone from the Trammell Crows and the Hunts to Mary Crowley and Mary Kay Ash; it embraces Tom Landry and Jerry Jones, J. R. Ewing, and his very live counterparts.

Fascinatingly, Dallas is more power than culture. Fort Worth, with less than half the population, is per capita more devoted to the fine arts. Dallas makes no bones about aesthetics for arts' sake; the most important art in Dallas is the art of the deal. No one in Dallas wants to be trumped.

First Baptist breathes the spirit of old Dallas. Power and money are taken for granted. Zig Ziglar once told me, "Criswell understands two things: money and power." However spiritual an aspirant to that pulpit might have been, it was impossible to separate the church from its setting. Every material security, emolument, perquisite, and fetish that a powerful city could offer belonged to the pastor of its biggest church. Front-row seats at the Reunion Arena for the Mavericks (basketball) and the Stars (hockey), luxury boxes at Texas Stadium for the Cowboys (football, of course), and the best private quarters at Arlington Stadium for Ranger (baseball) games were not even the beginning of entertainment. Add to this a warm welcome at Mrs. H. L. Hunt's home, membership in the most exclusive clubs in Texas, and constant invitations to the finest eateries in the Southwest, and the atmosphere was heady for a Baptist preacher who started in the slums and worked his way up through inner-city churches. The church is Dallas. Dallas is the church.

∾

THE BAPTIST MOUNT RUSHMORE

YET IF FBC were not located in Dallas, it would have its own irresistible aura. For almost one hundred years the church has had two pastors. Dr. George W. Truett served from 1897-1944. He died in July and Criswell came in September. Truett was and is without contest the greatest pastor/preacher in American Baptist history, and arguably the most influential Protestant pastor, with the possible exception of Henry Ward Beecher, who had other problems.

Truett's life story reads like a fairy tale. He is the Horatio Alger of Baptist success stories. A mountain boy from North Carolina, he moved to a Texas farm with his family. By the time he got to Texas he had already wowed folks with his natural oratory, piercing eyes, broad Anglo-Saxon face, and imposing presence. To look at his picture fifty years after his death made one feel as if one needed to comb his hair, if not check other things.

Truett went to Baylor, the world's largest Baptist university, in Waco, Texas. It was there that he attained a legendary status among Baptists, akin to George Washington among Americans in general. Before he even enrolled as a freshman, he saved the school from bankruptcy. When Baylor was almost broke in the late nineteenth century, Truett stumped the state for Baylor, enthralling the mostly rural Baptists with an unassuming, natural oratorical power. Eyewitnesses stated that it was impossible to resist his appeals for support. He raised the money that saved the university.

After that, he enrolled as a freshman. He wanted to be a lawyer, but against his will was ordained to the gospel ministry and became the pastor of a church in Waco. He never went to seminary. The Texas of the 1890s did not have one, and he could preach better than anyone at Louisville, the only Baptist seminary in the south. When the First Baptist Church of Dallas needed a pastor in 1897, Truett was obvious.

Immediately, the young man riveted the attention of the city. He was genuinely pious and supernaturally gifted as a speaker, and his church attracted the civic leaders of Dallas. The attendance skyrocketed for the first twenty-seven years of his ministry, leaving him much in demand to speak throughout the nation and later the world. Before such church-state separation as today, Truett spoke at every major state and private university in the south. John D. Rockefeller tried to buy Truett to become pastor of Riverside in Manhattan. Baylor offered him its presidency. He presided over every level of Baptist life in the state, nation, and world, ultimately becoming president of the Baptist World Alliance.

Truett was the first citizen of Dallas for the first half of the twentieth century. When stricken with bone cancer, he tried to resign, but the church refused. So he spoke to the congregation by telephone patched to the P.A. system, an innovation in 1944. When he died, the city shut down to attend his funeral. Baptists in America will never see his kind again.

When Truett died, it was common wisdom that the church would die, too. It is very rare for a Protestant church to have two gigantic figures. The shadow of one eclipses the next. The comparisons are so invidious, the weight of an encore so cumbersome, and the burden of history so unbearable that it seldom happens. Lightning did strike twice at FBC Dallas. Just when dandy Don Meredith would have sung in the fourth quarter, "Turn out the lights, the party's over," a tornado named Criswell blew onto the scene. He was, to say the least, a dark horse.

Criswell was born into Texas Panhandle poverty. His father attempted to homestead a farm outside Texline, a dusty border town set in a moonscape on the desolate boundary between New Mexico and Texas. Criswell grew up under the domination of a doting mother who desired a medical education for her son, so she moved with him to Amarillo for the better education he would receive at Amarillo High. Criswell excelled as a student and played the trombone in the high school band (an accomplishment which, for some unknown reason, he often mentioned from the pulpit sixty years later).

There was only one place for such a promising Baptist boy to go—dear old Baylor. So he was off to Baylor where his mother also went to see that he did well. His father, a barber, remained behind in Amarillo. The dominant influence of Criswell's mother marked him for life. Criswell-watchers, of whom there have been legion, are fond of noting the dominance of women in his life. The apparent psychological outcome on Criswell was a respectful reserve about women, who daunted him. Any man who crossed Criswell on the FBC staff could pack his bags. The tenured women of the staff, however, would sometimes address him like a transient who wandered into the facility. His curious inability to handle women often caused ponderous discussions among Baptist cognoscenti.

After finishing Baylor, Criswell faced a choice of going to the nascent Southwestern Seminary in Fort Worth or the illustrious and more scholarly Southern Seminary in Louisville. He opted for Southern because, in his own words, "that's where the scholarship was." He would spend the better part of a decade in Kentucky, earning a Ph.D. at Southern Seminary while pastoring rural churches in Kentucky. There he met and married Betty, a pianist in one of the churches. The First Baptist Church of Chickasha, Oklahoma, called him out of Kentucky, followed by the FBC, Muskogee. He admitted later in life that he almost despaired that his classmates were moving to great city churches while he was mired in the country.

That soon changed. After Truett's death, the attention of Dallas, Texas, and a good part of the South was on the nominees as successor for First, Dallas. Most felt it would be a death sentence to follow the inimitable Truett. As Criswell tells the story, it was an implausible series of unlikelihoods that brought him to Dallas. Some of his contemporaries at Baylor and Southern, however, remember the story somewhat differently. They contend that Criswell aimed at Truett's post from the day he matriculated at Baylor.

Criswell has often recounted a striking "dream" that afflicted him while he was in Muskogee.

Criswell has often recounted a striking "dream" that afflicted him while he was in Muskogee. He was sitting in the auditorium of First, Dallas, at the funeral of George W. Truett. As he peered into the casket he saw the waxen face of the Baptist icon. Then he felt the press of a hand at his side. He looked beside him and saw the face of Truett. The grand man told Criswell to take over. There is no question that Criswell now believes this story.

43

What Criswell believes he believes with all his heart at that moment. Having observed him invent reality by the yard, however, I grew somewhat skeptical of such anecdotes.

At any rate, he was gloriously called to the pastorate of the church in September 1944. What he found, however, was a shrinking congregation of older people who had stood by Truett during the decline of the world figure. Most of them lived near the downtown area and expected that Criswell would preside over the decline of a once-great institution. They had not reckoned with the indomitable Criswell will. He set out to redirect the old church. Criswell knew that the future of the church rested with attracting younger families. It took him five years to convince the leadership that the church could reach couples with children from the suburbs of the burgeoning post-war Dallas.

Criswell contended to me that the widow Truett did him great harm. Some long-time members told me quietly this was not so. According to W. A., she could not stand the fact that anyone might successfully follow her husband. One of the strangest conversations in my tenure at the church involved Betty Criswell damning Mrs. Truett for her relentless opposition to W. A. There I sat, the target of Mrs. Criswell's tireless efforts to undermine me, listening to her bemoan her husband's trials forty-seven years before at the hands of his predecessor's wife. While she raved that such insidious treachery should never befall a poor young preacher following a great incumbent, her minions were eating away at me like termites. As Robert Burns said in *To a Louse*, "O wad some pow'r the giftie gie us/To see oursels as ithers see us."

Mrs. Truett went on to her reward. This was the first instance of many in which Criswell simply outlived and outlasted opposition. He steadfastly believes that time is on his side. After fifty

Reverend W. A. Criswell, senior pastor of First Baptist Church, Dallas. (Photo by Norm Tindell, *Fort Worth Star-Telegram*)

years, it is hard to argue with that assessment. Criswell began to increase in power and stature, in spite of a blatant contrast with Truett. George Truett was a granite-faced, white-haired, black-suited embodiment of dignity behind the pulpit. His latter style was a mellow sunset of soothing southern oratory. In contrast, Criswell was like an atomic explosion. Red-headed, rock-jawed, screaming at the top of his voice, pounding the pulpit, and exploding before the congregation, he provided an astonishing contrast to Truett.

Through political influence, Criswell finagled the steel to build the Criswell Building during the Korean conflict. By force of personality and unbending perseverance, he molded the church into his vision. It would be a seven-day-a-week center of life for his people. Far ahead of his time, he hired divisional directors for every age group of the church. These full-time workers ran the nursery, toddlers, creepers, elementary children, youth, young marrieds, middle-aged folks, and old folks. Most of them were women, a number of these unmarried. They would fondly be called "Criswell's nuns." They would labor for the pastor at small salaries and wearying hours, but they produced.

Criswell began his stunning acquisition of downtown Dallas real estate. He simply bought out the dying First Christian Church with money provided by the heiress of an oil fortune. He proceeded to build a gymnasium and parking building over the ruins of the former church, altogether to the surprise of the congregation. This was the first of Criswell's famous "end-runs" in which he used private sources of financing to obtain another building, only to announce later to the congregation that they had a new piece of real estate (which they were obligated to use and care for).

By the sixties the church achieved an astonishing spiral of growth. The old Southern Baptist Convention had never seen anything like it. Three thousand and then four thousand people poured downtown to hear W. A.'s fiery oratory and listen to the enthralling music of Leroy Till, a businessman-turned-musician. W. A. was the envy of the denomination. Everything he touched turned to gold.

By his twenty-fifth anniversary in 1968, he was the acknowledged master pastor of the Southwest. Uninhibited, possessed of a photographic memory, he did the unheard of. His fundamentalism was a new phenomenon in the denomination. Many fundamentalists were red-necked, rural, bucolic, illiterate fanatics afraid of education, urbanity, and sophistication of any sort. In W. A., the right-wing of American Christianity had a genuine Ph.D. who could quote Shakespeare and Browning by the mile from memory as well as he could the Apostle Paul. His combination of intellect and emotion mesmerized his hearers. Shouting Greek verbs one moment and bawling like a baby the next, he attracted both the intellectuals and the sentimentalists of the city. He made *Time* magazine by preaching a long series against "godless evolution," one moment conjugating Hebrew verbs about fiat creation, and the next analyzing embryology and the geological record. No pulpiteer in the nation had done such a thing in living memory.

Fundamentalist Christianity must have an enemy, and Criswell excelled in the political arena by becoming a tireless anti-communist. Along with liberalism, evolution, and integration, Criswell scorched the communists weekly. With Joseph McCarthy finding a communist under every rock, W. A. joined the right-wing fusillade against communists and all their

"fellow travelers" (to use a phrase from J. Edgar Hoover, popu-
larized long before he was discovered to run around in his apartment in pink chiffon dresses). Criswell's bellicose anti-red
rhetoric attracted the late H. L. Hunt, who brought his family
and considerable fortune to First Baptist. The Hunt family genuinely loved the church and its work. They were very kind to
me and belonged to the most genuinely concerned Christians
in the fellowship.

By the late 1960s, Criswell had achieved the pinnacle of
respect, but had not consented to be nominated for the presidency of the Southern Baptist Convention. There was one very
good reason: FBC Dallas was segregated. Criswell had stood
before the South Carolina state legislature and cried, "Anyone
who believes integration, is dead from the neck up." In post-
Kennedy America many still believed this, but few shouted it in
front of state assemblies. Suddenly, Criswell had a change of
heart, publicly repented of his segregationist ways, declared the
doors of the church opened to everyone, and was shortly thereafter elected president of the Southern Baptist Convention.

That Denver Convention happened to be the first I attended
as a young, Baylor preacher-boy. I had just married and was a
junior at Baylor University in my first pastorate. I was over-
whelmed with the persona of W. A. Criswell. I was already mad
at the overt theological liberalism in the department of religion
at my alma mater. It would be years later when I learned of the
equally great danger of mindless fundamentalism. At the tender
age of nineteen, Criswell was the epitome of what I wanted to
be—a spellbinding orator, a doctor of philosophy, a historian, a
Greek scholar, and a defender of the faith. It was in my twentieth
year that the thought first entered my mind that the Criswellian

mantle could fall on me. Twenty-two years later it did, but it fell right over my eyes.

♋

WHO'S NEXT ON FIRST?

DURING THE 1970S, W. A. became the lightning rod for the controversy that would inevitably divide the denomination. Criswell excoriated liberals in our colleges and seminaries. The polemical Dr. Paige Patterson was brought on board to head up the Criswell College, a preacher college to turn out "green berets for the faith" in Patterson's metaphor. Weary of the unending burdens of a super church, Criswell openly spoke of finding a successor and retiring at sixty-five. Thus began a long fishing expedition with the stated public intention of finding a successor for the Great White Father, as W. A. was irreverently called by less-awed colleagues in the ministry.

No one can count the number of young men Criswell intrigued with the idea that they might follow him. Since my precipitous resignation, at least six I did not know about have come forward to indicate that they were offered the same bait I would swallow. Dr. James Bryant, for example, was the pastor of a tiny, blue-collar church in Fort Worth. During that time, he organized a west Fort Worth crusade at which W.A. would preach. Criswell was fetched with the energy of young Bryant and catapulted him into a role as associate pastor, dangling before Bryant the possibility of taking over the empire.

Years later Jim Bryant recounted a conversation with W. A. Standing outside the enormous facilities of the church plant, W. A. told Jim, "Young man, if you do exactly what I say, someday this could all be yours. But if you do not, you will regret that you were ever born." Bryant remembered waiting for a smile, a self-mocking gesture, or some other indication that this was only a Texas-style, good-natured joke. Instead, Criswell peered at him with a serious demeanor. Obviously, W. A. meant what he said. James Bryant wound up in Albuquerque, New Mexico.

By the mid-1970s, W. A. was tired enough that he wanted serious help. Dr. James T. Draper, Jr., now president of the Sunday School Board of the Southern Baptist Convention and twice its elected president, was a successful young pastor in Del City, a southern suburb of Oklahoma City. Jimmy Draper was and is walking compassion, one of the true princes of the denomination. Sincere, well-meaning, and affable, the young Draper resigned his booming church and moved his family to Dallas. It was explicitly understood that the young associate pastor would follow Criswell.

The congregation fell in love with Draper, who preached on Sunday nights while W. A. continued in the mornings. Soon people were coming an hour early to reserve seats on Sunday nights. More people were added to the church on Sunday nights than Sunday mornings. The energetic Draper began to capture the hearts of people who still loved Criswell, but who were wanting to hear a more contemporary voice. Not surprisingly, such popularity enraged and threatened Mrs. Criswell, who set in motion her formidable machine inside the church. Any threat to the public persona of W. A. Criswell put Draper on the spot. He was the man of the hour and the vulnerable target if W. A.'s reputation was diminished or tarnished.

One incident guaranteed Draper's ouster. Criswell agreed to debate the atheist Madeline Murray O'Hair on state-wide radio.

The entire state of Texas licked its chops at the very thought of a public shoot-out between its number one pastor and the nation's most hated atheist. Wiser heads at First Baptist begged Criswell not to do it. O'Hair was a visceral, obscene street fighter who would stop at nothing to undo him on the air. Always courtly toward women, W. A. was the perfect setup for the cussing atheist. Criswell could never comprehend a woman like O'Hair.

What happened was a rout. O'Hair skewered W. A. by quoting letters she attributed to First Baptist members. She alleged that such letters contained vile things and unmentionable by-products. The very thought of such things undid Criswell, who stammered and stumbled in the debate. During a commercial break, O'Hair taunted Criswell: "You don't have any balls at all, do you?" No one, but no one, in human history had ever mentioned such a testicular deficiency to Criswell.

It was merciful when the program was over. It also spelled a death-knell for Dr. Draper. He was reaching enormous and unprecedented proportions of popularity in the church and with the people. If there was even a remote chance that he could have such popularity that the people would call for Criswell's ouster, that must be addressed long before it happened. Criswell's embarrassment led to an insecurity that caused Jimmy's ouster. Criswell's public humiliation at the hands of the nation's chief atheist created an insecurity at "Swiss Avenue" that had to be assuaged. Typical of First Baptist politics, Draper was asked to do something he could not do in church administration regarding the abrupt dismissal of a colleague. A man of impeccable integrity, Draper drew the line at violating his own conscience and valued friendships. The result was swift. He was out on the street. It made headlines in the *Dallas Morning News*.

Thousands in the congregation were outraged, but Criswell simply hunkered down and waited it out. Still, the Draper expulsion opened the eyes of many members. Hundreds left the church; many who stayed were permanently cynical about the intention of Criswell and his wife. So beloved was Draper that he went on to an enviable ministry and became a statesman in the denomination. He is today the most beloved figure among Baptists.

Criswell never intended that Draper would follow him. Older, wearier, and wanting desperately to equal George Truett's forty-seven-year tenure, Criswell knew that he needed a younger man to energize the situation. Yet the presence of such a man provided a threat to his own tenure. It was a Catch-22. What he needed he couldn't have because it could keep him from having what he needed.

Leadership in a Baptist church is somewhat like having a stack of poker chips. Every act that displeases the congregation spends some leadership chips. When your pile of chips gets low, you had best wait awhile before you displease the folks again. You win more chips by pastoring them, caring for them, preaching appealing sermons, and generally laying low from controversy. Every Baptist preacher who lasts has an intuitive sense about how many chips he has left. Criswell is a genius at such pastoral poker. He knows when to hold and he knows when to fold 'em. (However, he has not yet demonstrated that he knows when to walk away.)

After the Draper debacle, W. A. decided he had better go on alone for a few years. Both Criswell and the church lost a certain buoyancy in the late seventies and early eighties. The congregation was growing tired of Criswell's typical approach to preaching, which was heavy on historical exegesis. Criswell seemed to live in a world where the Temple of Diana in Ephesus was a greater reality than the problems in modern Dallas. Under heat to get contemporary, Criswell launched a Sunday evening series on marriage and sex.

Everyone awaited eagerly the pastor's observations on sex. Keep in mind that Baptist folk do not normally look at their pastors as capable of sexual intercourse. Evidently they consider the pastor's children to have sprung full-grown from Zeus's brow or to have been born by miraculous spontaneous generation. On the appointed evening, Criswell mounted the pulpit with a list of quotations from, of all sources, *Redbook* magazine. Since that periodical hardly graced the coffee table on Swiss Avenue, everyone wondered how the elegant pastor had happened on such a primary source.

In his best form, Criswell quoted an article on sexual perfor-mance which claimed that evangelical women enjoy sex more and are by a greater percentage orgasmic than non-evangelicals. In full voice, Criswell explored the article with the congrega-tion. Since he is seen as hopelessly naive by most FBC folk, it was a real rarity to hear him expound from the sacred desk on the relative likelihood of female orgasms.

Warming to the subject, Criswell asked the congregation why any young man in the church would go to a bar or club to look for a young woman. Reaching the peroration of the ser-mon, he intoned, "Young man, marry one of our First Baptist girls and she will love you so much they will carry you out in a wheel barrow." The congregation sat stunned for a moment and then burst out in a howl of laughter. The sermon was soon dubbed "The Wheel Barrow Sermon" and received national attention. One footnote: When Mrs. C. was interviewed about the sermon, she gave this incredible response: "W. A. doesn't know what he's talking about." Everyone left that one alone.

When the dust settled from the Draper incident, Criswell started what would be called "the parade of preachers," flying in the elite of the denomination to occupy the pulpit for one Sunday evening. More than twenty made the pilgrimage to Dallas. There was a great unspoken agenda, the favorite kind of agenda at FBC: Would the congregation be ignited by one of these visiting preachers? As they came, one by one, they all disavowed any interest at all in the most powerful church in the nation. As the Bard would say, "Thou does't protest too much." On Monday morning AT&T could have declared a dividend from the instant analysis of the previous Sunday evening's sermon by Baptist preachers all over the country. Who would win this beauty contest became a matter of nationwide speculation.

∾

A CALL FROM CRISWELL

IT WAS AT THIS POINT that my own path intersected with W. A. From 1977 until 1982, the First Baptist-owned KCBI-FM had aired my sermons from the Gambrell Street Baptist Church. In order to be a Dallas-Fort Worth station they needed to play a tape from a Fort Worth church. At 5:00 P.M. Saturday, they had played a tape of my sermon from Gambrell. This is about the deadest time of the week to air any sermon tape, so I expected that no one had listened. To my surprise, a number of FBC folk had listened and liked what they heard. They leaned on Criswell to invite me to preach at the end of the parade. Also, it was perceived that some of the contestants were less than loyal to the denomination as it was then. I was a seminary professor, a part of the establishment of the Southern Baptist Convention, and a "rising star" in the preaching firmament. So it was that in the fall of 1983, I received a call from W. A. Criswell.

Once again, the nonBaptist reader may not understand what a shock it is to a Baptist preacher to be called by the Great White Father. First, there are a number of pranksters who emulate W. A. on the phone. One of the best is a Louisiana pastor and professional impersonator named Dennis Swanberg. From time to time he calls fellow pastors, pretending to be Criswell, and does such a credible job that most folks think he really is W. A. When I received a call in our modest southwest Fort Worth home from "Criswell," my first response was to say, "Swanny, stop fooling around." It was a rather inauspicious first conversation with the Great One. Criswell replied, "It is I."

By this time W. A. was used to people not believing it was really him on the phone, just as nobody believes it when the president of the United States calls them. The dead giveaway, however, was the use of the nominative pronoun "I." Swanberg would have said, good-old-boy style, "It's me." So it was he, the genuine article. I bolted upright in my chair and wondered what could precipitate a call from the Baptist Pope to a lowly assistant professor.

Criswell is as disarming as he is charming. He related to me how his members had listened to me on the church's radio station. A great groundswell had arisen for me to come preach to the people. This conjured up the image in my mind of thousands of chanting Baptists standing on Ervay Street in front of the church crying, "Gregory, Gregory, Gregory." Then he made the first, but by no means the last, proposal that he would make to me. Baptists have a practice called "The January Bible Study." From headquarters in Nashville it is decreed that a given book of the Bible will be intensely studied by all sixteen million Baptists in January. How this book is selected always intrigued me, but the mystery remains unpenetrated. Somebody in Nashville declares that a given book is the divine intention for that year. As a result, thousands of Baptists brave the icy weather of January to gather in a study of the book. The year Criswell approached me the book was I Corinthians. That was a stroke of good fortune for me. I had made several intense studies of that epistle and was armed to the teeth with information.

This conjured up the image in my mind of thousands of chanting Baptists standing on Ervay Street in front of the church crying, "Gregory, Gregory, Gregory."

Criswell asked that I occupy his pulpit each Sunday evening of January 1984, in a series of four messages from I Corinthians. The church would gather, I would preach, and we would "see what God does." That statement was just titillating enough to make me wonder if he had more in mind than just one month's study. That possibility was confirmed by other sources in the church. At that time an energetic young man named Thomas Melzoni was running the church. He had risen meteorically in Baptist administration and in his early thirties found himself the chief operating officer of the Criswell empire. Tom insinuated that more could be afoot, and I might well do a good job. Wide-eyed with wonder, I pondered the possibilities of leaping from an assistant professorship to the Big One, FBC of Big D.

The first Sunday night of January 1984, I showed up certain I knew more about I Corinthians than Paul himself. I was ushered

into "the minister's room," a holding chamber for guest preachers. Affable deacons sat around the antique table where W. A.
presided at the other end. No guest waiting in the "Green Room"
before taking the stage at the Carson show could have been more
nervous. This was the Baptist Super Bowl, the Grand Prix of
preaching, the Kentucky Derby of divine declaration. I was about
to stand in George Truett's and W. A. Criswell's pulpit. My heart
racing, my breath abated, and my heart pounding, I walked with
Criswell down the historic hallway into the sanctuary. There
they sat, the members of First Baptist. I thought they must be
some special superspecies of Baptists, aglow with a supernatural
hue just because they belong to the church.

After Criswell's generous introduction, I took the pulpit. I
had spent all day in final preparations, not even attending
church in the morning (a luxury of being a professor at the
time). I launched into an exposition of I Corinthians 1 in what I
thought was the best Criswellian form: heavy Greek exegesis,
historical illustrations, purple rhetoric, and a stirring conclusion.
The people appeared to listen, but no lightning struck. I ended
the sermon, gave a public invitation for response, and several
people "walked the aisle," publicly declaring their spiritual decisions. After a few handshakes, I found my car and drove the
thirty miles back to Fort Worth.

Early that week Tom Melzoni called me. After some preliminary remarks, he proceeded to help me with my preaching. He
indicated that the people were tired of preaching that was too
scholarly, that they wanted more practical application and less
obtuse theology. In so many words he told me that I had better
get off my professorial high horse and do some down-home
preaching if I had a snowball's chance in hell of being asked

back after January. Always one to respond to such subtle counsel, I assured Tom that I would do better. Looking back on it ten
years later, mine was a pathetic response. So daunted was I by
anything having to do with the church that I let a young man—
a man soon to be fired—intimidate me with unsolicited and
patronizing advice.

Armed with this insight from Tom, I warmed up on the subject of Christian love from I Corinthians 13. Abandoning illustrations from classical history, I added some syrupy anecdotes
about Christian love. The sermon was indeed a masterpiece.
Even Betty Criswell said that it was the best exposition of
I Corinthians she had ever heard. I had found the balance
between scholarship and mush! The next week I went further in
the same direction.

Then it was over. Strangely, we had not been invited to anyone's home after the services or entertained in any other way.
That is rare for Baptists in Texas. I had been received, heard,
and after four weeks it was finished. I felt like a football player
might feel after playing to a tie in a national championship
game. A curious sense of incompleteness fell over me as I drove
back to Fort Worth at the end of January 1984.

My more pedestrian duties as a professor beckoned. Teaching,
writing, and flying around the country preaching at various
venues replaced the weeks at the super church. I distanced
myself from the entire episode emotionally. I had been to the
Big Time, stepped up to the plate, hit the ball, but had no feed-
back on whether it went out of the park or drifted foul. Soon I
would know.

~

CRISWELL CALLS AGAIN

I RETURNED TO THE ROUTINE of an assistant professor with a grim determination that my future must rest in the ranks of academia. I had been to the mountain, tasted the rarefied air, and descended again to the valley of the ministerial common-place. The effect of such a trip, however, was to leave me with a certain case of "what-might-have-been."

It was approximately a month later that I was once again in my small study in our Fort Worth home. The phone rang. It was W. A. This time he began the conversation by asking me, "Lad, are you sitting down?" Presumably, this was to brace me for the life-changing announcement that was to follow.

He continued by telling me that he had invited more than twenty preachers to the church across the preceding months. The reaction of the church to this parade of preachers had varied. But he assured me that not in his entire tenure had the church reacted to a guest preacher as they had reacted to me. Then came the proposal. Would I be willing to come for a series of Sunday evenings as the guest preacher? In his remarkably ambiguous way, he once again said, "We'll see what God does." He asked me if I owned a house in Fort Worth, what size the house was, and what it cost. The implication was clear—W. A. was considering moving me to Dallas for some Bigger Thing. What that thing was—associate, permanent night-time preach-er, possible successor to the empire—was never exactly spelled out. That is part of the Criswellian style. Get the thing going, leave it ambiguous, and let Criswell guide it the way he wants it to go in the future. Criswell had the right hunch that I was ambitious enough to take the bait. How could an assistant professor resist the opportunity to grab the ring?

There was a nit-picking financial detail. Young seminary professors in the denomination are not paid a living wage. One must constantly hustle speaking engagements in order to provide a strained middle-class existence for the family. As a young professor, I had been rather successful in having several such engagements per week. In fact, I was making six hundred dollars a week outside my modest seminary salary, which meant I was making more money outside the school than inside. I had a lifestyle that was based on that inflated gross income. Not only did this provoke the jealousy of senior colleagues, it had me in debt. Consequently, I had to explain the situation to Criswell. He was at first taken aback, but then assured me that the ten-million-dollar-a-year institution would find some way to rise to the occasion. Only later did I find out that this tidy sum irritated some of his chief lay leaders, as well it might. So it was agreed that I would be a six-hundred-dollar-per-week Sunday night preacher with a promise of some nebulous Larger Thing at the end when we all saw "what God would do."

∾

SOME LAYMEN SPEAK

WHATEVER GOD INTENDED TO DO, several lay leaders in the church had their own agenda. Tom Melzoni, the whiz-kid administrator, presented himself to me as an inside interpreter of "what was really going on" and postured as an adviser. I was never sure of exactly what he was doing, but I took it at face value. He called to tell me that certain powerful lay leaders were upset at the idea that Criswell would give the pulpit to a presumed heir of the pastorate. In Baptist polity the congregation elects a pulpit committee that searches on behalf of the church after the incumbent has retired. That is, the former pastor is supposed to keep his paws off the entire process and have nothing to do with the election of his successor. It is also proverbial that he is supposed to be off the scene—either dead or otherwise removed to another place—for his successor to have a ghost of a chance. The one certain congregational prerogative in a Baptist church is that the folks in the pew get to select the next man in the pulpit. Certain laymen at First rightly discerned that W. A. had another thing in mind. They did not like it.

So it was that in the spring of 1984, I was summoned to the Fairmont Hotel to meet with two deacon leaders of the church. Both of them had chaired the board, were distinguished Dallas attorneys, and were unhappy with Criswell's present direction in the church. As we ate our lunch, Tom Melzoni sat in with us as the arranger of the meeting. The men were kind, but minced no words. The senior of the two told me that he had admired my preaching. He had heard me in Pittsburgh, Pennsylvania, the previous year when I had spoken to the assembled Southern Convention five times in fifteen-minute theme interpretations. He assured me that he had told himself at the time "that young man might be for our church." I was heartened to hear this.

Then the other shoe dropped. He informed me that the congregation had no intention of letting W. A. choose his successor. If I came for the proffered four months of Sunday evening preaching, I would have "three strikes against me." To my astonishment, he was telling me that powerful lay leaders in the church did not want me to do what their pastor was asking me to do. In hindsight, I should have asked that we all sit down together with W. A. and find out what was going on, but I was so stunned at the development that I could hardly speak. Here I was at thirty-five years of age sitting in the grill of a five-star hotel being told by two powerful attorneys that the only chance I had at the church was to turn down the invitation of W. A. Criswell. It was akin to being asked by a second-term presidential candidate to be his running mate and at the same time being told by party bosses that you have no future if you do so. The meeting came to an awkward and indeterminate conclusion.

Driving back to Fort Worth from that curious meeting, I recognized that I was close to the Big Time and that the stakes were high. Would I end forever my chances to follow Criswell and Truett by speaking on Sunday nights? Would I dash my hopes by listening to two contrarian deacon leaders who had made an end run? Who could I talk to about it? In Baptist life it was the equivalent of being considered for pope. There just are not too many former popes around to confer with about how things go when you get elected.

In the absence of ex-popes, I turned to the best inside sources I had, Tom Melzoni and Paige Patterson. Melzoni rode the fence. He was shrewd enough to recognize that I just might wind up his next boss. Paige Patterson was more forthcoming. He reminded me of the horror stories of Criswell's other pastoral candidates. In his usual florid way, Patterson said sympathetically, "I am tired of picking up bodies on San Jacinto Street," the street running through the church property.

Ultimately, it came down to my own holy hunch. Brimming with ambition to follow in the Criswell-Truett tradition, I bet on

W. A. After all, he had been there for forty years. You don't last that long in a big Baptist church if you rode into town on a load of turnips. He was Teflon before Ronald Reagan. Nothing ever stuck. I thus decided to accept W. A.'s invitation. I would tee up the golf ball of destiny, pull out my best homiletical driver, and bash it down the great fairway of life.

It was several months before I began the assignment. I had other preaching responsibilities and was advised by W. A. not to break my commitments. This allowed him to do the internal groundwork necessary for a good reception. It was agreed that I would begin the four months' assignment in August 1984.

❦

FOUR MONTHS ON DISPLAY

THE AWAITED SUNDAY in August arrived. I drove with the family to the First Baptist Church of Dallas from our southwest Fort Worth home. Since Criswell always made a fetish of preaching without notes, I had crammed down the sermon for the evening verbatim. Now I felt that if a note of paper touched the top of the sacred pulpit of Truett and Criswell the whole antique structure might collapse. A nonpreacher might not understand the pressure of this approach. It is the equivalent of a student taking an oral on his doctoral dissertation without having the thing in his lap, or a young attorney arguing the biggest case of her life without a brief in her briefcase.

We parked somewhere in one of the garages. In retrospect, it was unusual that no provision was made for our parking. We weren't even told which door to enter. This was the first of a number of not-so-subtle putdowns that would characterize the four months. Yet I was so caught up in a holy haze that I did not even recognize the signs of the times.

Suddenly, I found myself whisked into the minister's room, where you wait with the platform party to enter the church. Here it was, the very holding room of big-time religion. By command performance of the Great White Father I had been asked back for four months of display "to see what God does." Yet there was a certain uneasiness in the room. One could sense it in the reserved greetings I received from the deacons, who in rotation would sit on the platform week by week. Normally a guest preacher is pounded on the back, given a hail and hearty greeting, and told "go get 'em." There was none of that. There was a rather icy reserve, a correct politeness that was just barely civil.

What I did not know at the time was that a significant minority of the deacons did not want W. A. Criswell to cram his self-appointed successor down their throat. And they were exactly right. They had the prerogative to choose. My own blind ambition prevented me from seeing that at the time.

We marched out to the historic platform of the famous church. A full house of two thousand Sunday night worshippers greeted me. The minister of music, one of several in a row to get the ax, fired up the church choir and orchestra. The choir extends from the lower level up to the balconies of the church. To sit on the platform is to be surrounded with thunderous orchestral and choral music; one feels as if he died and woke up inside a stereo. It is an exhilarating feeling; the floor of the nineteenth-century building vibrates beneath your feet. If you did not already have enough adrenaline to send you through the roof, you would soon get it from hearing the loud music. After a sonorous introduction from Criswell, I sprang to the pulpit. I had been working on the initial sermon for months. Eisenhower could not have been more prepared for D-Day.

I preached and several people "walked the aisle." Every Baptist preacher faces a visible vote every time he preaches. If a lot of people walk the aisle he hit a home run. If no one moves a muscle, God did not move. Of course there is not a single instance in the New Testament of anyone walking an aisle after the apostles preached, and Baptist preachers and lay people spend an inordinate amount of time denying that this is in reality a weekly vote on how good the preacher is doing. But when the aisles freeze up and no sinners repent, you had better pack your bags. The greatest Baptist of them all, Billy Graham, owes much of his fame as the greatest evangelist in history to the fact that so many people walk the aisle when he preaches.

Every Baptist preacher faces a visible vote every time he preaches. If a lot of people walk the aisle he hit a home run. If no one moves a muscle, God did not move.

Fortunately for me, every Sunday evening of the four months an appropriate number of people walked the aisle. I would only find out much later that at First Baptist this was largely prearranged, not due to the power of my delivery. I could have read the stock quotes and the same number would have walked.

So my four months of Sundays unfolded. I would study all week, even all day Sunday, and make the thirty-minute drive to Dallas chock-full of the evening's message. And from the start, there was a clash of agendas. Melzoni advised me not to look too eager, but W. A. asked me repeatedly, "Why don't you come over during the week and let the people touch you?" He was in effect asking me to run for office, an incredible thing in the context of a Baptist church. I imagined myself standing in the crowded hallways of the super church with a sign around my neck, "Touch me." Melzoni advised me that I should do no such thing. A lot of the people already had kidney problems about the very idea that Criswell would try to impose an assistant professor on them as the next pastor. For me to stand in the hallways kissing babies would only further disenchant them. In that instance I took Melzoni's advice rather than Criswell's. For me to hang around the church during the week looking eager for the job was a repugnant prospect even for someone with my outsized ambitions.

From the prospect of ten years later, the whole episode seems bizarre. There I was, being touted by Criswell as a possible successor. I was held out in front of the congregation like meat on a hook to see if they would bite. When I did not run for office, Criswell felt that I was not socially adept. He told Dr. Russell H. Dilday, Jr., my boss and president of the seminary, "Why don't you help the boy?" It was during these months that I made a discovery that would be made again six years later when I finally became the pastor—to be around W. A. Criswell is to be hurled into one situation after another where you are caught dead center between a rock and a hard place, while he walks away.

By November 1984, speculation was rife in the church and across the country that I would be elevated to the status of potential successor to Criswell. He had asked me into his inner sanctum and pushed me to choose a house in Dallas. He wanted to know how soon I could move, whether I could sell my house in Fort Worth, and related questions. At the time I did not notice what should have been apparent: he never said what it was I was moving there to do.

It was clear to me that Criswell was in a bind himself. He was aging, tired, and needed someone to take some of the weight off his tiring shoulders. He had to have a great pulpiteer to be acceptable to the church, but he knew that it was a delicate operation to impose a potential successor.

Providence, fate, or fortune took it out of our hands. Jack Brady, a Dallas lawyer and chairman of the board at First, intervened. I never knew exactly what happened, but Criswell was put on notice by powerful people in the church that they would not let him choose his own successor. All of this happened behind closed doors and with no notice to me until one sudden, breathless moment. Late in November 1984, Criswell leaned over to me on the platform during the service: "Meet with me in the office after the service." I thought that this would be a meeting to seal the deal. I was in for a surprise.

After the service, he escorted me to his office on the second floor of the Criswell building. Obviously uncomfortable, he related to me a visit from the church leaders who had informed him that he was not going to force a potential successor on the church. For perhaps the only time in my experience with Criswell, he really leveled with me. I could move to Dallas and he was willing to force me on the church, if I wanted to take that risk. He could not really advise that given the present circumstances. He left the decision with me.

∾

ENTER REALITY

IN THAT MOMENT all of the dream dissolved and I crashed down to reality. I had been an experiment, one of many over the years. With all my personal ambition to follow the two great men, I saw the handwriting on the wall. Only a fool would thrust himself into such a circumstance. What I did not know I would find out years later. Criswell was fighting for his life with a faction of deacons. Jack Brady, Clarence Bentley, and some other Dallas lawyer-deacons had challenged W. A.'s divine right to run the church as a divine-right monarch. The subject of their crusade ultimately focused on the half-million dollars Criswell had amassed in his private "pastor's fund." This was a separate fund from other church moneys gorged with gifts from wealthy patrons of the church. Most pastors of large churches have such a fund for discretionary use for any cause; it is a necessity to meet immediate needs encountered by the pastor. Years later when I was the pastor I was amazed when a member would contribute ten thousand dollars at a time to my own "pastor's fund" for use in whatever project I wanted. But a half-million dollars was another matter. At about the same time I was being touted as a successor, these lay leaders were attempting to strip Criswell of the perks he had enjoyed through the years, the enormous pastor's fund being the chief among them. They were successful both at squelching my candidacy and removing the money from Criswell's personal fund.

Jack Brady did meet with me. He was kindly, even fatherly in his statement. Jack recognized that I had been a test case. He told me that Criswell would not choose his own successor. Seeing that I could be shattered by the experiment, the good deacon affirmed, "When the time comes, rest assured that we will pray about Dr. Gregory, but not now."

That was it. It was over. I had been to the top, breathed the heady air, and was now dismissed. I went back to the seminary, the classroom, and my students. In light of W. A.'s offer, I had canceled my calendar for the spring of 1985. Not only did I find myself without the dream of Dallas, I had to scramble to fill my calendar in order to meet my obligations. Ambition has its own rewards and punishments. "Hubris" is the Greek term for the overweening pride that reaches too far. Like the Greek figure of mythology, I had flown too close to the sun and my wings melted.

At that moment no one could have made me believe that six years later I would be the pastor of the First Baptist Church of Dallas. How that happened is even more incredible to me.

Chapter Three

❧

The Search for a "Successor"

*I*t happened, he said, when a vision struck him in London—a vision of a co-pastor coming to join him in the work. The city that witnessed so many epochs of civilization seemed an appropriate place to launch the most epochal change at First in forty-four years.

Every summer for many years Dr. and Mrs. C. took an antique-buying trip to the British capitol. The owners of antique shops knew them by name up and down the cross streets around Picadilly Circus. As an experiment, I once went into an antique emporium in Regent's Street. The owner immediately recognized the Criswells when I called their name. Without question they both have an uncanny knack of identifying coming values in antiques. Just after World War II they began to acquire British nineteenth-century portraits when they could be had for the hundreds of dollars. W. A. must have told me ten times across twenty-one months that these paintings were now worth tens of thousands. I never knew what to say at these revelations of financial prescience. I usually mumbled a ministerial, "What a blessing."

On one of these pilgrimages to the antique mecca, God gave Criswell the vision of the future. Upon his return, he told the congregation of it—not on a Sunday, when most churches would have been given such a history-making announcement—but on Wednesday, when a few hundred of the faithful were there.

Not surprisingly, the vote to find a co-pastor was "unanimous." Every vote since 1944 had been unanimous, for one very good reason: Criswell never asked for an opposing vote. He would simply call for the vote, witness the show of hands, and declare by fiat, "That's all of us." Most folks thought the floor of the old sanctuary would fall through if anyone ever voted no. Observers noted, however, a growing number of abstentions over the recent years.

W. A. had thought about the succession for years. Senior deacons told me they had tapes of Criswell in his sixties, ruminating from the pulpit about his successor. He had often said in private conversation that he would never do what Dr. Truett had done, that is, stay until his seventies. Thus, on an August Wednesday when he was seventy-eight years old Criswell called on the church to get him a co-pastor. His statement contained themes from earlier conversations with me as well as more recent decisions.

Criswell told the church that they needed a co-pastor to prevent any "hiatus" in the church's ministry if he were disabled or died. When I read this statement in the weekly issue of the *Texas Baptist Standard* it conjured up memories of my conversations with Dr. C. five years before, when he attempted to install me in a similar position. At that time he waxed on and on that the church could not survive a long interim, a "parenthesis," a "lacuna," or his favorite word, "hiatus." He had speculated to me in 1984 that his sudden removal would result in an "exodus" of members to the suburban churches.

"By the thousands people have told me that they are only here until I am gone," he said. There was no question that W. A. Criswell considered himself the glue that held the thing together. Without his presence he thought it would fly apart like some vast machine unable to control its own centrifugal force. W. A. can spin a tale. As he related this to me in 1984, I pictured armies of people marching out of the old church four-abreast headed to the greener pastures of suburban churches in north Dallas.

Actually, that exodus was already happening. During Melzoni's tenure at First Baptist some two hundred families left First Baptist to join the burgeoning Prestonwood Baptist Church. First Baptist had hemorrhaged for years, losing powerful and gifted members to the suburban churches. Criswell and those around him may have fooled themselves that losing members such as Ken Cooper of aerobics fame, Dallas Mavericks owner Donald Carter, and a long list of other Dallas leaders did not hurt the church. It did and it does. I spent my twenty-one months meeting people who used to be members of First Baptist. At times it seemed to me that every other person in Dallas either had been, was, or might someday be a member of the church.

Whether or not Criswell actually thought he was the magnet keeping the thousands there I cannot know. We all fool ourselves in one way or another about our indispensability. Perhaps it was a needed rationalization to convince himself that he must hang on endlessly. When he made his Wednesday evening appeal for a co-pastor, he presented it to the congregation as the first consideration in his new vision.

Then Criswell dropped the bombshell. He had brought twenty-two Southern Baptist pastors before the church in the recently preceding years. He stated that the man he had in mind for the post and with whom he had talked informally about it was among that group, but he declined to name him. Criswell avowed that the man would be a "fundamentalist" because the church was that way. He stated that the man would be forty years or more younger than Criswell. His next statement was aimed directly at those in the congregation who had continued to tout my candidacy for the pulpit: the man he had in mind would not be from Texas or the Southwest.

ॐ

DUMPED

I REMEMBER THE CURIOUS FEELING I had in reading that statement on an August summer day. Criswell and I had not talked in several years. His last conversation with me before my hasty exit in 1984 had been a heartening encouragement that "the day will come." It was with a combination of detachment, shock, pain, and relief that I read his words.

I was up to my eyeballs at the Travis Avenue Baptist Church in Fort Worth. The church had thrived and now had eight thousand members. It was in my hometown, enjoyed about as much peace with its pastor as a big Baptist church can enjoy, and appeared to be a place to retire. We were on television locally and nationally. I was the "permanent" radio "Baptist Hour" preacher heard on five hundred stations every Sunday across the nation. I had served as president of the five-thousand-church Baptist General Convention of Texas, elected twice without opposition. I had more than I could ever say grace over. So when I read W. A.'s latest pronouncement, it was with a semi-detachment that bordered on amusement. It felt like hearing about the latest romantic involvement of a high-school girlfriend from years before—somewhat interesting but of no immediate personal concern.

Yet in another way I was shocked. Few people get to a big Baptist pulpit without a large dose of ego. My old friend Bill Lucas, the Tarrant County Baptist denominational executive for thirty years, had watched thousands of preachers come and go. Bill theorized that Baptist preachers have about as much ego as they need. They have to stand and claim to speak for God. Think about it. That is an audacious claim. Added to that is the constant criticism that belongs to every pastor in every church. One SBC guru vouchsafed that the most successful pastor in a Baptist church had 20 percent of the people after his hide at any one time, and that's in a good situation. If a man did not have some ego, he would simply collapse under the weight of the obligation and the criticism of dissatisfied members. I certainly have my share of ego. Whether I had more than I needed to survive pastoring is a judgment best left up to other observers.

I certainly had enough ego to feel stung when I read W. A.'s words intended to slam the door on my candidacy for the church. Although by then I knew enough about the internal lunacies of FBC, Inc., to keep me from lusting for the position, it was nevertheless a pain to be excluded. I had been told by others inside and outside the church for years that I was the man.

Without any question the church presents too great a temptation. It has a seductive power of its own that weaves a spell, even on someone who ought to know better. I should have.

Yet in the complex of emotions I felt when I read of my own exclusion, there was also a sense of great relief. Someone once wrote, "Whom the gods would curse, they call promising." With reference to Criswell and First, Dallas, I had for some years felt like the golfers must feel who are tagged as "the next Jack Nicklaus." That burden fell on Johnny Miller, Tom Weiskopf, and Tom Watson. They are living out their pro careers knowing of the constant gallery and press speculation that they were heirs to the Golden Bear. Every tournament, drive, and putt has been at one time or another under that kind of scrutiny. The burden affected their games and their lives.

I had spent five years under that kind of speculation from people at Travis Avenue, at the nearby gigantic Southwestern Seminary, at First Baptist, and among Baptists and onlookers generally. Although reflection on that may appear arrogant and effete, such constant speculation about one's future becomes a burden in the day-to-day work of ministry. "Will Joel go?" was a whispered word passed up and down the pews at Travis and among other Baptist observers. A feeling of relief settled over me when I read W. A.'s definition of the next pastor. The onus was off of me. I could settle down to a long and happy ministry in my hometown without the brooding worry of my next destination affecting me and my hearers. Detachment, shock, pain, and finally relief competed with the natural amphetamines and endorphins in my brain. The endorphins won and I settled down to a sense of security and stability where I was.

Criswell told the church that Wednesday night that he wanted things to move on. He is like that. He does not like to wait for an elevator. He will tell you to pick him up at 8:03 A.M., and he means it. He told the church that the search would be carried out by a committee to be named by the church's committee on committees. That was safe, since no one is added to a committee at First without the pastor's approval. He intended the committee to be composed of fifteen or more people representing every area of the church's life, noting that was the procedure in 1944, when he was called to succeed Truett. W. A. wanted the search done quickly. When Truett died in July he came in September: "The idea that it takes forever and ever to find a pastor is folly wide of the mark. We don't have to take forever." As he has habitually done, he was giving public instructions to people before they were even named or in a position to do what they were supposed to do. Since he already knew by the London vision who God had anointed, the committee would simply serve as functionaries to present that man to the church, iron out the details with the moving van, and find the new parson a Dallas house.

ॐ

THE AGENDA

THE NEXT CRISWELLIAN UTTERANCE implied more than it said. The committee would seek a co-pastor with whom he could work. "If they brought in a man who was not congenial with me and in rapport with me, I would have to quit." That statement really said it all. That I should have missed it when it sat there quivering on the page of the *Baptist Standard* in black-and-white, cold, inerrant print is astonishing. In the years after, I consider that I must have been like the man who stood by Niagara and asked, "Roar? What roar? I don't hear anything." W. A. put it right out there: he had no intention of getting off the scene. Whoever came would help prolong his tenure, not end it. The agenda had nothing to do with finding a new leader for a declining downtown church that desperately needed new leadership. The agenda was finding someone who could work with W. A.

To the nonBaptist reader this might not sound strange at all. Churches find preachers, priests, pastors, ministers, or whatever you call them by a variety of ways. In monarchical churches with a hierarchy of bishops a church might be assigned a preacher whether they want him or not. In synodical churches or presbyterial church government there are various kinds of collaboration between the local parish and the higher-ups. Most folks in those kinds of churches do not harbor a sense that they alone can name their next preacher. Methodists move them around about every two years, an exchange planned by their bishops along with ecclesiastical bureaucrats. Even a Methodist church may get stuck with someone imposed from an outside structure.

In a Baptist church, however, there is one carefully conserved pristine perquisite of the people in the pew—they get to choose the next preacher. However long or short the incumbent has held forth, when he is gone the choice of the preacher rests solely with the congregation. They elect a pulpit committee to their own tastes and send them out across the country to look for the next pastor. Even the smallest Baptist church jealously guards against interference at this point from the previous pastor. However beloved he may have been, he is to keep his cotton-pickin' hands off the process of choosing his successor. Baptists have a congenital fear of apostolic succession, hierarchies, lowerarchies, or any other kind of -archies. Every Baptist kid has it drilled into his earliest memory that a local Baptist church is "an autonomous body of baptized believers." That means when it's time to find the next preacher, nobody outside the church had better mess with the choice. Outsiders can send "letters of recommendation" and make discreet phone calls, but they had better not do too much of that or they will be dismissed as pressuring and interfering.

But this prospect of interference is especially onerous if it comes from the previous preacher. In my observation, most churches are in a love/hate relationship with a long-term pastor. He has baptized their kids, married their young adults, buried their grandparents, and visited them in the hospital before heart surgery. Many of the members have eaten with him, traveled with him, and gone to endless "fellowships" with him. He is part of the landscape of life. On the other hand, they have put up with his own peccadilloes for decades. He has told them every Sunday what they ought to do, pulled off some pastoral power plays, forgotten some key occasion in their life, or neglected to visit aunt Millie when she contracted terminal ingrown toenail. He has, in short, both blessed them and bothered them. He has shown them, warts and all, that he is what every preacher is, a human being among human beings who claims to have God's call on his life.

In my observation, most churches are in a love/hate relationship with a long-term pastor.

However much they love him, there is one thing they are not about to let him do—choose the next man who does the same thing he did.

In his announcement, Criswell contradicted that tradition for First Baptist, Dallas. He had outlasted his opposition, asserted his will, and intended to name the co-pastor. Without question a good portion of the congregation rejoiced in that prospect. Over the decades most of the people who did not like his style simply left. Yet at this one point there were thousands of members—and as he would find out, a paralyzing minority of his own hand-picked pulpit committee—who would not go along with him. Criswell concluded his remarks on Wednesday, August 24, by prescribing the very process the church would use to call the new co-pastor. The co-pastor would not be asked to preach for the congregation before their vote, the normal Baptist custom. "We won't have a preacher race," he said. "The committee will just bring a recommendation." That the new pastor would have no exposure to the church before they decided whether to call him flew in the face of all Southern Baptist practice. Criswell further indicated that the new man would become the pastor of the church should W. A. retire or die, if the church wanted him. That sent a mixed signal to the congregation. The man would come as a co-pastor. When Criswell died the church could keep him or not. Obviously he would have an inside track. But at the same time the move set up a potential disaster: a divided congregation over the succession. I doubt that was uppermost in W. A.'s mind at the time. He wanted help. He wanted someone to extend his ministry to the fifty-year mark or beyond.

Criswell indicated that the "reason" for recommending the co-pastor was the load of preaching, pastoral, and administrative responsibility. He continued: "Another thing that is obvious is that I am seventy-eight years old. Before the year is out I will begin my eightieth year. It is obvious that the church ought to bring in a man who could work with me and be with me instead of waiting until I die or have a stroke or a heart attack that disables me and the church enters into a hiatus. Instead of doing that, let's call a man now and let him come in and get acquainted and then whatever happens to me we will carry right on—only better."

Anyone who swallowed that last line—that Criswell really thought someone would do better—is a candidate for some ocean-front property in Arizona, to quote a country ballad. Criswell ended his remarks with a characteristic line of humor and carefully crafted self-deprecation: "I still preach as loud as ever. All you have to do to hear me preach is open the window of your house toward the church on Sunday morning."

It was homespun, Will Rogers-style quotes like this that endeared Criswell to his people. Every occasion would end with a genial bonhomie regardless of the bombshell he had dropped on them. To this day I confess a begrudging admiration for his ability thus to handle people. He is irresistible.

As an undergraduate at Baylor I was assigned to a church at Purdue University in West Lafayette, Indiana, for a brief engagement. My host was a professor at Purdue, Dr. Wallace Denton. He was a member of the national executive board of the Southern Baptist Convention. Denton was obviously a left-winger whose every instinct in the late sixties was to despise what Criswell embodied. He had written a scathing letter about Criswell's right-wing denominational activities and intended to confront the board with it in Nashville. Before that time, however, he met Criswell. After five minutes with the Great One he trashed the letter and was eating out of his hand. Incidents like this abound. Those qualities helped Criswell do what he did in the pastoral change.

Following this announcement, word sounded forth across the Baptist Zion. The greatest question among Baptist preachers—who would follow Criswell—would soon be answered. The faxes whined their mating calls. The phones buzzed. The letters flew. Everyone recognized the Great Unspoken Designation. The mantle would be placed on Dr. O. S. Hawkins, pastor of First Baptist Church, Fort Lauderdale, Florida. He was the man of Criswell's vision, an affable, friendly "people person" whose interpersonal skills and pastoral dynamics had propelled him to the front rank of the new wave of young fundamentalist leaders.

Ironically, Hawkins also is a native of Fort Worth, Texas. O. S. grew up on the east side of Fort Worth in an enthusiastic, down-home congregation, the Sagamore Hill Baptist Church. O. S. had done well in two Oklahoma churches before the summons to the Florida coast. There he revived the old downtown, beachfront church. He was distinguished not only as a churchman but as a civic leader as well. At his side was a lovely and charming wife, devoted children, and a blue-blooded Baptist heritage. Beyond argument O. S. was a strong candidate with the credentials, personality, and general streetwise savvy to follow Criswell. I doubt that Hawkins had any more or less ambition for the job than the rest of us. Although he and I were often seen as rivals, I considered him an able man with an excellent track record and fully able to take on the job. In fact, O. S. got caught in a twenty-seven-month-long meat grinder.

༄

THE BEST-LAID PLANS

EISENHOWER ONCE WAILED that appointing Earl Warren to the Supreme Court was the worst decision of his life. Criswell may have later felt that way about his committee on committees.

One nonBaptist once quipped to me, "Only a Baptist church would have a 'committee on committees.'" Someone defined a committee as a group of people who individually could do nothing and collectively could decide nothing could be done. Criswell actually had no tolerance for committees. He bellowed from platforms across America, "Show me a committee-run church and I will show you a dead church." Such sentiments caused more suspicious members to wonder why he wanted a pastor search committee at all.

What actually happened in the selection of the pastor search committee rests beyond my ken. Since I was the outcome of their twenty-seven months of deliberations, they hardly told me of their untoward origins. Hallway gossip at First Baptist had it that a novice convert chaired the committee on committees. It was evidently thought he would do the Criswell bidding without turning to the right or the left. Somewhere in the process the pastor search committee wound up with twenty-two members.

I can only imagine the arcane, Byzantine political trade-offs that resulted in the committee selected. One thing is certain— there was a minority on the committee strong as horseradish who had absolutely no intention that W. A. name the next preacher. Some of them had waited a lifetime for this moment. They intended a total change in the church's direction and wanted nothing to do with a Criswell-installed successor. They did not oppose O. S. on his own merits; they were unalterably opposed to him from the beginning because he was "Criswell's man." They rightly assumed that the committee charade had nothing to do with choosing a successor and ending W. A.'s reign at the church. The whole thing was only so much holy smoke. The real agenda was to find someone convivial to Dr. C.

and most particularly to Mrs. C., so they could both stay in the saddle.

The chairman of the committee was Dick Clement. A short, stocky white-headed man with a florid face, Clement had come to the church two decades before from the East Grand Baptist Church in east Dallas. He had joined the ranks of ardent Criswell supporters and heartily embraced the theology that the pastor rules the church. He had served as the deacon chairman and most other chairs of power in the fellowship. A real estate man, he had endured the depredations of the slump while maintaining an active real estate group in the city. I later found him to be a man of compassion, honesty, and impeccable attention to detail. I did not have a better friend at First Baptist than Dick. He was really done no favor by being installed as chair of the soon-to-be deadlocked committee.

The vice-chairman of the committee was Ralph Pulley, a Dallas lawyer and long-time lay leader in state and national denominational affairs. Ralph is Mr. First Baptist. More than any other man, he seemed to embody the spirit and love for the church. He knew every story behind every building, every battle, and every victory. He was above all publicly identified as second-to-none in his lifetime loyalty to W. A. Criswell. In every setting of the church life, formal and informal, Ralph honored the office and person of the pastor. Like E. F. Hutton, when Ralph Pulley spoke, the entire church listened. This had also placed him against the opposing agenda forwarded by Criswell's detractors.

The secretary of the committee was a young lawyer named Kenneth Stohner. Ken was a graduate of Baylor and Baylor Law. His father was a long-time Baptist preacher in New Mexico. An

invariably intense and serious man, Ken took the burden of the
pastoral selection as personally as anyone on the committee. We
shared a similar background at Baylor, as well as awareness of life
in the ministry—he as a pastor's son and I with two sons in the
same role. With an impressive office atop the NCNB building in
the gigantic Jackson and Walker law firm, he specialized in
issues related to petroleum law. From the start of the process he
had a definite opinion that I should be the next pastor. But it is
a byword among pastors that the person who most supports you
on the search committee may at the end not do so. Sadly, this
was the case.

The other committee members presented a cross section of
the church's membership. Dr. Charles McLaughlin was actually
on the staff of the church as an associate pastor. A revered figure
in the Texas Baptist denomination, he was one of the few
denominational bureaucrats who had remained with Criswell.
After retiring from denominational executive service, he had
joined Criswell at the latter's plea. A long series of administrators had been eaten alive by First Baptist's insoluble problems.
"Dr. Charlie" was called in to rescue the situation several years
before my coming. A tall, erect beanpole of a man, he sported
an impressive head of snow-white hair. Shot down in World
War II, a prisoner of war, he had returned to a four-decade career
as a Baptist denominational executive. He loved Criswell, but
also knew the Old Man's clay feet. McLaughlin was as smooth
an operator as I ever saw in a Baptist church. Pastoral, kindly,
personable, and affable, he could be a velvet-covered brick when
needed.

It is unusual to have a staff member of a Baptist church on the
pastor search committee, because in a sense they are hiring their

own boss. However, Charlie was held in such esteem by everyone, including the candidates, that no one much worried about a conflict of interest. He turned out to be an unflagging help to me, although I expect he knew what would happen.

My closest friend on the committee was the late Dr. Carlos McLeod. He was the director for evangelism for 2.2 million Texas Baptists in five thousand churches. As such, he was among the most beloved figures in Texas Baptist life. He and I had been friends since early in my ministry. Carlos really wanted me to be his pastor, although he respected Criswell enough to listen to all sides of the debate. During the twenty-seven months of the search, Carlos would often give me an insight into the internal workings of the committee. He was careful, as he should have been, not to break any confidences. He did let me know in general terms how the search was going.

There were a number of old-line, long-time members on the committee. Mrs. H. L. (Ruth Ray) Hunt was named to the committee. A genuinely pious and devout septuagenarian, she had poured her fortune into the church for years, giving entire downtown buildings to First Baptist. Most recently, she had led the Hunt Foundation to give the Criswell College $3.5 million as a matching gift in order to move the school to a new campus. An unassuming and quiet woman, she virtually kept open house for the church at "Mt. Vernon," the estate of H. L. Hunt overlooking White Rock Lake. I found her to have a natural intuition into Criswell and a compassionate understanding of my impossible situation in the church.

Curtis Baker was another committee member with a high interest in the Criswell College. An oil explorer with other business interests, he was a wealthy man who lived in East Texas.

He had helped Criswell troubleshoot many projects and was a brilliant, persistent analyst of the college and the church. Jim Bolton, a Dallas entrepreneur, had served as chairman of the deacons. Jim had been a trustee at Southwestern Seminary and Baylor University. He was constantly concerned with liberalism in the denomination and had served as a stalking horse for the conservative political-theological concerns of Criswell and Paige Patterson. Patsy Wallace further represented a high interest in the Criswell College on the search committee. She and her husband Bob were heirs of a Dallas wholesale plumbing fortune and occupied a palatial mansion in Highland Park. A genteel lady of Southern charm, Patsy was a gifted interior decorator who had "done the college" with impeccable taste. After I came, she decorated my office. As much as anyone, Patsy embodied the tension of divided loyalties between a beloved senior pastor and the man who was supposed to take his place. She obviously adored Criswell, but wanted to be loyal to me. As it did with others, Criswell's unwillingness to get off the scene left her walking an uncomfortable tightrope of loyalties.

Carolyn Wicker represented a family whose roots in the church preceded Criswell. She also felt more support for the denomination and less for the insurgent fundamentalists led by Criswell and Patterson. She helped to balance out such members as Bolton and Pulley who were warriors in the fundamentalist battle. Her presence on the committee represented the delicate balance of people and issues sitting in the pews of First Baptist.

There were several on the committee who appeared to be there because they spoke for several age groups or special interests in the church. Marian Ashwill worked with younger married people. Lee Roy Tredway chaired the personnel committee and was a Criswell loyalist. Leon Howard had a perpetual, public concern that the church be more evangelistic. Doris Greene was the wife of the current deacon chairman and a member of the always powerful sanctuary choir and orchestra.

Among the younger members of the church, John Thomas began the committee process as a representative of the single adults, but married before the committee brought its report two-and-one-half years later. Scott Wilpitz must have been placed on the committee because of his overwhelming concern that the church was not prayerful enough. During my entire tenure Scott fretted that the church was not spending enough time in prayer. Mark Goode, a young deacon, was another representative from both the musical program of the church as well as their work with teenagers. A member of the well-known Goode-Taylor Pontiac family, Mark seemed to spend as much time working for the church as for the dealership.

The most impressive younger leader of the church was Mark Lovvorn. A banker and real estate investor, his late father had been a church leader for years. Handsome, articulate, and steeped in the traditions of the church for his entire lifetime, he brought to the committee a firm conviction that I should be the next pastor. Although he respected Criswell as his pastor for the three decades of his life, he had an independent judgment about the committee's work.

The loyal opposition on the committee was represented by Ed Drake and Ed Yates, the "two Eds." It was no secret that these two men wanted W. A. out and someone else in the saddle. Both were attorneys. Drake had a prestigious practice and had been pastored during his childhood by George Truett. I had the feeling that Criswell had never replaced Truett in Ed's heart.

Yates ran the famous Highland Park Cafeteria with several Dallas locations. They belonged to a shadow parliament of deacons who constantly looked for ways to thwart the Old Man and bring in new leadership. Drake was ice-cold toward me during the process and after I came. Yates unexpectedly became a good friend and confidant.

The committee originally had two more members. One of them, a novice convert, became so disillusioned with the highly politicized process that he stomped out of the committee meeting, declaring that he was "abandoning First Baptist and organized Christianity." Another member also resigned in disgust over the antics and manipulations on and of the committee.

These people lived with a heavy burden of destiny. They were the elected ones who would search the country and name the next pastor of the nation's most powerful Protestant church. Thousands in the church would have gladly taken their place. To make a mistake in their decision could leave the church in a vulnerable decline. To succeed would gratify them to no end in the present and cast a warm afterglow of achievement on the remainder of their lives. The stakes were high. Most of them, even the powerful and wealthy, would consider it the most significant achievement of their lifetime.

THE SEARCH BEGINS

IT WAS INTENDED that the anointed twenty-two would make the pilgrimage to Fort Lauderdale, announce the vision to Dr. Hawkins, and bring him back in a triumphant entrance to Big D. Considering what happened over the next four years, that might have been a good idea. To quote wee Bobby Burns again, "The best lay'd plans of mice and men often gang agly."

The actual minutes of the pastor search committee are confidential documents. Somewhere in the archives of First Baptist, or possibly in a deacon's law firm safe, they sit unopened until some remote date, when we are all off the scene. There were not too many secrets, however, about the committee. It leaked like a baptistery in a West Texas country church. What the committee did in their weekly meeting was reported via the Baptist grapevine on the East Coast the next day. In exasperation some of them thought their room was being bugged (it may have been).

Instead of the desired, immediate proclamation of a new co-pastor, they would take twenty-seven months screening pastors in sixteen states. They would travel millions of miles, spend hundreds of thousands of dollars, and at the end of it drive to Fort Worth and ask a lad from Cowtown to make the thirty-mile trip to Big D. God must have a sense of humor.

It became apparent early that the committee had some disinclined members who had no intention of installing the Criswells' choice. This had little to do with Dr. Hawkins's ability to do the job. The immediate deadlock of the committee also reflected a desire on the part of some that W. A. get off the scene altogether, the usual order of business when a Baptist church finds its next preacher.

I took the whole thing with a great deal of detachment until someone sent me the Sunday, October 8, 1988, edition of the *Houston Chronicle*. There was a screaming headline which read, "Fiery Dallas pastor ready to train protégé." Among other things, that was an interesting public perception of what was happening. The Great White Father would bring in a wet-behind-the-ears novice and train him for the Baptist papacy. The article continued:

"Speculation focuses on two young Baptist pastors—one a Floridian, the other a Texan.

"The Rev. O. S. Hawkins, pastor of First Baptist Church of Fort Lauderdale, Florida, and a former president of the Southern Baptist Convention's Pastors Conference said: 'All I can tell you is I'm pastor of First Baptist Church, Fort Lauderdale, and that's where I think I'm supposed to be.'

"The Rev. Dr. Joel Gregory, pastor of Travis Avenue Baptist Church in Fort Worth and president of the Baptist General Convention of Texas, could not be reached for comment."

Indeed not. I avoided press scrutiny about the subject by refusing to answer any call even remotely related to it. That was not noble; it was an act of self-preservation. I had led the Travis Avenue Baptist Church into a seven-million-dollar debt on the basis of my intention to take them into the next century. We were about to raise the money. Any whisper of departure could maim the program, create church-wide anxiety, and undermine what I was doing where I was.

The paper continued: "The twenty-two-member search committee of First Baptist, Dallas, spends its weekends visiting prospects, then meets once a week and reports regularly to Criswell. Some say they've narrowed the field to a handful of finalists. Criswell had hoped the committee would announce a co-pastor today."

The article then quoted North Texas State University religion scholar Joe Barnhart: "Criswell is going to be watching him, and making certain he's going to be as much in his image as possible. That almost never happens in a Baptist church.

Most Baptist churches would not put up with it because Baptists traditionally don't think the next pastor is the preacher's decision. It's the church's."

That a Houston paper would give a two-page story to the matter, accompanied by a three-column wide, ten-column-inch long color picture of W. A. in full pulpit declamation, demonstrated the Texas-size interest in the whole ordeal. It was slightly amusing to me that I would be mentioned. The committee had already been told, "Go to Florida." I had already been excluded in the very first announcement on the matter two months before.

About that time I did an incredibly childish thing that demonstrates the enormous attraction of First Baptist despite my own schizoid ambivalence about going there. While in downtown Dallas for other reasons, I went to the church complex. I made my way up the stairs of the Criswell building to his office. He was not in so I left a copy of my business card with a note scrawled on the back: "Dear Dr. C., whatever happened to me?" I thought that a cute couplet of poetry might take the edge off an altogether inappropriate question, an intrusion that today makes me cringe with the thought of it. It would take Freud and Jung to untangle why I would make such a sniveling, pusillanimous inquiry. Why did I care that he had cast the mantle on a Florida pastor? Did I want an explanation? An apology?

He shot back a letter. It was the usually unctuous, gushy prose of a Criswell missive. The upshot was that he had wished things had worked out in 1984, but things change. The letter was clearly dismissive in tone. I was stung by the note, ingratiating though it was. With the reception of that note I turned my attention toward Travis Avenue and deliberately attempted to shut it out of my mind.

For months I would catch straws in the wind that the committee was still considering a potpourri of aspiring candidates, including yours truly. Dr. Paige Patterson, associate pastor of First and president of the Criswell College, professed great insight into the machinations of the committee and avowed that he had been asked to give them a "short list." He assured me that I was in the "top five." Since it was widely believed that Patterson wanted the job himself, I took that with a grain of ministerial salt. I just wanted it all to go away. Like Poe's *Tell Tale Heart*, however, the thing just kept beating under the floor boards, and I couldn't get the thump out of my head.

&

THE FIRST MEETING

THUS I WAS SURPRISED to receive a sudden call from the committee. They phoned to ask the privilege of visiting Travis Avenue to hear me, followed by a luncheon at the place of my choice. They would attend a Sunday morning service and audition my sermon. Would I please accommodate them?

Well, of course I would. To turn them down would be arrogant. Thumbing your nose at FBC Dallas would be an act on the level of Charles Colson's turning down a full scholarship to Harvard because no one had ever done so. It would at least be a slice of history to meet and eat with the chosen ones.

Actually, they did not have to come to Fort Worth at all. I was on television and radio Sunday morning, on radio Sunday evening, and on the ACTS Network (the Southern Baptist TV network) several times a week. But for the same reason football fans will endure a blizzard to sit in the stadium when they could

93

be watching in front of a toasty fire at home, pulpit committees like to see the game itself. They just get a "feel for things" by visiting a prospective preacher's home turf. They can watch whether the congregants sit in mesmerized wonder at the latest word from the pulpit, or whether choir members are falling out of their chairs in a somnambulistic stupor.

The visit of a pulpit committee, however, can stir up the ire and suspicion of members in the invaded congregation. If they like their preacher, they emphatically do not want anyone coming to town in an attempt to woo him away. If they do not like the preacher, they secretly pray that the committee will call him on the spot. At either extreme, the visit of a pulpit committee occasions comment in most churches. The members of FBC, Inc., were widely enough known that they would be spotted at Travis immediately. Indeed, every time they visited, a wave of gossip swept over the church. I would get visits, letters, and remonstrations that I had "promised to stay." Travis Avenue had not lost a preacher to another church since the 1920s. That a pastor would leave Travis Avenue to go to another church just was not thought to be a way things were done.

Some folks at Travis would have been gratified to see me hit the road. In the Southern Baptist denominational war, I had, to the horror of some of them, fallen down on the right side of the aisle, with the fundamentalists. This raised the hackles of virtually every seminary professor in the church. I had a steady stream of letters, calls, and visits from the seminary crowd and their lay groupies admonishing me that I was too cozy with the fundamentalists for their liking. The appearance of the FBC pulpit committee only confirmed their darkest suspicions that behind my mild-mannered facade there lurked a screaming fundamentalist.

Dr. Joel Gregory, the author, standing in front of First Baptist Church, Dallas. (Photo by Richard Michael Pruitt, *Dallas Morning News*)

Baptist life abounds with jokes about pulpit committees. One pastor had so angered his congregation that they were thrilled when a committee showed up to hear their embattled parson. In the providence of God they invited him to become the pastor of another church. He accepted their call. In the final sermon to his alienated former pastorate, he took a pious parting shot: "Jesus called me here and Jesus has led me away." The minister of music then asked the congregation to stand and join in singing, "What a Friend We Have in Jesus."

It is also customary that a pulpit committee will join the prospective pastor for a noon meal following church. Travis Avenue had given me a membership at the Fort Worth Club, the century-old private club presided over by Amon Carter and other Fort Worth notables. In anticipation of their visit, I arranged a private room for the after-church lunch. I figured folks from a sophisticated church like First would appreciate the dowager among Fort Worth clubs.

Like a lady agonizing over what dress to wear to a special event, a preacher agonizes over what to preach when a committee shows up. The temptation is to pull out a "sugar stick" (the trade lingo for a red-hot sermon, the best in the preacher's barrel). Most committees are wise to this, so they like to ambush a preacher and hear his typical Sunday effort cooked from scratch that week. Committees correctly suspect that every preacher has one or two dynamite sermons anomalously better than anything else in his quiver. They would rather hear the typical discourse that their congregation would receive weekly, just in case anyone held them

Like a lady agonizing over what dress to wear to a special event, a preacher agonizes over what to preach when a committee shows up.

responsible for foisting a terminal bore on the church that deputized them to find a new preacher. That was no problem with
me. I was in a long series from the Psalms, announced weeks in
advance. It would have appeared odd to everyone to depart
therefrom with some special pulpit pyrotechnics to impress the
folks from the east.

They came; that is, part of them came. So large was the committee that they visited in platoons. By sending a third of them
to three venues each they could cover more ground. Since they
professed interest in hearing up to seventy preachers in sixteen
states, such a division of labor appeared wise. They entered
Travis and dispersed themselves among the congregation, as if
they were innocuous visitors who just happened in. I saw them,
though. No member of the Audubon Society searching for a rare
bird is keener-eyed than a visited preacher surveying the congregation for a pulpit committee.

On Sunday morning the sanctuary choir and orchestra—
nearly two hundred strong—rattled the rafters with triumphant
praise music. Visitors to the church would literally sit with open
mouths at the resonant strength of the choral and instrumental
music filling the massive, Corinthian-columned sanctuary.
There is no more impressive worship place in the South or
Southwest than the imposing auditorium at Travis. Without any
question, all of this is a mighty help to a preacher when he is
under consideration. When it comes to consideration by a committee, it is better to be a sparrow roosting in an eagle's nest
rather than an eagle roosting in a sparrow's nest.

The music before one preaches sets a mood, an expectancy,
and by the time I walked to the pulpit, the congregation at Travis
was almost always in a great mood. My sermon that day was a

rather pedestrian effort, certainly no spellbinder. It was a typical craftsman's work of a busy city pastor. When I invited would-be converts to "walk the aisle," enough did so to constitute a vote of confidence in a large Baptist church. During the benedictory prayer, I scooted toward the towering vestibule to greet the guests and shake hands with the members. As soon as it was seemly, I hurried to the car and the drive to the Fort Worth Club. On arriving I found the contingency of the pulpit committee already seated in the private dinner room on the twelfth floor.

Unbeknownst to me, where so many oil deals had been struck over the decades, a big Baptist deal was about to begin. You would not have guessed that from the luncheon. While we were served, we engaged in the strained small talk that typifies such settings. We all knew what the meeting was about, and that the southern protocol required chitchat throughout lunch. You did not get down to business until coffee was served.

The conversation followed a very familiar format to one who had talked with Southern Baptist pulpit committees scores of times. In that regard I was far more a veteran than the folks across the table. No one at First Baptist had been on a pulpit committee for forty-four years. I had talked with dozens. They asked me to rehearse when I was "saved," "called to preach," and what kinds of churches I had served. They wanted to know the kind of interest I had in different age groups in the church. Did I support missions and evangelism? What size budget did Travis have? How many staff members? What did I think about the inerrancy controversy in the denomination? Did I believe the Bible was inerrant? How would I feel about the Criswell College and the First Baptist Academy, a K-12 school? I answered these expected questions in a low-key, direct manner.

What I did not do was ask them the question: What is W. A. Criswell going to do? Does he have a definite date of retirement when he will get the gold watch, have the farewell dinner, and ride off into the ministerial sunset? No question was more pertinent and obvious. Compared to that issue everything else we discussed was idle talk. Yet it stuck in my throat. It was the great unsayable.

At about three o'clock in the afternoon we parted. The meeting left one, distinct impression: Some of them had a real interest in me and others were obviously going through the motions to appease the ones who did. That could not have been more obvious if they had worn name tags labeled "Hmmm" and "Forget It." The talk had obviously been preliminary, superficial, and inconclusive. I rightly discerned that it was a required agenda to accommodate some members who wanted to talk with me, a kind of due process before doing what Dr. C. actually wanted to do.

Following this meeting, the committee simply disappeared for many months. I heard nothing from them. This behavior was rather rare for a Baptist pulpit committee; they usually do not leave you in the dark for months after a visit. But this was not the usual committee.

❧

GRIDLOCK

I HEARD NOTHING OFFICIAL from the committee. Unofficially, news about the committee was no harder to find than a Cowboy fan at Texas Stadium. My good friend Carlos McLeod gave me just enough indirect insight to keep me in context. While he could not in good conscience tell me verbatim what the members were saying, he insinuated enough that I knew the committee was developing terminal gridlock.

Mark Lovvorn and Ken Stohner also provided interim insights. On more than one occasion at their initiative we joined for lunch. The two young men wanted me to be their pastor. In the committee meetings they stated just that. They would call me, eat with me, and otherwise encourage me not to give up on the situation. They implied that the committee was under great pressure to go elsewhere, having uproarious meetings and Herculean confrontations, and that I should sit tight. The remainder of the committee was not aware of these meetings, to my knowledge. This sort of sub rosa contact with a candidate is normally out of bounds, but others on the committee were actively courting several candidates of their own. I suppose that turnabout was fair play.

Dr. Paige Patterson was another source of inside information. From time to time when we were thrown together, the talk would invariably turn to "the search." Paige generally expressed his sympathy for anyone coming into the situation. Again he would say, "I've picked up too many bodies on San Jacinto Street" and generally question the sanity of anyone with aspirations to go to First Baptist. (As it turned out, he was dead right.) A master politician who would make LBJ look like a candy striper, Paige played his cards close to the vest. He always told me the truth, but not always all of it. He recognized that any one of several among us might wind up as the head honcho and thus his boss.

After months of official absence and silence, I suddenly and without explanation received another call from the committee.

Could a contingency of them come for a second visit? By this time I had reason to be somewhat guarded in my response. With less enthusiasm I accepted their proposal to attend church and then meet me at the Fort Worth Club for lunch with another squad of the committee. There had been a sharp reaction from some members at Travis to their first visit. High-stakes financial issues, such as a seven-million-dollar bond program, were underway at Travis. Anything that upset the equilibrium of the situation threatened projects involving thousands of members. At this stage I felt as if I were a second-string high school football player being visited by a major college coach who really had no interest in me.

They came, I preached, and we ate. It was obvious that these new searchers were there for a perfunctory visit. Their questions were shorter and their manner nonchalant, to be charitable. One officer continued looking at his watch in a conspicuous, and to me, irritating way. It was scarcely disguised that they were there on a secondary mission and the real interest rested elsewhere.

At this point one could well ask why I continued to be a shill. Even members of the committee had privately confided in me that the entire process was manipulated. Why did I continue to be a pea in the shell game? Even now, from the perspective of four years later, I cannot answer that question.

According to our idealized version of our calling, ministers are perceived to be men of God, humble servants willing to go where sent. The chance to hold forth in the nation's strongest and most influential Protestant church should not raise a single covetous desire on the part of a candidate. The opportunity for a worldwide influence that might last for centuries should be discounted as an inferior blip on life's screen, to be dismissed in a fit of Christian humility.

But ministerial ambition is a slippery thing. The seductive power of the nation's super church traps you in a jarring collision of the ideal and the actual. On the one hand there is a desire to be God's humble servant, wherever. On the other hand there is the stark recognition that no other venue presents an opportunity to maximize personal gifts and influence in the same way. For those complex reasons I allowed myself to be demeaned by the obvious charade that was underway. It was a hand that had to be played out and I could not fold. "Why climb Everest?" Sir Edmund Hillary was asked. "Because it is there," he replied. So was First Baptist.

The seductive power of the nation's super church traps you in a jarring collision of the ideal and the actual.

The reason may be more mundane and pedestrian. In the middle years most men recognize they will either take a final risk or remain at the level of achievement they have obtained. Some men graciously accept the lot life has cast while others must throw the dice once more. By any reasonable interpretation I should have been satisfied where I was. It was a huge church in my own hometown with great love for its pastor and a strong future for any possible tenure I could reach. Thousands of brethren would have traded places with me at Travis. Yet for some reason, an attraction as mysterious as gravity pulled with a seductive power. In no other context have I ever suffered fools or allowed myself to be degraded. Yet in this instance, like Ulysses tied to the mast, I listened to the siren song. Unlike Ulysses, I steered my craft right into the rocks.

The more pious may ask, "Does it not all depend upon the will of God?" As long as I can remember I have heard people speak of finding and doing the will of God. It is a Baptist obsession, an evangelical way of life. "What is God's will?" I frankly have witnessed so many inanities, absurdities, and even injustices attributed to the divine will that I speak of it only with reluctance. I never belonged to the school that seems able to peer over the divine shoulder and thus discover the will of God. The actual term "finding the will of God" does not even appear in the New Testament. If you follow Paul around in the Acts of the Apostles he seems to be the victim of circumstances and chalk them up to providence. It gave him a cheerful and charitable view of life that whatever happened God would work it out for his purposes. Paul seemed to see the will of God in life's rearview mirror rather that its periscope. Where God's will fit into my experience with the First Baptist Church of Dallas belongs to a higher venue than presently available. I have yet to learn how God's will directed my days at First Baptist, although I believe such illumination will someday come my way.

Following that second visit, the committee turned its attention elsewhere. Reportedly gridlocked between the Criswells' desire for O. S. Hawkins and the steely determination by some committee members to block the Old Man, the committee shifted its focus to Dr. James Merritt, a rising star in the Atlanta suburb of Snellville, pastor of its First Baptist Church. Under his pastoral leadership the church had exploded, with a strong emphasis on evangelism. Merritt held the doctor of philosophy degree from the Southern Baptist Theological Seminary in Louisville, Kentucky, the same degree earned by Criswell at the same alma mater. Commanding in the pulpit, immaculately tailored, and thoroughly committed to the fundamentalist cause, Merritt presented a formidable presence to the committee. Ed Yates and Ed Drake, the two Dallas attorneys on the committee, formed an unyielding alliance on behalf of Merritt.

Standing with them was one of First's few remaining world-famous members, Zig Ziglar. Although not on the committee, Zig carried a big stick. These stalwarts believed Merritt was God's man for the hour.

Weary of the gridlock, other committee members began to feel the same way. At some point in the negotiations young Merritt was brought to Dallas for a delicate meeting with the Criswells. A member of the committee told me that Merritt was scarcely inside the house when Betty Criswell slammed him with a question: Why did he have the temerity to think he could follow her husband? It was the Baptist equivalent of visiting Buckingham Palace and being asked by Elizabeth II why one felt he should be the next occupant.

Now, James Merritt is nobody's fool. It did not take him long to size up the situation. He demanded to know the specific time and circumstances of W. A. Criswell's full and total retirement. That was the most manly, obvious, and significant thing he could have asked. He saw through the holy haze with sharp vision. That question, however, enraged the Criswell partisans on the committee. That anyone would dare have the gall to ask the most necessary and significant question was interpreted as an unforgivable slap at the Criswells' dignity and an offense violating their very persons.

Although the specifics are locked in the annals of the committee, Merritt ended the courtship. He wrote a rather cheeky letter to the effect that he felt he was God's man for the post, but this was not God's time. Added to his earlier unforgivable indiscretion of asking the obviously pertinent question, this further forthright statement pushed him over the edge. Being obvious and up front is not a favored strategy when dealing with First Baptist. In ministerial terms he told them to "go fly a kite." I admire his candor and should have emulated it.

ⱨ

A SURPRISE LETTER; AN APPARENT END

SOMEWHERE IN THE FUZZY CHRONOLOGY before or after the Merritt ordeal, I was surprised to receive a letter at my residence:

Dr. and Mrs. Joel Gregory
2124 Pembroke
Fort Worth, Texas 76110

Dear wonderful friends:

How very, very pleased we are that you are willing to fellowship with our Search Committee on Monday, November 27, at the Radisson Suite Hotel-Arlington, 700 East Avenue H, telephone number, 817/640-0440. Many of our committee will be able to come as early as 4:30 P.M. at which time I requested you to be present. We plan to have dinner at 6:00 P.M. and shall certainly be sympathetic with the necessity of Linda's leaving in time to make her engagement at 7:30 P.M.

Both of you know our church, and I feel that both of you love our church. We earnestly solicit your prayers for our committee and the important decision which is ours to make. We know that we shall be blessed by our visit with you and look forward to this experience.

Gratefully yours,
Charles P. McLaughlin

This letter accompanied a telephone call to the same effect. If a carrier pigeon had dropped a misplaced communiqué from World War I on our porch we could not have been more surprised. Here it was, sixteen months into the process, and we were asked to meet with the entire committee for a plenary session halfway between Fort Worth and Dallas. By this time two members had quit the committee, one leaving the church and declaring that he was abandoning organized Christianity altogether, so disgusted was he with the whole intrigue. The leadership of the sixteen-million-member Southern Baptist Convention had followed the escapade with a mixture of awe and amusement. The speculation over who had the upper hand—Hawkins, Gregory, or Merritt—had almost reached the book makers on the Las Vegas strip.

With a renewed anticipation we eagerly attended the meeting. Seated around a horseshoe of tables, we discussed for hours the questions facing the downtown church. How would I lead the staff? How would I pay the multi-million-dollar debt recently acquired with no notion of how to pay it? Would I support the Criswell College? Would I lead the church into a new era of evangelism? Would I support the denominational cooperative program? (This came from a distinct minority on the committee. First was not famous for shipping money off to headquarters.) Would I support the church's thirty ethnic missions spread all over Dallas and start more of the same? How would I break up the huge, personality-centered Sunday school classes into smaller tactical units? (This question led to a rather rancorous debate among the committee members themselves about the merit of such classes. First Baptist literally had two competing adult Sunday schools.)

In short, I was asked how I would continue Criswell's existing programs and at the same time solve problems he had not addressed in years. The church was such a whirling vortex of insoluble problems that there was little conversation about my own distinctive vision for the future.

The committee by this time in the meeting was friendly, animated, and engaging. They had been through battles, sifted through candidates, and were under increasing pressure to get on with it. The evening ended with a genial feeling of momentum toward something.

Then they simply disappeared. Nothing happened. No decision was made. Finally a member confided to me that their votes were hopelessly deadlocked. It was a real possibility that Criswell or the church would dismiss them.

It was to me 1984 all over again. By this time I had been to the lip of the cup with First Baptist twice. I wanted nothing else to do with it. It had become distracting, demeaning, and even threatening to the work I was doing at Travis in Fort Worth. I was finally pleased to put it out of mind.

It would have been well had it stayed there.

Chapter Four

∾

The Clash Between Divine Will and Human Ambition

*M*y confusing, back-and-forth relationship with First Baptist caused me to think often on a subject pastors tend to mull anyway: Why do human beings fall into repetitive, nonproductive conduct? It's an old question, at least as old as the second transgression after Adam and Eve took the bite. The first bite led to such a catastrophe one would think the human race had learned its lesson. Then, when Cain rose up and slew his brother Abel, an obvious perversity had entered the human psyche, bloodstream, or environment.

That tendency to bang our heads again and again on the wall, refusing to learn from past experience, permeates every life, family, decade, and civilization. The rare person learns from past mistakes. Most of us go on our way like Sisyphus, pushing the rock up the hill until it rolls back upon us.

Religion seeks to understand the mystery of human behavior with a variety of explanations. Hindus see our misery as a law of karma, a reincarnation in our present life which pays the bill for the previous life. Confucius interpreted the human predicament as an inability to learn from history, which is certainly true as far as it goes. The insurgent faith of Islam understands all life as a direct expression of Allah's will. The caricature has it that a Muslim walking down the sidewalk was beaned on the head by a flower pot falling from a second floor window. His response was to praise Allah. In the Islamic world every happening is a direct expression of providence.

The Bible sometimes emphasizes divine determinism and sometimes human freedom. Augustine, Calvin, and their followers emphasize the inscrutable will of Almighty God. Pelagius, Armenius, and most modern Christians come down on the side of human free will: We make our own messes.

The above is not a digression. It underscores the mystery of human behavior, which includes the small sub-mystery of why I got further involved with W. A. Criswell and FBC, Big D. I really should have known better.

After the sum total of experiences with FBC, Inc., in the 1980s, one would think I might have avoided further involvement. Yet there was still something that propelled me into the process. Divine will, human ambition, the momentum of history, the manipulation of a situation, or manifest destiny might all be in the mix. Why did I do it? I could not tell you to this day. A second bite of the apple was not enough for me. I had to have a second, then a third...

ॐ

A MANDATE

BY THE END OF 1989, events frustrated W. A. Criswell to the boiling point. His hand-picked committee had in his estimate dawdled away seventeen months. He took his crusade to the pulpit, basically giving the pastor search committee a tongue-lashing from the pulpit in front of the assembled congregation and, through the press, much of the denomination. His tirade was about as un-Baptistic a statement of polity as was ever uttered from a Baptist pulpit.

On January 7, 1990, W. A. Criswell gave his annual "state of the church" sermon. It was more a comment on his own state of mind. He set an Easter deadline for the search committee to find a co-pastor. In one of the more curious examples of pulpit exegesis, he cited numerous instances in which biblical figures had appointed or anointed their own successors. Jacob, Criswell said, gave his birthright to Joseph and his blessing to Judah. Moses appointed Joshua to take command. Samuel poured anointing oil on a surprised young David. Elijah placed his mantle on Elisha. Peter chose John Mark. Paul indicated that the young Timothy would help him.

Roared the agitated W. A., "There is no exception to that in the word of God...these men chose their successors. And my word to the search committee is this: Listen to the word of the Lord. Follow the example of these men of God." By this everyone listening knew what Criswell meant: Go get the man I want. It had been in January 1986, that he revealed his prayers for a younger man to come serve beside him. The committee had been at work since October 4, 1988.

At no time in his forty-five years at the church had Criswell so sought to manipulate a process without result. His frustration was volcanic. Even for him it was an extraordinary act to put the committee on notice before the church that elected them. He even dared to set a deadline: "The time has come when an ultimate decision must be made. It must be made soon. It must be made by Easter. I am now eighty years of age. I would like to be called senior pastor. I would love for him to be designated as pastor. And we'll work together, pray together, serve God together, build this lighthouse for Christ together."

One can only imagine the cringing committee members being berated in front of the assembled congregation. Most of them would have known the story about Criswell once being late for a wedding because he could not open the newly installed automatic garage door at the Swiss Avenue mansion. The solution? He put his car into reverse and bashed the door off its hinges. A man who does that has little patience with deadlocked committees. No one had the temerity, I suppose, to point out that Moses and Elijah may possibly have been sui generis in history, constituting a class of their own. After all, in the New Testament the former two stood on the mountain of transfiguration with Jesus.

At least it clarified the league in which W. A. saw himself: Moses, Elijah, and Criswell.

The upshot of Criswell's statement was to reverse theoretically centuries of church government in the Baptist tradition. Baptists have always rejected the Roman Catholic and Anglican traditions of apostolic succession. In those communions it is of paramount importance that there be an unbroken line of succession in which one bishop anoints the next. This can be traced, in their polity, back to Christ Himself through the Apostle Peter. Without questioning who is right and wrong in the matter of church government, it is undisputed historical fact that heroic Baptists were martyred for their opposition to the very plan Criswell now endorsed. As a brilliant student of history with a photographic memory Criswell knew this himself. He should also have known that it was questionable biblical exegesis to rely on nonbiblical traditions, for example, that Peter chose Mark to follow him. This explosion only indicates the frustration that motivated Criswell. He knew better than he said.

Another major change in this address was indicated by his preference for the title senior pastor. The committee was charged to find a co-pastor. Now Criswell changed the charge from the pulpit. The church would call a "pastor." He would remain "senior pastor." In American church terminology that meant one and only one thing: W. A. Criswell was still in charge. The senior pastor in any church is the leader. By that very statement on January 7, 1990, Criswell ultimately guaranteed the failure of anyone who attempted to follow him. Deep into my second year at the church Dallasites would still ask me, "How long have you been Dr. Criswell's assistant?" I found out firsthand that Criswell wanted just such ambiguity. When it came to authority, he still wanted it all. When it came to responsibility, this Teflon titan wanted me to have it all.

After my resignation, indignant Criswellites accused me of proud ambition. They caricatured me as a grasping young man who could not wait to take charge. Why couldn't I let the Old Man keep his title as senior pastor for fifty years or until he died? But titles had nothing to do with it. For all I cared he could be called High Pope, Head Honcho, or Big Kahuna. The unvarnished fact is that no one can lead the First Baptist Church of Dallas effectively while there is ambiguity about who is really pastor. As long as Criswell kept that title, ambiguity would vitiate the church. By the time I resigned members were constantly preoccupied with figuring out just who was actually leading the congregation. And keep in mind that First Baptist is not just a church. It is a huge business concern with crushing debts, enormous property management, a then-five-million-dollar personnel budget, and incredibly complex problems.

A bemused if not startled Dick Clements, chair of the committee, told the press that Easter "was not a deadline as such" and expressed doubts that the committee would reach a decision by that date. Clements indicated that Criswell simply wanted the church to move ahead. Clements further stated that he did not take seriously Criswell's right to choose his successor.[3]

Still, Criswell's explosion called for something to happen. In the Baptist tradition, you can at least have a prayer meeting. Thus a "call to prayer" was issued for Wednesday, January 31, 1990, for the hours 7:00 P.M. to 12:00 midnight. The program for the evening informed the congregation of the agenda:

"Welcome to the 'call to prayer' extended by Dr. Criswell and the co-pastor search committee. The search committee and the pastor earnestly desire that our entire church family join together in this focused and extended time of prayer to empty ourselves before God and to know and do his divine and perfect will for our church. Your presence and participation reflect your belief in God's faithfulness to respond to the fervent prayers of his people and to reveal to both our church and to his anointed man the person he desires to become co-pastor of our church.

"Following our Wednesday evening service which will be focused on prayer, we will join together in a time of prayer from 8:00 P.M. to midnight. The members of the search committee will be situated in different locations throughout the auditorium. A placard will be placed by each mem-

---

[3] Ken Camp, "Criswell Challenges Search Committee," Baptist Standard (January 17, 1990): 4

ber to facilitate your locating the members. Throughout the prayer time, you are encouraged to move to the individual members of the search committee and vocalize a prayer by their side for them and the work of the committee. After completing your prayer, you may move to another member of the committee or you may simply move back to a place at which you continue to pray silently to the Lord.

"At the beginning of each hour, there will be a period during which we will sing together and a member of the search committee will share a brief testimony. At 11:00 P.M., the entire search committee will gather at the altar and each member will offer a public prayer. Our prayer time will then be concluded with closing remarks and prayer by our pastor. You are free to leave at any time you desire: however, it is hoped that as many of our church family as possible will be able to stay and pray and worship during the entire period. May God visit upon us an unusual outpouring and anointing of his Holy Spirit."

Perspective makes all the difference in perception. The kingfisher bird has two kinds of vision, one for above the water as it hunts for prey and another for under the water when it dives. My reaction to this prayer meeting depends on which vision I bring. On the one hand it was a moving time for a beleaguered group of church members trying to find a pastor for the nation's most powerful Protestant church. I was told that some committee members wept openly as church members poured out their hearts to God. For thousands of people this decision had more personal significance than any national election. Generations of their families had sat in the same sanctuary. Their babies were dedicated, their children baptized, their couples married, and their parents buried in the historic room where they now prayed. It mattered very deeply to thousands of members that God's will be found in the matter of the next pastor.

Seen another way, a pathetic charade was going on. Both before and after the genuine prayers of common people in the pew the committee had a loaded agenda. The reason for their delay was a resistance to constant pressure that they do what they had been told to do. What was arguably the most powerful single local church congregation in the twentieth century limped under institutional paralysis because of this double agenda. The terminally weird and inexplicably bizarre incongruity is that everyone in the active membership not in a catatonic state knew what was going on. So great is the will to believe that people can practice a collective denial in such matters that would never mark their individual lives. In a zombielike way thousands of people went through the motions of this arabesque. It is frightening the utter trust and suspension of belief that people will render to powerful religious leaders. This prayer meeting embodied the ironic clash of genuine devotion and human manipulation that is First Baptist. To understand this admixture is to understand the human soul. Indeed, angel and ape we are.

I was sent a copy of the prayer agenda in the mail with a note from Kenneth Stohner, Jr., the secretary of the search committee:

"Pursuant to our telephone conversation, enclosed please find a copy of the prayer guide distributed at our prayer meeting on January 31, 1990. I believe the prayer meeting was used by God and hopefully will be the beginning of a new attitude and practice of prayer by our church. May

God continue to bless and direct you in your ministry and this search process."

The letter with the enclosed statement on the call-to-prayer left me with no particular impression at the time. I had other fish to fry at Travis. To me it was another item in a dreary parade that had become personally draining to watch.

About this time the pastors of the largest Baptist churches held their annual "mega-metro meeting." To qualify for this annual club meeting your church had to have two thousand people in average Sunday school attendance and a budget of at least two million dollars. For years there had been a "metro meeting" including less-big Baptist churches. The really big boys, however, had problems and challenges they deemed more peculiar than their brothers in lesser churches with only a thousand souls showing up. Also, the "mega-metro" pastors belonged virtually to a man to the fundamentalist wing of the denomination. During the Baptist civil war of the eighties this made for some explosive meetings at the old "metro" conference. The two conferences split with the biggest churches having an annual shindig at some resort while the left-wing group of smaller churches did their own thing, mostly grumbling about the predatory fundamentalists who had taken over the SBC. I have heard a rumor that there is now underway a "super-mega-metro meeting" of pastors from churches with four thousand in attendance. (In less reverent moods I now ponder a future "superbly-super-mightier-mega-metro meeting" of pastors with churches having ten thousand in attendance. The Lord knows, we may run out of adjectives before we run out of thousands.)

These all-day sessions featured the tenured leaders of the nation's largest nonCatholic denomination giving mentoring

advice to the "young Turks," men in their thirties already building huge congregations. Men such as Adrian Rogers of the
gigantic Bellvue Baptist in Memphis and Edwin Young of the
colossal Second Baptist in Houston are logistical geniuses of
church growth. I could sit with mouth agape for hours as they
gave their philosophy for building a big church. Although I was
one of the stronger pulpiteers in the group, I had no such administrative genius for building a huge congregation. I took notes
furiously at these meetings and later tried to apply them.
Compared with the big boys, though, I just limped along.
Quality preaching is only the minimal ticket for admission to
the club of big-time church builders. The personal qualities
needed in time and people management, financial resources,
plant construction, media ministry, and a score of similar apti-
tudes belong to a very few men. They build the super churches.

For two years the hallway gossip of the thirty or so at this
exclusive clerical coffee klatch centered on the search at First
Baptist. Although to a man everyone in the room denied it, I
expect every man in the room would have gone to First Baptist
if called, even the most tenured and powerful. O. S. Hawkins,
James Merritt, and I took no end of good-natured kidding about
the ups and downs of such involvement. O. S. and I spoke
together about our relative roles in the search several times,
both of us averring that we had no interest in such a place.

During a break time in the mega metro conference we joshed
with one another about the extended search process, both of us
in a self-deprecatory mood. O. S. suggested that we draw aside
and share a word of prayer that God's will be done in the matter.
As subsequent events unfolded, that prayer may have been
answered. O. S. has admitted to me in private conversation that
his way has been made easier because of the bumps I absorbed in

my fast ride at FBC. The older members of the group—Rogers, Young, John Bisagno of First, Houston—told us individually and collectively that we were out of our minds for even considering the situation. We all had better churches where we were, they said. Adrian Rogers even commented, "I could not succeed there myself under the circumstances" (meaning the continued presence of W. A. and Betty Criswell).

The Germans have a word—schadenfreude—that denotes a joy at the misfortune of others. One of the sad notes about ministry is the relish with which some practice schadenfreude. Even in anticipation, a few brethren lick their chops at your possible future undoing. What this has to do with following the crucified one I cannot discern. Like I say, it's a few brethren that smile at another's misfortune, although in my case, most were supportive as far as I knew.

~

ANOTHER FLIRTATION

Just when I thought it was over, it was not. I had not heard from the search committee in months. Then a call came out of the blue: the committee wanted a copy of my academic transcripts, church balance sheet, and a short-form personal financial statement. In twenty-five years of dealing with Baptist pulpit committees I thought I had seen it all, but this took the cake. No one in recorded history had been asked for these documents by a pastor search committee. The committee well knew that I was a graduate of Baylor, summa cum laude, and had earned a doctor of philosophy degree from the same institution. The materials on Travis were available from Baptist headquarters. My credit rating could have been obtained by any member from the reporting agencies.

On March 27, 1990, I received a formal letter from the committee over Stohner's signature giving me the actual addresses to write for the transcripts and the desired format for the church and personal financial statements. I was assured that the entire committee would not see my personal financial statement, only the four-man executive committee of the search committee. Given the national leakage of information from the weekly meetings of the group, that was cold comfort.

The same request had been made of O. S. Hawkins. who was also amazed that the committee would ask such a thing at this point in the process. By this time we were both equally jaded by the ongoing public gyrations of the committee that had made both of us the butt of national, denominational jests. At a subsequent post-presidential election bash during the Southern Baptist Convention we were actually lampooned in a good-natured skit. Hawkins indicated that he had no intention of sending the requested materials.

Perhaps emotional investment in something creates its own momentum. For a now implausible reason I consented to the request. I felt indignant and degraded in doing so. The search committee by this time had a literal book on each major candidate. This request was as demeaning as asking the president of a university to produce his high school diploma immediately before his inauguration. Clearly something else was going on other than a desire for information.

This insulting request may have come from one part of the committee desiring to harass the other. Or, having run out of anything else to do, perhaps they were simply killing time. Or, perhaps some thought they would frustrate one of us into a flat rejection of such a gratuitous request not called for by any traditional circumstances and thus end our candidacy. One member of the committee privately told me it was simple harassment.

If I did not want to send the materials, why did I do so? The explanation rests in the schizoid attraction/repulsion that characterized my relationship with the church from the first. When Eve looked at the apple she could scarcely have felt more ambivalence than did I in dealing with FBC. So I took another bite. They got their transcripts and balance sheets in April 1990.

Following that, they again disappeared without explanation for nearly eight months. Informal leaks suggested a terminal case of deadlock. For one more time I resigned myself. It seemed that the months of mental turmoil, vocational uncertainty, and disturbance at Travis Avenue because of First's flirtations were all for naught.

The Baptist grapevine being what it is, I began to feel increased pressure from inside Travis to disavow publicly any further dealings with First Baptist. One member in Travis, Rev. Bill Swank, sent me a letter which typified the feelings of many. Bill had been an official with the Tarrant County Baptist organization and a long time observer of the Dallas/ Fort Worth church scene. He wrote:

April 6, 1990

Dear Joel,

There are fresh rumors that the committee of First Baptist Church of Dallas has determined that they will actively seek to call you to the 'co-pastor' position of their church. I of course have no way of knowing this is so, but the Baptist grapevine is usually pretty reliable. You will recall we discussed this a couple of weeks ago when we had lunch together. At that time I believe I heard you to say that you were not a candidate for the position, and that you could not see yourself as being interested should you become a candidate. However, things change rapidly, and I don't know what your current thinking might be.

If what I hear is true I want to pledge my prayers to you as you seek God's will for your life, and for the life of the churches involved. While praying that God's perfect will be done I don't mind telling you that at this point it is very difficult for me to believe that He would have you leave Travis. So much of the growth at Travis during the past five years is still very much tied directly to your personal ministry, and would be very hard to sustain without you. The church's debt was incurred in order that the church's growth could be accommodated. For you to even consider leaving at this critical time would cause many church members to feel that you deserted them. I fear that the results for Travis would be tragic.

I also fear for your own ministry should you go to First Baptist Church under the present conditions. I know all about what is said concerning Criswell's plans to run the school, and to turn major responsibilities over to the co-pastor. I would remind you, however, that such plans have been advanced before, but James Bryant, Jimmy Draper, Tom Melzoni and a long list of others have found out that such plans simply do not come to pass if they begin to reduce the power and prestige of W. A. Criswell.

I heard Criswell interviewed on a Sunday morning program on KRLD two Sunday's ago. He stated that the plan was for the co-pastor to preach the early Sunday morning service, the Sunday evening service, etc., but that he, Criswell, would always preach the 11:00 A.M. worship service. This, of course, is the service that is televised. I know that he is now eighty years old, but until he dies or is forced into complete retirement I can see the position of co-pastor being a dead-end job that may never result in you becoming "senior" pastor. I believe that the only way that you, or any other pastor, should accept an invitation from the First Baptist Church is on the condition that Dr. Criswell announce his complete retirement from the pulpit ministry before you announce your acceptance as pastor. It is quite possible that my concern is completely unfounded. I think, however, that I can say truthfully that until the whole issue of the First Baptist Church position is settled it is going to have a negative effect on Travis Avenue. The concern is not limited to people such as myself who have access to large amounts of information from a wide variety of sources. I hear the concern expressed by the average laymen in our church who cannot help but be aware of First Baptist's search. The very uncertainty of the situation could become a detrimental factor in many respects of our church life—including the proposed bond issue.

If, as I believe, the committee does make a serious offer, I hope that you will make a very quick decision—and stick to it. If you come to the conclusion that it is not God's will for you to go I hope that you will make a public announcement to that effect. On the other hand, should you choose to go nothing would be gained by either church by delay.

Again, I apologize if I am speaking out of turn. I did want you to know, however, of my deep feelings for both you personally and for the Travis Avenue Baptist Church. I have a complete confidence that you will seek and do God's will. I just thought that, should the need for a decision on your part arise, it might be helpful to know that one of your church members is praying with you about the matter.

Sincerely,
Bill Swank

This letter typified scores of such approaches verbally and in writing from people in the context of Travis Avenue. In hindsight many of them had an uncanny insight into what awaited me. There is no question that the prolonged, intermittent forays of the search committee had a paralyzing effect on the good people of Travis Avenue. I felt that keenly and lived with it daily in both major and minor decisions of a church with eight thousand members. I faced inquisitive looks at the Rotary Club and the gym where I exercised, in the neighborhood where I walked my bulldog, and not the least from my own family who wondered where we would be next year.

Yet it would have been a precipitous act of arrogance to turn down publicly a position I had never been offered. The folks of First Baptist could readily tell the press that they had never offered me anything. I would look ridiculous on all fronts. So I simply kept my own counsel and ignored all requests to do otherwise.

The summer of 1990 distracted me from any such considerations. I began the summer by speaking for a week to two thousand lay people gathered at a Baptist camp in New Mexico. My wife and I flew to France for a vacation at a favorite chateau/hotel south of Dijon in the Cote d'Ore. While there I visited the famous Cistercian monastery at Citeaux, the mother monastery of the Cistercian and Trappist traditions of silence. I would sit for hours and listen to the plain-song chant of the monks who lived and worked in silence. While sitting on the grounds of the chateau outside Nuit St. George amidst the vineyards of the Burgundy region, I read Father Henry Nouen's *Genesee Diary*. Nouen was a professor at Yale who submitted himself to months of silence at a Trappist monastery. The words leaped off his pages and grabbed me by the throat. They spoke of the emptiness of a merely busy life, the sea of words in which modernity drowns us, and the need for long periods of recreating silence. I felt that my life had become a mile wide and an inch deep. Those days in central France were the last such time I would have before the changes that undid my very life. It was an intersection. I could have taken the road less traveled.

After returning to Texas, I was obligated to speak to the Baptist World Alliance in Seoul, Korea. The BWA is the worldwide organization of Baptist bodies that meets in a loosely fraternal setting. I was scheduled to bring an address to the plenary session meeting in the basketball arena at the site of the Olympic Games. Because of numerous out-of-town engagements, I felt I could not take any more Sundays away from Travis. I flew directly to Seoul on Monday, spoke on Wednesday, and flew back to Texas the next day. I had never felt wearier of life or ministry. The pressure of big-time religion had maxed out. Perhaps the lay reader will not understand this. Clerical experts agree that constant ambiguous demands fall on all pastors, those with large churches and those with small. There is no way to measure whether or not a pastor has done his duty. There is always one more sick person to visit, one more in need of pastoral counsel, one more call to make, one more prospect to visit, or one more hour to spend improving the sermon. I had an added burden. By the consent of some people I was a "great" preacher. I did not and do not say that. I am not able to listen to myself on tape, radio, or television. My sermons always seemed banally predictable to me. But the opinion of others concerning my "great" preaching put me under unyielding, relentless pressure. I could never let people down, in my own estimation. Psychologists speak of CEOs who suffer from "encore anxiety," a feeling that every year must be better than the next. That is why so many CEOs check out.

Not long after returning from Korea, I kept a speaking engagement in Boston at a national denominational meeting on reaching the urban areas. Southern Baptists were strategizing on how best to reach the northern Irish Catholic stronghold and similar urban sites. I walked around Boston Common in a detached frame of mind, wondering what kind of role I should have in Baptist life. At the same time, the national law school fair met in a nearby exhibition building. I spent hours talking to the representatives of major and minor law schools. After purchasing a kit on learning to take the LSAT, I began to consider a radical change in direction altogether. As the jet rolled out at Boston's Logan International, I was taking sample LSAT tests. After twenty-five years in ministry, three degrees, six churches, and thousands of sermons, I was on the brink of chunking it to be a lawyer. That whole Twilight Zone episode (it didn't last much past getting back to Texas) suggests to me the toll that ministry in general and the stress of prolonged uncertainty about the future had taken on my own psyche.

∾

ONE MORE TIME

ALL OF THAT suddenly evaporated when the folks from First showed up again. This time the feelers came from Dr. Carlos McLeod, who had befriended me in the late seventies when he pastored a prominent First Baptist Church in the Texas Panhandle. A personable, warm, perpetually enthusiastic man who came from roots in rural Texas poverty, by faithfulness to his calling and boundless energy he had become the favorite leader of 2.2 million Texas Baptists. He moved from the Panhandle church to Dallas as an executive with the denomination in the influential post of evangelism director. Carlos covered Texas like a blanket, ubiquitous in his presence. His bright smile, constant positive demeanor, and remarkable gift for encouragement lifted the drooping spirits of many a beleaguered Texas pastor. Some denominational officials have their positions because they like power; Carlos held his because he loved people and everyone knew it.

The church elected Carlos as the denominational representative on the search committee. Even before his election to the committee he expressed to me his dream that I become pastor of the church. Carlos admired W. A., but also had a realistic view of the shenanigans in the church and on the search committee. Throughout the search process he stayed in touch, characterizing the goings-on generally while honoring the confidentiality of the committee.

Dismayed by the deadlock of the committee and expecting their imminent dismissal by Criswell and the church, Carlos called me in the autumn of 1990. He asked that we meet for lunch half-way between Fort Worth and Dallas at the Atchafalaya Cajun restaurant near Arlington Stadium where the Texas Rangers played ball. Eating our blackened redfish, we discussed the future of First Baptist. Carlos felt the committee must make some decision or dissolve. He proposed to me that he move the committee to give sole consideration to my becoming pastor. Given their imminent dissolution, there was nothing to be lost. By this stage I met such a proposal with a curious sense of detachment, but I told Carlos that would be fine. I wondered what they would actually do after twenty-seven months of a futile process in which I had been repeatedly dismissed.

Carlos went off on his mission. Then things suddenly changed. On Wednesday, November 14, Dick Clements, the chairman of the committee, called me. He reported that for the first time in twenty-seven months their committee had voted unanimously by secret ballot to give sole consideration to me. This, he said, had come out of a spirit-sent time of revival on the committee. God had come down and brought them to an experience unlike any they enjoyed across their extended task. The committee as a whole considered it an act of God that eighteen of them would so agree. He jokingly related that they had not even been able to agree on when to meet. In fact, the committee had met in some raucous sessions in which some of the men had almost come to physical blows. One member confided to me that had some of their meetings been in a non-church context he would have flat decked one of the other committee members. I suppose in that Christian context a unanimous vote had a certain refreshing quality.

I was so astonished at this that I did not give him an immediate answer. Along the tortuous trail of twists and turns relating to First Baptist since 1984, I had no real basis to believe this was anything more than another mirage. I asked Clements for a day's time to consider the request. After the desultory series of meaningless meetings lasting twenty-seven months, I had no desire to sit through another one.

The next day I called Clements to ask for a face-to-face meeting with Dr. W. A. Criswell, alone in his office, to find out what he really wanted. He wanted another man to have the job. After all, they were asking me to move in down the hall from him and work out a relationship more delicate than doing brain surgery on a high wire with the wind blowing. We also arranged a meeting with the deacon officers of the church and the chairs of various significant committees. In addition, I requested that my wife and I have a private meeting with Dr. and Mrs. Criswell to discuss our relative roles should anything develop.

But any meeting in Criswell's office always posed a question: Which office? You see, W. A. Criswell maintains four offices. The east wing of his Swiss Avenue mansion provides a spacious resort where he spends his mornings studying while wearing his robe and pajamas. The shelves accommodate thousands of volumes. Antiques and oil paintings complement the room which connects by a hallway filled with more antiques to the house proper. The church added this to his parsonage early in his ministry. He decided to stay home to study in the mornings, going downtown at midday. On the second floor of the Criswell building at the church he maintained a pastoral office. Modest in size, it consisted of an outer waiting room and his inner sanctum. Criswell used this office from 4:00 to 6:00 P.M. for appointments with church members. The walls of the room were hung with credentials, diplomas, and recognitions. It was also furnished with antiques, prints, and oils.

At the Criswell College in the newly acquired Gaston Avenue property he had a third office. More impressive than the other two, it was sumptuously furnished with appointments of exquisite taste. As a centerpiece of the office was a desk given to Criswell by an attorney in the church and reputed to have been used by Napoleon himself. Even the statuary in the office was worth a small fortune. It was estimated by the irritated faculty of the Criswell College that his office cost $250,000 with furnishings, but Criswell never used this office. To my knowledge he never sat at the desk during my tenure as pastor. The college office had been prepared to appease the Hunt family who insisted that he move to the college in exchange for their $3.5-million gift to buy the college location.

Criswell's fourth office was on the thirty-second floor of the Lincoln Properties high-rise building across the street from First Baptist. This was his "business office" shared with Jack Pogue, Criswell's alter ego and chief financial advisor. This was the most impressive office of them all. Western bronzes, huge European oils, priceless ceramic paintings, and rare china adorned the ornate office. As in the Swiss Avenue mansion, rococo does not begin to be an adequate description. During my tenure as pastor, some visitors to this office were openly outraged at the excess. I declined to tell those folks that this was one office of four.

It was in this fourth office that a meeting with W. A. Criswell was arranged the week of Wednesday, November 14, 1990. Criswell and I had held no private, face-to-face conversation since the inauspicious end to my 1984 stint at the church. I was ushered into the office where Criswell sat behind a rather delicately ornate desk in front of a window with a view of north Dallas. We both knew this was high stakes conversation, that the outcome of it would be formidable for the church, for him, and for me.

After pleasantries, he recounted his version of events over the last few years. He wanted a younger man to become pastor. The committee had taken unconscionably long in doing its work. He just could not understand why they had taken so long. As he dilated on that subject, I sat in dumb-struck wonderment. Did he have no idea that it was his own manipulation of the committee that had paralyzed the process? From the moment he first had his "vision" in London, through the attempt to hand-pick the selection committee, in his pulpit coercion of the committee to let him chose his own successor, and in countless private conversations with the committee members, he had made himself clear. I would find over the next two years that talking with Criswell was often to enter a fairy-tale land in which reality was whatever he felt at the moment. In that sense he is a pure existentialist who would make Sartre and Camus look like idealistic Platonists. Reality is the reality of that moment.

I asked him just what kind of relationship he had in mind with me as "pastor" and him as "senior pastor." He painted the picture of a transition time during which he would do "less and less" and I would do "more and more." In order to "keep things going" he would preach at the 10:50 A.M. televised service and I would preach the earlier 8:15 A.M. service, the 7:00 P.M. evening service and the Wednesday evening service. Then he made a crucially ambiguous comment about time. This would all go on for "a few months just to keep things going." He would devote "more and more time" to the Criswell College in light of his promise to the Hunt family that he would become the "CEO" of the college. The church would be "mine" and he would simply stand by to help.

By any honest, forthright, manly understanding of language he stated in no uncertain terms that he would be off the scene at the church within a "few months." There was no written record of this conversation, no stenographer or court reporter preparing a verbatim account. It did not occur to me that I would need one, that I would be totally misled. It did occur to me that he might have some difficulty letting go, but not that he would make a covenant he had no intention of keeping. In truth, however, it would have made no difference whether I had a written document or not. We could have chiseled an agreement on the wall of the church, but unless he willingly left the scene it would have created an uproar. The arrangement itself could only work if W. A. Criswell by his own free volition kept his promise to me

Recently, the rock star Madonna was a guest on David Letterman's CBS show. He never had a night like it. She simply refused to leave the guest's chair. Sitting in the chair and smoking a cigar, she blew smoke in his face and refused to leave. Letterman did not make her go and neither did anyone else. She was making the statement that she was so big she could do whatever she wanted, and she knew it would only make them look bad to evict her from her chair. I had a strange sense of déjà vu in watching her performance.

The time came to ask The Question. With more deliberative calmness than I would have thought I could have summoned, I looked W. A. in the eye and stated, "You wanted another man.

What has happened?" With a grandiose, dismissive gesture and in full vibrato he replied "No, no, no." He then gave his interpretation of the last six years. In 1984 he had wanted me, but "circumstances" intervened (meaning the church's refusal to let him name me to the post). He had then turned in other directions. Since the church could not have my services in the pulpit, he thought he should look for a "people person who would encourage the people." Then in a mighty self-revelation he intoned, "It was you I wanted all the time."

Some pop psychologist observed that there is an "adult" and a "child" in all of us. At that moment I wanted to believe Criswell. I had admired his pulpit prowess and leadership skills since my teenage years. His combination of biblical conservatism, historical grasp, and persuasive pathos had been my primary model. I looked past him at the high-rise buildings looming around the thirty-second floor of the Lincoln tower. Nestled beneath them rested the five city blocks of the First Baptist Church, Dallas. Before me sat its pastor of forty-six years. Behind us both was the legacy of George W. Truett. Around us was the opulence of downtown Dallas. Above us was a God who I hoped had something to do with all of this. Waiting for us was the search committee. I said, "Yes."

∽

PREAMBLE TO THE PRESENTATION

MORE MEETINGS BECKONED. I had not met the current lay leadership of the congregation. The deacon officers wield enormous power at FBC, Inc. Outside Criswell's thirty-second floor office awaited a conference room overlooking the Trinity Valley and the western metroplex. The pastor search committee officers and the principal lay leaders of the church met me around that table. Eugene Green was the avuncular chairman of the deacons. He was thirteen years old when W. A. Criswell became his pastor. He had seen the whole five decades with W. A. Like so many long-tenured members, for Eugene, Criswell was Mt. Everest. He was so much a part of the landscape of life there was no imagining life without him. Eugene headed up a Dallas printing empire and was the incarnation of an upfront, outspoken, go-for-it Big D businessman. His wife had been on the search committee.

Around that table I met Bo Sexton for the first time. He was vice-chairman of the board and would succeed Eugene as chairman. Bo was currently serving as chairman of the board of trustees at the Criswell College. Unknown to me he was in an all-out war with President Paige Patterson. I would not learn that until my first week as pastor. Trim and athletic, Bo projected a sense of take-charge confidence combined with a respect for the church and what it represented.

Kenneth Stohner was secretary of the deacon body as well as secretary of the search committee. The young lawyer had veritably lived for this day. From the beginning he desired to have me as his pastor. Now we sat at a table in a final conversation with church leadership before the public presentation of a new pastor. Ken must have felt it was the end of a long road. Other leaders gathered around the table were representative of the church's vigorous and varied empire.

During the conversations with the search committee I had discovered that the church had a large debt with no specific plan to repay it. First Baptist had matched the Hunts' contribution to buy the Gaston property for relocating the Criswell College. But they had done more than that. Beyond the initial 3.5 million dollars, the church had spent another two million in the refurbishing of the old classical revival Gaston Avenue property. Given its location, it was a gardenia in a garbage can. The church had attempted an abortive fund-raising program in which the people by the thousands had voted "NO" with their pocket books.

In addition to that five million, some months earlier Criswell and Pogue had engineered the purchase of the 511 building, so called because it bore the address 511 Ervay. An unattractive high-rise, its bottom floor had housed a popular yuppie bar. When Criswell pushed the deacons to buy the building from the Criswell Foundation for the church, he met hot resistance in one of the more raucous deacons' meetings in his tenure. He had bellowed to the assembled deacons that if the church did not want it they could stay there and die; the Foundation would keep it and make money. After his polemic the deacons hunkered down and bought the building. But the imposition of this additional debt for an unwanted building in the midst of a capital campaign to pay for the new college site outraged hundreds of members. The church owed about another million dollars for the high-rise. It would also cost $150,000 per floor to make it usable for church purposes. Unless there was an explosion of growth unlike anything in the last three decades the church had no conceivable need for the building. I spent my tenure as pastor defending what I knew was an indefensible purchase out of loyalty to W. A. and Jack. The other church buildings were disintegrating. They had overwhelming deferred maintenance problems. They could not even raise the money to pay for the Criswell College. Now they had a million-dollar white elephant.

If that were not enough, there was another million dollars due at an unknown time. Shortly before contacting me, the church had bought a million-dollar warehouse from a local wheeler-dealer who subsequently bellied-up in federal court on a fancy check-kiting scheme. When we paid for his building depended upon when the federal courts untangled the web of his scheme. We could have in fact bought the building for much less had the church simply waited for a federal auction, but in an impetuous moment they had signed the note. This housed the "Dallas Life Foundation," a five-hundred-bed night shelter for the hungry and homeless of Dallas.

To me that was a legitimate investment for a huge, wealthy church. W. A. always professed a soft spot in his heart for the homeless. He often recalled going down to the church one morning early in his tenure. A crowd of people had gathered at one of the entrances. After Criswell pushed his way through the crowd, he found a man dead, having expired in the act of reaching out for the doors of the church. Since that time he desired to have a place for the homeless.

Criswell's dream took place in time for me to figure out how to pay for it. Lest that sound as if I took the debt too personally, permit me to explain the situation of past incurred debt and the present installed pastor at a Baptist church. When a church gets into financial trouble, they do not hunt up the finance committee from years of yore or the former pastor (or in this instance the senior pastor). They put the whole thing squarely at the feet of the present pastor as if he had forged the check without benefit of lay approval. The church may not do this immediately, but they will do it ultimately. I knew going in that I would live with the six-million-dollar-plus debt W. A. had run up before I got there.

During my twenty-one months, to my astonishment, W. A. spoke of the debt as if some horde of Visigoths had overrun the church and signed the notes while he bravely fought to stave them off!

The lay leaders around the table put the best construction on this fiscal mess. Not one of them would have run his own business affairs in that way. Yet collectively they had permitted Criswell to run up a debt that would choke the church program with no known plan to pay the debt. They were brim full of optimism that the new pastor would lead the church into halcyon days financially. Had the new pastor been permitted to be the pastor that might have been so.

The months ahead would be one astonishing discovery after another of the financial disaster into which I had walked. The men at the table told me as much as they knew at the time. At my first deacons' meeting I would discover that the church had overspent its 1990 operating budget by one million dollars and had borrowed from restricted designated funds to pay its current bills. The church already had three committees to oversee its money. There was a budget control committee, a finance committee that looked after investments, and a special deacons' committee that oversaw the endowed funds of the church. Yet these three committees together did not know for sure what the church owed. A fourth special committee to discover the debt was chaired by a young lawyer named Louis Cole. Far into my tenure that committee discovered that the church actually owed nearly nine million dollars, including a debt to the Criswell Foundation. Oh well, to paraphrase former Senator Everett Dirkson, "What's a million here and a million there?"

As we sat around the conference table that day all of these known and unknown millions seemed far away. The church leadership felt they were reaching the end of a marathon. We just had to push toward the tape and good things would happen. In my own naiveté I thought, "This is the First Baptist Church of Dallas. They must have money buried in coffee cans under every building."

With prayer and a handshake all around, we dismissed from this discussion of debt for a time of informal fellowship in which I got to know the men better with whom I would toil in the months ahead.

ᘏ

FINALLY AT FIRST

ONE MORE most significant meeting awaited. My wife and I needed to meet with Dr. and Mrs. Criswell. Pastoring a Baptist church is a family matter, especially at First. No one questioned the power of Betty Criswell at First Baptist. By the scores, members inside the church, former staff members of the church, and Baptist observers attributed the professional demise of a goodly number to the work of her minions and sycophants. It was alleged that she never attacked openly, but worked through a network of minions on and off the staff who did her bidding. Although enough people had finally caught onto the situation to limit her antics, she was still capable of sudden, blind-siding skirmishes. When she got it in for someone, she could take decades to get rid of them. Ask Paige Patterson. Allegedly she worked to expel him for the better part of twenty years. Her influence on her husband's opinion was seldom immediate but often effective.

The worst-kept secret at First was Mrs. Criswell's desire that O. S. Hawkins become the pastor. In one very frank conversation with me, Paige Patterson attributed this desire to her belief Hawkins could raise money to save the college that bore her husband's name. In reality, her agenda was and is the continuation of her own power and influence in the church. With her class of three hundred in attendance, broadcast on the church-owned station, and its contribution of a million dollars to church causes, she carries a big stick. I thought it best we sit down and break bread.

Lest I appear overawed, I never feared Betty Criswell. Old, increasingly ill, and petulant, she had been shorn of most of her power. A radical core of her Sunday school class were still faithful operatives, but these consisted of newer members in the class unaware of her previous power-plays. Before I jumped ship, I actually wanted an open confrontation with her. I had heard so many accounts from staff and laity alike of her antics at the church that I thought it would be interesting to go down in history as the one who finally confronted her. I was restrained from doing so by wise staff members.

Since we needed privacy, the venue was a private dining room at the church. Situated on Old San Jacinto Street is an anomalous building called Braden Cottage. To enter it was to enter a 1960s middle-class suburban living room, still boasting gold shag carpet and eclectic decor. It was to that room my wife and I went to meet with the Criswells. In any other Baptist setting imaginable we would have been invited to their home. Had I not been in a somnambulistic state I would have given that snub more thought at the time.

Mrs. C.'s greeting was less than effusive. She was always proper to Linda and me, but in a chilly way. No one accused her of personal warmth. At least she did not greet me with the "Why do you think you could follow my husband" routine that marked

Betty Criswell, "first lady" of First Baptist Church, Dallas, delivers some well-chosen words at the podium with her husband, senior pastor W. A. Criswell, looking on. (Photo by Matt Brunworth, *Fort Worth Star-Telegram*)

her meeting with James Merritt. I expect the only reason she tolerated the situation was a certain insecurity about what would happen if the committee were dismissed. Without any question I represented at the best the least of several evils. She knew that Merritt and possibly other shadowy figures being considered would demand that the Old Man quit. Above all, she knew that her own power base was tied to his.

In the arcane casuistry by which some fundamentalists rationalize their behavior, the only way Mrs. Criswell could continue teaching a mixed class of men and women was to be "covered" by her husband's preaching ministry. The right wing of Baptist life does not suffer a woman to teach men in the church. Yet at Right Wing Headquarters a woman did just that for decades. This was rationalized as an "extension" of W. A.'s ministry because she was "under his authority." This latter remark led to gales of laughter in the back halls of First Baptist. Just before I resigned W. A. justified his continued presence to me as necessary "so Betty can go on with her class." I considered this more holy smoke. If W. A. went onto his reward, all the deacons in the church could not peel her hands off the microphone in Coleman Hall.

We were served by white-jacketed kitchen workers who brought the food across the street from the massive kitchen in the basement of the Truett Building. The meal was uneventful. At that time and place, Mrs. C. seemed to me a grandmotherly, if somewhat aloof, figure. In the months ahead when she started in on me she reminded me more of the wolfish grandmother in "The Three Little Pigs." That night, however, she seemed tame enough, if not thrilled with the proceedings.

Following the meal we moved to some over-stuffed sofas surrounding a small cocktail table. On the table had been placed a gigantic bowl of popcorn. W. A.'s eating habits are among the more curious of any public figure I have known. When we sat down to discuss business, he pulled out his glasses, perched them on his nose, bent over the huge popcorn bowl, and studied it like an augur examining the entrails of a sacrificial animal for some sign of the future. This continued for an uncomfortable amount of time. In fact, I began to peer into the bowl of popcorn myself like a reader looking at tea leaves. So strange was this ceremony that Linda and I asked to take the popcorn bowl home as if it were a relic radiating light from some Epiphany. One would think that this historic prelude to the passing of the baton at FBC would leave some other memento than a plastic popcorn bowl. I guess you had to be there.

When this culinary seance was concluded, Criswell in one quick movement pulled out his calendar and asked, "When will you come? The church will call you Sunday evening, November 25. When can you move? Do you own your house?"

His questions took me by surprise. We had not even decided yet whether we should go; this meeting was part of that decision. Yet in Criswell's mind it was a fait accompli. I suggested that the Sunday in question was the Sunday following Thanksgiving, historically a low day in church attendance. Would the church want to call a pastor for the first time in forty-six years on a Sunday with a low attendance? Criswell replied that the people would be there aplenty. He did not want me to preach or even be present that evening. The church would simply vote on me in absentia. The search committee would nix that; they wanted to present me live and in person to the congregation. After considerable such detailed discussion we drove back to Fort Worth. I had not yet been given a formal invitation from the search committee itself.

॰

THE WORD COMES DOWN

AT 5:30 P.M. SUNDAY, NOVEMBER 18, 1990, Richard E. Clements, Chairman of the Pastor Search Committee of the First Baptist Church, Dallas, called Dr. Joel C. Gregory, pastor of Travis Avenue Baptist Church in Fort Worth. His first words were, "Our committee wants to present you to the church to be called as pastor. How soon can you come?" With those words of promise and omen the decision became mine. After twenty-seven months this had all happened in four days. It seemed to me to be too hasty. It was not until Wednesday, November 21— the night before Thanksgiving—that I released them to present my name to the church for the church's vote the following Sunday evening.

The *Dallas Morning News* scooped them. On November 21 in a copyrighted story, Religion Editor Helen Parmley predicted that I would be called as "co-pastor" at First Dallas on November 25. By this time the actual title was "Pastor" with W. A. assuming the title "Senior Pastor." The deacons, hastily assembled in light of these developments, voted to change the church bylaws to create the office of "Senior Pastor." Without a unanimous vote the deacons could not change the bylaws in one session. That they did so was extraordinary in light of the tone in immediately preceding and following deacons' meetings. The committee assured me that a unanimous vote by the deacons was an act of God, especially such a momentous change. Obscured in all of this was one pivotal question: How long would Criswell remain with his title, in his office, preaching at the church? This was the paramount question that should have been officially addressed. It would have saved the church, the Criswells, and the Gregorys enormous heartache and a historical crisis.

It was unfortunate for me that the news story broke in the papers before I could personally tell the leaders at Travis Avenue. A devoted young architect, Larry Foxworth, was Chairman of the Deacons. Even though he was one of the youngest to hold that office in the church's history, he performed with poise during the sudden crisis at Travis. I had kept him informed of events from November 18 onward. He and I decided together that it would put an unbearable strain on the congregation and the pastor for me to attempt preaching on the morning of November 25 before speaking at Dallas that evening. I called my two living predecessors at Travis to inform them of events. Dr. James Coggin had preceded me at the church. A princely man of great dignity and presence, he had been nothing but an encouragement to me during my nearly six years at Travis. I asked him to take one of the Sunday services. I then called Dr. Robert E. Naylor, the eighty-year-old patriarch and President Emeritus of Southwestern Seminary. A legendary leader, the ever-alert Naylor had been a good friend during the Travis days. He agreed to take the other service on Sunday. Both men wished me well. I did not have to explain what I faced. They understood.

I went into seclusion with my Bible, Greek Testament, sermon notes, and private thoughts. A trial sermon should be a demonstration of what the people can expect from week to week from a new preacher. There was never a question that the church would call me on the recommendation of the committee. The sermon was more of an inaugural address in which a theme for the days ahead would be articulated. I chose a text from the apostle Paul, II Corinthians 10:3-5. Paul there presents the Christian life under the figure of warfare. The thesis of the message concerned how the Christian fights, where we fight, and the enormous potential for victory. At the heart of the message was an appeal to the church that was more prescient than I knew. I would tell the church that:

> "...in the conflict to tame ourselves within and to take the world without we are not dependent on anything that human nature can afford us. The church does not conquer on the basis of any kind of human strength—intellectual, physical, economic, institutional, or cultural. We do not win because we are sharper thinkers, stronger fighters, richer spenders, or greater builders. We will not even make a dent in the world unless our weapons come from a supernatural source."

I marinated myself in that theme for the next several days. I felt that the church must hear a new call for reliance upon the spiritual rather than the temporal.

During those days I was not without advice. Dr. John Bisagno, the popular pastor of First Baptist, Houston, called me personally. We had preached together on programs across the country and had a real affinity for fellowship with one another. John warned, "Do not go unless the Old Man has fully retired, accepted his gold watch, and gone on a cruise around the world. You will regret it if you do." Of course, John was dead on target right. In the anticipation of such great events as rested ahead, however, I waved away his words of warning. It was too late anyway.

I felt it best to get to Dallas before the event. The church checked our family into two rooms at the luxurious Fairmont Hotel across the street from church property. Looking out the window of the Fairmont up Ervay Street and the five blocks of the church property, it suddenly crashed in upon me that this was really about to happen. Suddenly, I felt the weight of history as if George Truett were sitting on one shoulder and Criswell on the other. The inevitable question came to mind: "What in the world are you doing here?" Fifteen years before I had been pastor of the Cottonwood Baptist Church in Central Texas sitting in the middle of a maize field. We literally chased rats out of the parsonage. It's a long way from Cottonwood to Dallas.

One thought gave me the confidence to face the hour. I had never politicked for the position. I never asked to be recommended, considered, or pushed forward. If I were called there, it would be at the initiative of the search committee and the people. I hoped that all of them together could discover the divine will.

I had bought a new postal-blue suit for the occasion. My wife wore a stunning blue dress. The boys sported new suits. At the appointed hour the officers of the pastor search committee appeared in the lobby of the Fairmont Hotel. We went through the underground tunnel for two blocks until we popped up at the First Baptist Church. The family was seated in the sanctuary while I was taken to the minister's room. The atmosphere in the room was electric. There was a different ambience from my 1984 experience. Joy, relief, and highest celebration marked the atmosphere. After prayer, I was rigged with a wireless microphone for auditorium, radio, and television sound.

The moment had come to walk from that room down the hallway into the historic sanctuary. If a man's life ever had a historical moment it would be this. Nothing of greater significance than this hour would ever take place in my life. We walked through the old wooden doors into the sanctuary. The orchestral music thundered as the choir sang a mighty anthem. The old hall was packed to the top of the balcony with no room for another person. Many people were openly weeping. I could not help bursting into tears as I made my way to the platform. When the people saw that, many of them wept as well. It was 1990. The church had known only two pastors since 1897. No hour in American religious culture could be more laden with destiny. The most influential church of America's largest Protestant denomination was about to call a new pastor.

After the thrilling music that always characterized the church, I took the pulpit. It took some moments for me to gather my composure. I preached the message intended. Some people responded to the public invitation. It was as if all were beside the point until the vote was taken. When I finished the church repeated a custom I had experienced in country churches and city churches six times before. Our family was ushered out of the sanctuary for the committee to make its presentation and recommendation. We were shown across the street once again to the anomalous Braden Cottage where we were served pie. I was so tense I could not eat.

We sat alone in the room for what seemed an interminable time. The process had placed the four in our family under considerable strain. My older son Grant would have to change high schools in his senior year. It was expected that both boys would attend the First Baptist Academy. My younger son Garrett had a premonition from the first that the whole thing would not work. He was a prophet. Linda and I had been married for twenty-three years. We literally grew up pastoring churches from the time I was twenty years old. She had been with me from the first slum church near Baylor until this moment. Life in the parsonage and the glare of public life had taken a heavy toll on our marriage. Yet she had a sense of destiny stronger than my own that I should be at First Baptist. Now we were alone awaiting the verdict of the congregation.

We seemed to wait forever. The committee decided that they would give a very full report. They had been at it for twenty-seven months and I am sure desired to justify their search to the church. Most of them had something to say. At the end of the presentation the church gave us a unanimous call by a standing vote.

After the vote we were ushered across the street into the sanctuary. The glaring lights of television cameras beamed on us as we entered. The congregation stood as one with a thunderous ovation of applause that seemed to shake the very floors of the place. Criswell embraced me. Our family stood on the platform during the prolonged ovation. People wept, shouted, and even whistled. I had never seen anything like it. I finally went to the pulpit and croaked out that I accepted their call.

It felt like the end of a thousand-mile journey. I was now the pastor of the First Baptist Church of Dallas.

Chapter Five

❦

Big-Time Religion

Welcome to Big-Time Religion.

First Baptist and everything about it had always intrigued the media. They gave full play to my call as pastor. The evening news, the morning metropolitan dailies, and lesser publications all wanted a word. On Monday, November 26, I left the Fairmont Hotel to meet the press assembled in the Hunt Youth Building of First Baptist. A table had been arranged for Criswell and me to sit in front of the assembled media. Radio, television, secular, and religious print media were all present. As I would come to find in the months ahead, Criswell was always seated beside me at public events. This was to be his occasion, too.

The questions in the conference centered at first on the location of the church in the future. Both inside and outside the congregation speculation was rife concerning a possible move. Many large Southern Baptist downtown churches had moved to the suburbs and experienced explosive growth. Criswell told the press that his decision to leave the church downtown was the "highlight of his ministry." At least once a year Criswell brought a message extolling the presence of the church in the center of the city. He would later sit in his office and wistfully recall for me his early days when "entire families came downtown every night. They would walk up and down the streets in front of the church, crowds of them."

Criswell seemed to live more in downtown as it used to be than as it was. In reality, people had been attacked in the parking garages, and the bill for vandalism in our buildings was enormous. For me to get a young couple to join the church from the growing edge of Dallas took a personal recruiting job akin to a major college coach wooing a blue-chip prospect.

In the press conference Criswell basically used the situation to put me on record before the press that I would not move the church. That was okay with me. There were too many other battles to fight before facing that one. Typically, a move kills the ministries of three pastors: the one who proposes it, the one who actually moves the church, and the one who follows him. I would find that among those who wanted to move the church there were three schools of thought. Some wished to move across Woodall-Rogers Freeway and place the church on vacant property immediately north of downtown. I was surprised to hear the deacon chairman suggest that option. Others wanted to consider property halfway between north Dallas and downtown, in the old EDS area or the Dr Pepper Plant property close to Southern Methodist University (SMU). Still others envisioned a move to the far north along the LBJ Freeway corridor. The church could have sold its downtown property for $200 million at the height of the real estate boom. It once entertained an option on land near LBJ Freeway and Interstate 35, but Criswell would not move. Now the property could not be sold for anything like that.

Reverend W. A. Criswell, showing a preacher's fervency, dedicates an office building. (Photo by Judy Walgren, *Dallas Morning News*)

Privately, Criswell would later tell me, "When I am gone some day in the future you will sell this and move the church." The Old Man knew in his head that the church could not survive long-term downtown, but in his heart he could not face it. He was right. The church will move in the twenty-first century or die.

The media pressed us about our mutual roles at the church. The Baptist press particularly had an intuition that this whole thing might not work. Criswell explained that he would continue to preach the televised 10:50 A.M. service and I would preach all the others. The press correctly sniffed out that this was an unusual deal, seeing how the church was calling a new preacher who needed the television exposure to get any momentum at all. Criswell rationalized his continued presence on Channel 11 "due to the church's commitment to KTVT, Channel 11" who had approached him in 1989 about televising the services. He left the implication that First Baptist's presence on TV was due to a special agreement with Channel 11 that he preach on television.

There was nothing of the sort. We were paying them twelve thousand dollars per week, one of the highest tickets to the airwaves paid by any church in the nation for a local VHS outlet. They could care less who stood there. Criswell did say, "As time goes on, we will do whatever he would like, maybe rotating it. He would preach and then I would preach." Turning to me, he asked in front of the press, "If that is all right with you."

That was a typically Criswellian touch. What was I supposed to say? "No, Dr. C. I am going to take the whole thing away from you in three months." This was the first time I sensed that he was already backing off from his specific promise to me made two weeks earlier that it would only be a "few months" before he was off the scene.

Otherwise, the press asked us about state and denominational affairs, including the recent defection of Baylor University from its roots. Baylor had presumptively belonged to Texas Baptist for one hundred forty-five years. In a unilateral vote, they violated the constitution of the state denomination and dared Texas Baptist to sue them in order to restore the relationship. We both declared that the denomination should sue them to get the school back. The remainder of the time was spent with my making laudatory remarks about Criswell and his heroic leadership of the church. The papers gave a lot of ink to the conference.

This conference proved a harbinger of the future. I would never be able to stand on my own and speak on my own as a forty-four-year-old man who had pastored for twenty-five years. Rather than getting off the scene so I could establish my own leadership, Criswell would be present at all public occasions. There would have been nothing wrong with this at all for a few months. It would have been appropriate for many years had I been called as an associate pastor to help the Old Man extend his ministry (which turned out to be the real agenda.) But I was called to lead the church into the twenty-first century and in order to do so desperately needed to capture the momentum of early leadership and be perceived by Dallas as the leader of the church. He would not let that happen.

ɔↄ

THE MUNDANE MATTERS

THE CHURCH HAD CALLED ME with no specific understanding concerning support. I had asked for nothing before accepting the job and had been offered nothing. After the call we sat down to work out the details. The church offered me a $165,000 package. The basis for this was a salary equal to Criswell's $90,000 plus a housing and utility allowance for a $450,000 home in the exclusive Lakewood area of Dallas. I had been paid $110,000 per year at Travis Avenue, but outside speaking engagements and publishing ventures brought my gross income close to the mark First Baptist offered. In going to First I had canceled twenty-two out-of-town speaking engagements that would have produced considerable income. I felt that I had to stay in Dallas without leaving town for at least a year in order to learn the situation and establish leadership.

To my surprise the church also offered a "signing bonus." They presented me with a $100,000 loan to be forgiven over five years of service at twenty thousand dollars per year. This would cover the purchase of a 1991 Honda Accord to be used in the service of the church as well as money for down payment on the house. There is a wide gap between the value of housing in Fort Worth and Dallas. The eighty thousand dollars was an equalizer to make me whole in the move. The church also presented me with a membership in the Lakewood Country Club and the downtown Petroleum Club to use for church purposes in courting prospects and holding meetings for church committees. There were also arrangements concerning a cellular phone, academy tuition discounts for my sons, etc. The church was, as I expected them to be, very generous.

The only thing I asked for and received was a severance agreement. In six previous pastorates I had never had such an agreement, but neither had there been a senior pastor on the scene. On November 30, 1990, I received a letter signed by three church officials:

Dear Dr. Gregory:

Persuant to your request and in conjunction with terms of employment with the First Baptist Church Dallas, the following terms apply to any future severance of your employment at the church:

If the pastor should voluntarily resign the church in order to accept the invitation of another church or entity, the church will have no obligation beyond that of normal procedures as outlined in the by-laws of the personnel manual.

If the pastor should be terminated by the vote of the church or resign as the result of a negotiated decision in any untoward circumstances, the church commits to care for his family under the following arrangements:

(1) 100 percent of salary and benefits will be paid for six (6) months duration, or until suitable employment for the pastor's gifts and calling is found; whichever is less.

(2) If suitable employment is not found by six (6) months, it is recognized that mortgage obligation constitutes the heaviest burden and encumbrance to the welfare of the pastor's family. In the event that the pastor's home cannot be disposed of within six (6) months the church will assume the mortgage payments of the home until it sells at a reasonable market value. The church will be reimbursed, at the time of the sale, from the net proceeds of the transaction.

Further, should any unexpected and untoward circumstances develop, it is recognized by the church that the Kingdom of God would be best served if the pastor could make a transition to another position without dismissal or resignation. In that regard, the church would do everything possible to retain the pastor's services until such a transition could be made. This transition period will not exceed six (6) months. May God bless you in His service.

This agreement was reviewed by a church lawyer and signed by Lee Roy Treadway, chairman of the personnel committee; Dick Clements, chairman of the search committee; and Eugene Green, chairman of the deacons. They presented themselves to me as having the authority to make this agreement. A newcomer to the scene, I had no reason to believe they did not have that authority. Had things gone as I had been told and Criswell got out of the picture, this agreement would have gone unnoticed in an arcane file of yellowing paper. One week before I resigned, deacon secretary Doug Brady asked to review this agreement. He asked this in the presence of the deacon officers. He told me, in effect, that the agreement as written might have no legal force. He rewrote an expanded version that was signed by the corporate officers of the church. As things did go, when I resigned, this agreement outraged deacons who did not know of its existence. Some of the very men who were aware of its existence from the beginning sought to change the nature of the document, challenging it at virtually every point.

We needed to get to the scene in Dallas, so the church leased us a three-bedroom executive apartment in north Dallas until we could close on a house. Our sons were duly enrolled in the First Baptist Academy. Dick Clements, the chairman of the search committee and a Dallas real estate executive, showed my wife and me fifty houses between the two of us. We settled on a new home ten minutes east of the church and not far from the

Swiss Avenue mansion of the Criswells. Such proximity to W. A. was not intended, but we really did like that house best of all. It also had the advantage of being in the closest neighborhood to downtown safe enough to inhabit. However, the house had no area for a study so deacon Ed Rawls, an architect and personal friend (I had pastored his physician brother at Travis) quickly drew up a $35,000 addition to the new home. This two-room study featured a fireplace, shelves for six thousand books, and an extensive filing area. FBC can get things done. The study was completed from the groundbreaking in three weeks.

The Criswells showed a distinct indifference toward our personal affairs, with a couple of exceptions. The day after my call to the church, he was on the phone.

"Lad," he said, "I have incredible news. There are seven thousand members at the downtown YMCA."

I did not understand why that was so incredible. Perhaps he was the chairman of the new member drive?

He continued, "You cannot get a locker."

I must confess that was not at the top of my list.

"But I got you a locker next to mine," he quickly added.

Sure enough, he had used his influence to get me a full-sized locker next to his. He expected me to work out at the Y, preferably at the same time he did.

To his credit, Criswell was aerobic before aerobic was cool. For decades he had worked out at the Y. The church had two gymnasiums, but it was impossible for the pastor to exercise there; the members would not leave him alone. Criswell told me a dozen times that the YMCA had kept him alive. I believe it. Six days a week he would work out at the Y. Even in important meetings he would look at his watch, gravely state that he had a commitment, and run to the YMCA . It was the one thing that he absolutely would not miss. He told me in the presence of others, "I may not pray, I may not study, but I will go to the Y." He even went when he was sick. Most winters Criswell would suffer from the flu, but he would go to the Y even when he was ablaze with fever. I remonstrated with the Old Man, actually fearing for his well-being. He told me, "I have found over the years that I get well more quickly if I exercise."

These joint sessions of exercise were not without some high humor. Criswell began his workout running in place on a small, round trampoline. After bouncing in place for awhile, he would do sit-ups on an inclined board. Surrounded by young businessmen one-third his age, he provided an admirable contrast to the generation gap. Doing his sit-ups he would sometimes groan to the point of creating concern. Following the sit-ups, he moved to an ancient machine with a vibrating strap. To improve his circulation, he began with the belt at the back of his ankles and worked it up to his head as the machine shook him furiously. At times he attempted to talk with me about church business while strapped to this thing. Even at rest, Criswell has a vibrato that would be set at No. 4 if he were an old Hammond organ. When the vibrations of that machine were added, his utterings were unintelligible.

These joint sessions of exercise were not without some high humor.

I distinctly remember one day when he told me, "Lad, it is of uppermost significance that we ah-ha-ha-ha-ga before the uh-uh-uh-uh. There is every reason to give immediate priority to the oo-oo-oo-oo." I could never quite interpret these vibrated dicta.

Other than the membership at the Y, he called to make one other request. Marcia Will had been the secretary of the second-in-command at First for years. She had served Tom Melzoni who had been forced out and Denny Dawson who had been shown the door. More recently, she assisted Charles McLaughlin as administrator before he retired. She had since served as the secretary for the search committee. He asked that I consider her as my secretary. On the surface of it, I had no reason not to do so. On the other hand, I thought his interest in that detail among all the others was most interesting. Perhaps it was out of loyalty to a long-tenured employee. Marcia turned out to be a loyal and competent co-worker. She knew the church well and understood the position I was in relative to Dr. Criswell. Incidentally, it became apparent shortly after I arrived that Criswell's secretary, Elaine Palmer, had every intention of protecting his turf. Until I left she answered Criswell's phone, "Pastor's office," which some considered a direct insult to me. Like others around Criswell, she understood him to be the head honcho. I cannot complain about that. A man's secretary should be his loyal fan or he has problems.

Other than those two requests, W. A. stayed out of the way in the earliest days of my tenure. Before I could get started at First, I had to say good-bye to Fort Worth.

ॐ

FAREWELL

BEFORE TURNING TO DALLAS, it was necessary to say good-bye in Fort Worth. The majority of members at Travis wished me well and regretted that we were leaving. As in any church, there were some ready to see me go. This included a small group that had recently attempted to seize control of the church through the nominating committee process as well as certain

Southwestern Seminary profs who despised my coziness with the fundamentalists. For the overwhelming number of us, however, it was a fond and sad farewell. I told them, "Let us affirm our vows and stand by the assignment. The hope of this church certainly doesn't live in this pastor, or any pastor." I assured them that a great congregation such as Travis would go on into God's future.

Some members felt that I had saddled them with a seven-million-dollar debt and was leaving town. I understand how they felt. When you lead a Baptist church into an expansion program, they feel you should stay to see it through. That is a fair assessment. On the other hand, a Baptist church seldom gives the pastor a no-cut contract. It is generally felt that you should stay committed to them, but they are not obligated to stay committed to you. Even so, I felt badly about leaving Travis with the debt. They could pay it, but the expansion program had been my vision. Fortunately, they have done well in the following years.

Across five-and-a-half years we had seen the membership grow from sixty-five hundred to eighty-five hundred and the giving of the church almost double. It had been an exciting, fast-paced ministry that demanded the best I could give. Yet I also felt it was time to go. I would not have been at Travis much longer had First Baptist not called me. There is a mysterious, intuitive process that goes on between a pastor and a congregation. It is a mix of the spoken and the unspoken, the subtle gesture, what is said and not said. The ministry of some pastors lends itself to shorter terms and others to longer terms. I had served my day at Travis and it was time for a different style of leadership there.

The church presented our family with a lovely reception the evening of December 9, 1990. With hugs, tears, and farewells, we were gone.

The *Fort Worth Star-Telegram* featured a second-front (in its metro section) story on the departure the next day. The writer gave an account of my preaching on the final day: "His style is a combination of storytelling and old-fashioned oratory, moving from bursts of booming commands accented by pointing and clenched fists, to loud whispers with his voice trembling with emotion, his moist eyes tightly shut and his head bowed and shaking slightly from side to side." His comments on my nonverbal communication left me wondering if I needed to see a physician for treatment of some kind of seizure. More than a characterization of preaching, I appreciated what some members said about my pastoral ministry: "But his theatrical preaching style is only part of what makes Gregory unique, longtime followers say. He also is a devoted pastor who is known for taking special care in comforting his congregation in times of great need." That was more positive than some members would have been, but it was good to have the affirmation in the leaving.

The church did what is typically done in such a loss. They elected a pastor search committee and retrenched financially by canceling our television contract with Channel 11. Travis had been on Channel 11 for thirty minutes at 9:00 A.M. We were scheduled to pay forty-six hundred dollars per week in 1991. Some in the church were already complaining that was too much. As soon as I left, they ended the contract. As it turned out, First Baptist also canceled their contract with Channel 11 the year after I resigned.

Were these wise decisions? I think not. The value of television to a local church continues to be debated by the laity who pay the bills. It's very expensive, but I feel that churches such as Travis and First cannot grow without it. When a large church is miles from the growing edge of the city, the only window the city has on the church is television. Where the preacher's personal ego and the needs of the church intersect is on no known road map. If one takes a reductionist approach, television makes sense in reaching people with a message. First Baptist had a ten-million-dollar budget to reach thirty-five hundred people sitting in the sanctuary on Sunday. Six hundred thousand dollars enlarged the sanctuary to include an average of fifty-two thousand who watched on television. In terms of dollars spent per person reached, it makes sense. For those who think it has more to do with the ego of blow-dried TV preachers, it does not make sense. The last two churches I left decided it was not worth it.

FIRST THINGS FIRST

WITH FORT WORTH IN THE REARVIEW MIRROR, it was time to concentrate on Big D. Criswell told me that it took him five years to launch his vision for the church. If it took that long for him to learn how to lead First Baptist, Dallas, I knew that I needed to get started immediately. There is no book written, no seminar held, and no model to compare with it. You learn on the job, and you need to learn quickly.

First Baptist has been one of the most studied churches in the world. In his heyday Criswell hosted thousands of pastors at an annual "School of the Prophets" to teach preachers how to build a large church. There is no salt for salt; I had nowhere to go to learn how to do it—we were the only place. I was handed an Arthur Anderson study commissioned before I came describing the current personnel structure of the church. It was in a bulging blue binder. The administrator asked for it in order to discern just how many employees the church had and what they were doing. I gingerly opened the binder and began to read. There was a chart in the book which diagrammed the church employee structure at twenty-two levels. At the top was a box with the word "pastor" and at the bottom were many boxes labeled "porters" and "maids." In between were the rest of the more than three hundred people to whom First Baptist wrote checks. The annual payroll was an astonishing five million dollars, 50 percent of the operating budget. There is nothing else like it in American Christianity.

With my twenty-two-level notebook in hand, I set out to meet the top tiers of the staff. At the highest level of the staff was the "church cabinet." This was a group of fourteen who met weekly on Monday afternoon. It included the major members of the ministerial staff. The minister of education was a jovial Italian-American, Jody Mazzola. The product of a Roman Catholic family on the Texas coast, he converted to the Baptist way and married a famous East Texas preacher's daughter. Jody had come from a lesser position at gigantic Prestonwood in North Dallas. At First, he had to preside over a fractious, fragmented, and tenured Christian education staff. No one in living memory had succeeded in his job and it was a struggle for him. Jody served me every Monday night as navigator when I groped my way around Dallas visiting prospects for the church.

Next in the Cabinet sat the minister of music, Fred McNabb. A team player, Fred had come from the largest Baptist church in Abilene, Texas, shortly before my arrival. As in most major positions at First, the two men before him had been dismissed and the man before that pressured out, some said, as a result of Mrs. C.'s intrigues. In 1994, Fred decided to head back to the church in Abilene from whence he came. He presided over a huge musical staff with their own building built by the famous Dallas businesswoman, the late Mary Crowley. The spiritually minded folks in the choir loved him. Those that wanted a big show were eating away at him like piranhas. The two groups would send delegates to my office to lean on me about Fred. With my backing Fred took the youth choir and orchestra to the Barcelona Olympics.

Next to Fred sat Dr. Charles McLaughlin, already introduced. The week I came, another church in Dallas tried to hire him away. On the spot I begged him to stay and head the pastoral ministries staff, because the care of "twenty-nine thousand" members at times of need defies all explanation. I needed him and he served the church and me well. He supervised the thousands of visits to hospitals, rest homes, shut-ins, as well as funerals, weddings and other pastoral emergencies. Charlie always knew the right thing to say in every situation.

Sherryn Cates presided over the massive business office. That office covered the entire first floor of the Criswell building except for worship and reception areas. Sherryn was a very young woman hired for the position by Dr. McLaughlin when he administered the church. When I first met her, I could not believe they had turned the business of the church over to her. Seasoned professional men had buckled under the enormous pressures brought to bear on the financial offices of First Baptist. Individuals, some of affluence and prominence, would simply show up and demand money for their church-related cause. The constant shortfalls because of debt had to be covered by endless interfund borrowing. In spite of my first impression, Sherryn Cates proved herself to be one of the most capable staff members I ever encountered.

Mart Cuttrell had the stewardship of the sprawling physical plant of the church. With five square blocks of buildings, for years First Baptist was the largest ground-level property holder in downtown Dallas. By 1990 the physical plant was very old and the problems of maintenance defied solving. With a large staff that included full-time carpenters, electricians, plumbers, and painters, Mart struggled to maintain the decaying buildings. He must have felt like the people who paint Golden Gate Bridge only to start over again.

As president of Criswell College, Paige Patterson could have sat on the cabinet, but he did not come. He sent a representative from the Criswell College. Although Patterson was titled associate pastor of the church, he had nothing to do with the church proper while I was there. The people either hated him or loved him. He had led the Baptist battle for twelve years, crossing the nation with Houston Judge Paul Pressler to fire up the fundamentalists and keep the denomination under their control.

From the beginning of my tenure Paige was embattled with the Criswells and his board. He would have been fired early in my tenure had it not been for my direct intervention, a fact he never acknowledged to me. The college, with its three hundred students, twenty faculty members, and new seven-million-dollar refurbished campus in the midst of a Dallas slum, is a lethal drain on the church, a constant burden to the pastor, and an institution with a diminishing purpose in the now fundamentalist-controlled denomination. At a time when the church desperately needed all its pastoral energies for a new day, the college siphoned off more wasted time and energy than everything else put together. With virtually no income but that provided by the church and the foundation, every dollar to the college competed with needed funds for church programming.

By the end of my tenure I was of the steadfast private opinion that either the college would survive or the church, but not both. Moody started Moody Bible Institute and Moody Church in Chicago. The church is almost gone, but the Institute lives on. Spurgeon founded both the Metropolitan Tabernacle and Spurgeon's College in London. The church has virtually vanished but the school lives on. Criswell knows this well. His bronze statue was placed under the dome of the College, not at the church. Privately, he expressed to me no confidence in the long-term future of the church. More than once he told me, "What if a liberal follows you and me here? He would kill it in a generation." I stifled the temptation to say that a liberal would have as much chance becoming pastor at First as Ronald Reagan would in being the featured speaker at the Democratic National Convention.

Fred Lively represented the First Baptist Academy, the K-12 school on two campuses, one downtown and the other in a suburb. With nearly a thousand students, the academy was the only enterprise we had that was in the black. Lively trumpeted that he was a businessman, not an educator. The academy was committed to a strict, fundamentalist view of education. Creationism, right-wing political and social philosophy, and a biblical interpretation of even Shakespeare's plays typified the school. (When the students studied *MacBeth* they were asked to categorize the various sins of the characters. That would be a long list.)

My older son Grant attended the academy his senior year. A gifted artist, he drew a Picasso-like mural on the art room wall.

This created no end of conflict with the uptight high school principal, Suzette Estes. She wanted those pagan images off the wall because "Picasso was not a Christian." Fortunately Grant's friend and art teacher prevailed and the paganistic bovine creatures remained on the wall until Grant headed for SMU. Basically, I stayed out of the way of the academy. There were too many other problems to tackle. When a group of parents came to our home to describe a covert snitch system with stooges among the students reporting to the administration, I waved it off as too much trouble. I should not have. They would later turn on my own son.

Dr. Polly Cooper represented the counseling center. First Baptist had two full-time Christian psychologists and could have had many more. They were booked all the time. Their offices were discreetly tucked away on the third floor of the Criswell building so that couples with problems could sneak up to the counseling office.

First Mark Eaves and then Ron Harris represented the media ministry. First Baptist had been on television off and on for years. Their equipment was antiquated compared with that of Travis Avenue and other churches. The church spent so much money for time that there had been no money for improvement of equipment. I brought Harris in from the church radio station to reestablish the program. He was responsible for the weekly local television and radio broadcasts as well as the national television broadcast on ACTS and Family Net. He taped my messages for the international Baptist Hour radio broadcast heard on five hundred stations. This was an extra effort, for each message had to be exactly fourteen-and-one-half minutes long—an awesome challenge for a preacher like me. They also had responsibility for the international distribution of tapes from the pulpit ministry of the church, as well as much of the print media. The church had a complete in-house printing plant with a number of full-time employees.

With a man of Harris's ability we put a toy piano in the hands of a Van Cliburn. He tried royally to produce quality products with inadequate equipment. This kind of anomaly could be found throughout the church. There was plenty of money, but it did not make its way to some key, visible areas of the church's life.

Elaine Palmer, Criswell's secretary, represented Dr. C. in the meetings. He no longer attended that Cabinet and had not done so for some years. She kept notes for him and checked off his calendar for major events.

Four major members of the Christian education staff under Mazzola also sat in this meeting. Libby Reynolds represented the church's work with children. Libby had known Criswell since she was a child when W. A. pastored her family in Kentucky. She had been with the church for more than three decades. A maiden lady, she was first at work and last to leave. Her capacity for hard work amazed me. I could never get there earlier or leave later than Libby. At ten o'clock in the evening I would leave my office and find her exercising by walking the second floor hall between her office and Criswell's. Generations had grown up under her watchful eye. Libby was always positive to me, although she was totally loyal to W. A. I trusted her.

The youth division was a disaster my entire tenure. When I arrived one young man stayed a while and decided to leave. I then invited Lee Mabry from Merritt's church in Snellville. Mabry was supposed to be the hottest thing going among

Southern Baptist youth ministers. He lasted a year and went back to Georgia to pastor. The youth minister lives in a pressure cooker of impossible expectations because the program really has no overarching rationale. There are four hundred teenagers who show up on Sunday from all over Dallas County. The spectrum of opinion about what the church ought to do for teenagers ranges from giving them a place to play to running a boot camp for Jesus.

The single adult program at First was only a shadow of what it needed to be. When I arrived it was virtually non-existent in a county where 51 percent of the adults are single. Before my time at the church, the Criswell's adopted son Cris had led a group to separate from the larger singles body and establish their own program in another building! I publicly announced from the pulpit that the church must reach out to the singles of Dallas. After a national search I imported a single's minister from First Baptist, Jackson, Mississippi, who was supposed to be the cream of the crop. After a few months at First, he threw up his hands and left us for the Park Cities Baptist Church, our competition to the north. Chris Elkins had never seen anything like First Baptist and wanted nothing to do with it.

Lee Hunt coordinated the adult work of the church. About to retire, he was a friendly soul who brought me ties and handkerchiefs.

Lanny Elmore was the minister of missions. He coordinated the thirty mission churches that First Baptist owned throughout the city. These points of outreach touched thousands with an aggregate attendance of two thousand every Sunday. Lanny had to deal with Japanese, Chinese, Koreans, Hispanics, Jews, blind, deaf, and other constituents. A former foreign missionary, he had the patience of Job. He also administered the church's huge relief program, doling out food and clothing to the thousands who wanted a hand-out from the huge, rich church. I always felt a closeness to Lanny. He expressed love and loyalty to me. After I resigned he was the only one of the tenured staff members at First who came to my home with an expression of concern.

If the aforementioned list seems unduly negative it is only because the problems brought to the weekly cabinet meeting defy description. Criswell had built his empire one piece at a time over forty-six years. He knew each building block, stress point, strength, and land mine. I inherited the entire thing in one week. The problems never, ever stop. I woke up with the phone ringing about them in the morning, dealt with them all day, and went to bed with them at night. The above description only touches the surface of the complex difficulties. Many of the persons named above had an entire staff himself or herself. It was not until I had been pastor nine months and brought in Tim Hedquist as administrator that we even began to find out how many people were actually on the payroll. People down the organization had been permitted to hire people beneath them. When we thought that we had found them all, we still found others on the payroll hiding in one of the buildings.

On Tuesday afternoon the educational staff met. For months I met with them just to find out what was going on in the Sunday school. Under Mazzola were ministers to mothers before children were born, for babies, creepers, toddlers, preschoolers, elementary children (one for grades one through three and another full-time worker for grades four through six), youth, singles, young marrieds, young adults, median adults, meridian adults, senior adults, and eventually crown adults (those about to go to heaven and get their crown). This did not count Mrs. Criswell whose class had its own full-time pastor and staff, Zig Ziglar's huge auditorium class with its own full-time pastor, and other master-taught classes for everybody from the president's class (for those who presided over their own company) to the medical-dental class for doctors and dentists. Many of these had their own multiple staffs or interns. If there was any task that could be done, the church had hired someone to do it.

To say that Criswell made spontaneous personnel decisions is to put it mildly. He seemed to think that immediacy of decision and quantity of personnel were more important than deliberation and quality of decision. He pounded into me again and again, "Lad, you get a good staff member and when they reach ten tithing families they have paid their own salary." That was of course true of major league home run hitters like Libby Reynolds. That was not true of three hundred people, half of whom could have disappeared without affecting the program whatever.

My first act in coming to the church was to book appointments with all the major staff members in thirty-minute intervals.

My first act in coming to the church was to book appointments with all the major staff members in thirty-minute intervals. It was a blitz technique I had read about in some management book. The guru who authored the book stated that what a boss did in the first twenty-four hours was the most important thing he would ever do. Swallowing that nonsense whole, I asked each person described above to spend thirty minutes with me, bringing a written report of his or her area. By the end of that process I had absorbed so much information that I sat in a catatonic state staring at my office wall.

Having met the people, I thought I ought to look at the place. I asked the building manager if I could have a key to everything, seeing as how I was now pastor. He looked at me in blank astonishment with the same look a parent gives a four-year-old who asks, "How high is the sky?"

"Key?" he said, mouth agape. As it turned out, there were rings with hundreds of keys. Some of the tenured staff members had personal fiefdoms to which only they had the key. Backing away from an obviously absurd question, I asked someone to lead me around the plant. The church had grown outward concentrically from its original square block. To the south stood the Veal Building referred to earlier. It had an ancient gymnasium, skating rink, garage, and assorted facilities. It connected to part of the Christian Education Building, which in turn had been wrapped around an early-twentieth-century office building, the Burt Building. These buildings in turn abutted up against the youth building given by Ruth Ray Hunt. The Mary Crowley Building connected the original buildings to these. Across the street was the Spurgeon Harris building named for the first pastor. It held still another garage as well as some of the First Baptist Academy and Sunday school space. The boondoggle 511 building connected with it to the south. On the north side of the original block of church buildings stood the Criswell Building, the Sonshine Building (an old office building) and north of that the multi-story Ross Avenue Garage.

If this sounds confusing, it was. These buildings had been acquired over forty years and connected to one another. The floor levels often did not match, and some hallways led to a dead end. In my first walk-through I discovered a Pandora's box of deferred maintenance. The Burt Building, used by the academy

and older elementary Sunday school students, had been so
neglected that I almost lost prospective staff members who did
not want their own children to go to Sunday school in such a
mess. When friends came to town I would attempt to give them
a grand tour of the five blocks. In every single instance of doing
so I got lost myself in one of the high-rise church buildings.
Finally I gave up and asked somebody to lead me every time I
had to go more than a block away from my office. It was some
comfort to learn that long-time members still got lost in the
place as well.

The deacons meet once a month in Coleman Hall, a cavernous half-basement dining room in the oldest building. Every
major committee consisted of deacons, all men of course. Since
the possibility of meeting "twenty-nine thousand" members was
remote, I decided to meet the three hundred deacons six at a time
for lunch. I sat the lunches up at Lakewood Country Club and
every week for a year met with six deacons for a lunch discussion.
Most of them were mild-mannered godly businessmen of long
tenure in the membership. Like the congregation, they tended to
be an older group who had raised their families in the church.

Until they discovered that I really would stop the uncontrolled
spending, each of these sessions turned into a diatribe concerning
the church's out-of-control deficit spending. Few of the men criticized Criswell directly. It was just not done to utter a critical word
of the Old Man. For those men to do so would have been like
cussing Granddaddy because he went on a sudden spending binge
and used up the family fortune. You would be mad as blazes at
Granddad, but you really could not talk about him; he was family.
This inability to confront Criswell made it seem that no problem
at First Baptist had any real cause. Many deacons were perpetually

disturbed because such-and-such had been done, but there was never any attribution to who did it. The church had a nine-million-dollar debt with no known way to service it, but some shadowy figure or figures unidentified had perpetrated this outrage. I always left these sessions with the sense of watching men fire live ammunition at a nonexistent target.

My first several deacons' meetings were uproarious sessions concerning church finances. It was discovered that the church had spent one million dollars more in 1990 than they had taken in. This deficit was covered by funds from the "wills and trusts" committee that oversaw the endowment funds that had been given to the church since 1868. Of course, the corpus of these funds was never to be touched. The purpose for most of them was supposed to be mission-related ventures. The earnings on the trusts had been intended to support various outreaches of a missionary purpose. In 1990, they had used them to help pay the light bill and everything else. This was news to me.

My immediate concern was more the future than the past. In spite of a one-million-dollar cash shortfall, the church had adopted a larger budget. They had not reached the previous 1990 budget in actual giving. Guess who would take it in the neck when they missed reaching the 1991 budget? It sure would not stick to Old Teflon himself. When I heard the ravings of powerful, conservative, self-made deacons, businessmen appropriately outraged about the church's fiscal irresponsibilities, I decided to act.

Based on current giving, the church would have at least a $750,000 shortfall in 1991 unless we acted to cut the budget by March 1. My very first week, I faced the egregious task of eliminating $500,000 from the program budget and $250,000 from personnel. W. A. abhorred this kind of retrenchment. He considered it the worst thing I could conceivably do at the beginning of my tenure. "When you cut back and down and retreat and retrench it means decline and death and disappointment," he remonstrated alliteratively. Part of W. A.'s distinctive rhetorical style featured copulative conjunctions to give length and substance to such pronouncements. When he thus complained, I listened quietly but went ahead with my plan. If we overspent another million in 1991, there were disastrous implications for the church. The financial leaders among the laity had spent a year putting together a loan from NCNB to cover the debt we could not pay. Fiscal responsibility was part of the loan covenant. Long gone were the days when W. A. could walk down the street to Republic National Bank where his good friend ran the show. The folks in North Carolina would not bat an eyelash at calling in a loan from First Baptist if we did not toe the line. There were very serious issues at stake that involved the financial survival of not only the church but also the college. Welcome to the ministry.

Added to this was a greater inanity. The Criswell College is a separate entity from First Baptist with its own charter, incorporation, trustees, and budget. For all practical purposes, however, it is an arm of First Baptist. Upon arrival I found that the college officials were simply showing up at the church financial office and asking for money to make the payroll. The college did not have the money to pay its own bills. Not only did I inherit a church that owed nine million dollars and that fell a million short the previous year, I now found that I had a college that could not pay its own professors. Sherryn Cates had simply been badgered into giving them money in order to run the school. That money was off the books; there was no line item for it in the budget. The college could just as well have been hauling it out of the church business office in wheelbarrows.

This led to some very delicate negotiations with Paige Patterson. I had to put an immediate cap on the amount of money the church could give the college from the 1991 operating budget. We were already $750,000 in trouble the day I started work. The church could not run a slush fund for the college. Although there was some tension in the conversation, Paige and I agreed on a cap and a declining schedule of draws for the Criswell College. But that was only the beginning of troubles about Patterson and the college.

∾

VISITORS

ONE OF THE FIRST VISITORS I invited to the office was the church's most famous current leader, the motivational speaker Zig Ziglar. Zig taught the auditorium class, the largest Sunday school department at the church. He gave some of his usual motivational material and ended the sessions with an appeal for Christian discipleship. Zig was the church's main draw for new, unchurched pagans. Salesmen and managers needing a boost would drive downtown on Sunday morning to hear Zig. After his "meet you at the top" boosterism, he made a genuine appeal for conversion. While Zig was at the church 20 percent of our adult baptisms came from his class. He would have as many as four hundred in the auditorium. His "class pastor" was Paul Gomez, one of the sharper young staff members. Paul worked full time caring for the members of Zig's class and working the prospects.

Some of the members criticized Zig's approach as "too secular." They did not like a man teaching sales motivation in Truett's sanctuary. I thought it was a good idea. Pagans do not come to church to hear sermons. Zig baited them with his motivational material and then gave them the gospel. He turned around hundreds of lives with that approach. I told one of his critics, "Halitosis is better than no breath at all." A censorious woman once told D. L. Moody, "I don't like the way you do evangelism." The Chicagoan told her, "Ma'am, I like the way I do it better than the way you don't do it." At least Zig was on the playing field, not in the bleachers. Until something much better came along, I was all for anyone who could put four hundred people in the sanctuary, many of them unchurched.

I wanted to see Zig because he had wanted James Merritt to be his pastor. Zig was apparently a friend to Drake and Yates on the pastor search committee. But more than that, Zig thought W. A. should retire and get out of the picture. Since Merritt had the temerity to ask for just that, Zig liked the idea. So I asked Zig to come to my office as the very first visitor. I sat down, looked the renowned speaker in the eyes, and asked him to support me. He was candid. He told me that he wanted Merritt. But he stated that the church had acted and I was now the pastor. He would support me. I felt relieved. I did not want the most popular teacher in the church leaving at the beginning of my ministry. (He would later leave, but not because of me.)

Months later, Zig would call me to his headquarters in north Dallas. He told me that I was being demeaned by Criswell in front of the entire church. He said, "Every time he calls you 'lad' I cringe." He predicted that the men of the church would ultimately hold me in contempt if I continued to play the sycophant to Criswell. He interpreted my tenure at the church up to that point. Up until Easter 1991, my ministry had gained momentum, according to Zig. We had ten thousand people in Sunday school that Easter and the auditorium filled three times. Zig allowed that things started to slow down after that. The people saw that W. A. would not go, that I would not preach the 10:50 A.M. service for some indefinite extension of time, and there would not be a substantial transition. At the time Zig told me, I thought he was presumptuous. In hindsight he was absolutely right in his assessment. The momentum of my new ministry began to slow when Criswell refused to get off the scene after the first few months.

Zig then made a bold proposal. He suggested that I announce a leave of absence for three months. Get out of there. Take a trip. Tell the lay leadership to settle the situation. He guaranteed me that things would change. He would help see to it. I was shocked speechless at the proposal. Here sat a bona fide national figure requesting that I force the issue with Criswell. It would have been interesting, to say the least, had I followed Zig's advice. Yet I knew to win that battle would be to lose the war. The Criswell fanatics would never forgive me. I would fight a war of attrition for the rest of my days. When I did quit and leave the scene for good, the Criswellites defamed me from that day forward. Had I left with the intention of coming back, God knows what they would have done.

But Zig had a larger problem with the church than any of that. He was a trustee at the Criswell College, one of the few that supported Paige Patterson at that time. He was outraged at what he perceived to be the Criswell's maneuverings to get Paige fired. So the first visitor to my office represented the largest ongoing problem of my twenty-one months: Paige Patterson and the Criswell College.

The second heavy hitter to visit my office represented the other side of that problem. Bo Sexton held the chair of trustees for the college. In addition to that he would be the next deacon chairman, then serving as the vice-chairman of deacons. After Bo settled into his chair he indicated a need to talk about the "problem at the college." I already knew there was a money problem. I had no inkling of what he was about to tell me. Paige Patterson was in trouble. Most of the trustees wanted him out. This minor piece of intelligence had not arisen in any previous meeting with the search committee, Criswell, the lay leadership, or with Paige himself. I would later find out that the cognoscenti among the fundamentalist leaders in the denomination knew this. Apparently a number of them begin the day in a round-robin phone marathon checking each other's pulse. I never participated in these tête-a-tête, having little interest or time for them. Among other things, this left me out of the loop in a great deal of denominational gossip. Apparently the knowledge of Paige's troubles was widely known among the insiders. I was the last to know.

When I did quit and leave the scene for good, the Criswellites defamed me from that day forward. Had I left with the intention of coming back, God knows what they would have done.

Leaning forward in the stuffed leather chair matching the one where Bo sat, I wanted to know more. Dr. Patterson, it seems, was out of town too much to manage the college. When he was in town, according to Bo, the place was in fiscal and administrative chaos. Added to that was a whole string of administrative faults alleged to have been committed by Patterson. The vice-presidents of the college did not support his leadership and some professors were of the same persuasion. I returned a blank stare to Bo, having heard none of this before that moment.

I suggested to Bo that it would be best my first days in office not to deal with this. He agreed, and said that it would be a trustee matter, but I needed to be informed because of the "possible fall-out in the church." No one is neutral on Paige Patterson, that fiery, polemical redhead. Bo had just laid on me the major problem in the church for the better part of my short career.

I could never get away from the Patterson issue. When I went to the YMCA for a brief respite of exercise, a towel-clad deacon approached me in my birthday suit demanding, "You are the only one who can save Paige Patterson." In the same facility shortly thereafter another church leader told me, "Patterson must go. You have to take a stand."

Of course, Old Teflon had nothing to do with it. Paige had been telling me for years that Betty Criswell wanted him long gone, but he had a board of trustees that would not let her get to him. Apparently things had changed on the board in recent times. Paige's account, of course, was different from that of Bo. Paige had built the college faithfully for seventeen years from nothing to a three-hundred-student institution with twenty faculty members. The school was in financial trouble, Paige said, because Criswell insisted on buying the new campus. The old campus using the church plant had been fine with Paige, who had nothing to do with the move and the nine million dollars spent on the new campus. To himself, Paige was the victim of a cruel conspiracy hatched by the Criswells, Sexton and other "worldly" trustees, and the ingrates who served as vice-presidents.

Over two years I heard enough plots in this story to confuse Agatha Christie. The accusations hurled by both parties ricocheted through the church like loose bullets. The issue divided the church, the deacons, the staff, and the major benefactors to the college. At a time when the energies of a new pastor should have poured into the church, the problems with an ancillary organization depleted not only my energy but that of the principal lay leaders. The problem became so entangled that I lost all interest in who was "right" and who was "wrong." Like Tommy Lee Jones in *The Fugitive,* I wanted to say, "I don't care." I just had to solve it and keep it from blowing up the church.

ௌ

FIRST ACTS AT FIRST

ONE WEEKLY RESPONSIBILITY was to write the "Pastor's Pen" column in the church's newsletter, *First Baptist Reminder.* While many mega-church ministers no longer write a weekly column, Criswell for decades had penned a rather lengthy potpourri of promotion, recognition of members, comment on current events and down-home humor. My first column was a paean of praise for Criswell:

> For more than forty-six years Dr. W. A. Criswell has written this column. In this church and across the nation, in city congregations and in country chapels, Baptists and nonBaptists by the thousands have read his words. I am among them. He stamps his charm, wit, passion, and inimitable style onto this page. His weekly words have been for decades a breath of air refreshing. At Dr. Criswell's request, this weekly responsibility now falls to me.

Dr. Criswell is in his forty-seventh year as pastor, now senior pastor, of this congregation. He is a hero and a legend, alive and yet larger than life. At his eighty-first birthday he is more with us than ever. From my earliest memories as a sixteen-year-old Texas Baptist preacher boy, he has been my model and mentor, a constant presence in my life and ministry. For me he has always been there. Like an Everest towering over the landscape he was rarely out of sight, and even when he was, he was still a presence to me.

Dr. Criswell has no living peers. As a preacher he stands alone. As a pastor his presence with his people is legendary. As an administrator of church growth he has been not years, but decades ahead of his time. The only names in Baptist pastoral life that can stand alongside him are those of Spurgeon and Truett. Even as Spurgeon's crowning days of ministry were in the last decade of the nineteenth century, so also Dr. Criswell's consummating days are in the last decade of the twentieth century.

Dr. Criswell cannot be replaced, may not be imitated, but must be followed. God who created heaven and earth made only one W. A. Criswell. As a First Baptist deacon of yesteryear said, "God broke the mold when He made Dr. Criswell." I am under no illusion that Dr. Criswell can be replaced. I cannot replace him, but by your call I must follow him. In one sense, the highest tribute to a man is that he can be followed. In nineteenth century England there were two great Baptist pastors, preacher, and authors—one in Manchester and Spurgeon in London. The Manchester man's church is now gone and his work reduced to books. Spurgeon's church, sermons, and college abide to this day. He brought forth fruit and his fruit remained.

Most of you understand the weight of history, the enor-
mity of the legacy, and the mandate for continuity that
now fall on me. Only a deluded man would consider himself equal to the task. My only sufficiency rests in God and
in your prayers. If I succeed, it will be because you beg God
to help me and overlook my inadequacies which will soon
be evident to many. If I fail, I shall fail gloriously pouring
all my strength and life into this task, for there is no other
task before me for the rest of my life. I have the confidence
in God to trust triumphantly that I shall not fail, but rather
that with God above me, Christ beside me, and the
beloved church gathered around me, we shall work till
Jesus comes.

Thus I began what would become almost a weekly panegyric of
elaborate praise to Criswell. From a later standpoint it appears
obsequious, as if I were a fawning sycophant or toady. At the
time it seemed the appropriate thing to do. The Old Man
deserved some praise. Some on the church staff and membership
objected about his giving up the weekly column. I frankly
thought all of my praise was appropriate to his going off the
scene as promised in a few months. When it became apparent
that he would not quit, I backed away from these elegant trib-
utes. It became obvious that such heartfelt praise from me provided a "fix" to him that encouraged him to stay. It was naive for
me to think that such praise would help smooth the way for the
Old Man to leave on a high note. The more he was praised, the
more he wished to stay.

The ego of W. A. Criswell became a fascinating study to me.
It is unlike the ego of Friedrich Wilhelm Nietzsche's "super-
man," the conscious, willful assertion that "man is god." That is

a raging, towering ego that vaunts itself. Then there is the ego of a movie or athletic star, gushy and newly achieved, without any real connection to long-term merit.

Neither of these represent the ego of Criswell. To me he is the victim of an "innocent" ego, more akin to that of a two-year-old. A two-year-old is without pretense the center of his own world. When you stroke the child with praise, he simply beams and smiles as if to say, "Give me more." I watched Criswell praised by me, the press, and the public. His ego was that of a child who simply expects to be the center of attention. He reminded me of my Yorkshire. When you scratch his tummy, he rolls over and waits for more, with a sort of innocence that makes one wish to rub him again. This naive egotism has a sort of attractive quality that makes the givers just give more. It also makes it very hard to give up the place where it all happens, in this instance, First Baptist, Dallas.

Chapter Six

∾

The Criswells and Me:
Conflicting Agendas

irst Baptist knows how to throw a party. The reception for the new pastor was on Sunday evening, January 6, 1991, at the Fairmont Hotel. Dick Clements, Patsy Wallace, the search committee, and Louie Mann of the staff planned the evening, which was to have been the biggest church occasion until W. A.'s complete retirement. Buffets, ice sculptures, instrumental serenades, strolling photographers, and thousands of members showed up. The church must have spent more than ten thousand dollars on the reception itself.

As guests of honor we were provided chairs on a raised dais at the north end of the room. Of course, there were four chairs. The Criswells were also on the dais. There was rarely an occasion on which all four of us were not present, usually seated at the same table or adjacent tables. I am sure that at first the church leaders felt that such recognition for the Criswells would help ease the pain of edging him out. It did no such thing. As I have noted, the more they got, they more they would get. I came to accept it as a way of life.

Again, I am not begrudging of recognition to Criswell. I gave him more of it than anyone else had in the history of the church. If it had been possible to lead First Baptist and at the same time allow him an even more conspicuous place for years, that would have been fine with me. But in event after event it became obvious that Criswell had no intention of yielding his place to another leader.

The difficulty rested in the dynamics of the situation. In that church in that city it was impossible to establish the necessary leadership while Criswell remained constantly visible at every occasion. I doubt that Lee Iacocca could have turned Chrysler around as he did if his predecessor had attended every board meeting and each significant public function in the company, looking over Lee's shoulder and constantly giving his two cents' worth. This was exactly where I found myself. It started at the reception and it never stopped.

This soon became even more obvious in the matter of a plaque commemorating the pastor search committee. Eugene Green composed an eloquent tribute to the hardy souls who spent twenty-seven months in the war for another pastor. Eugene proposed that a plaque be placed in the sanctuary thanking God for their work. When Mrs. C. got word of that, she responded hotly that there had never been a plaque honoring the committee that brought Dr. C. in 1944.

Now consider the situation. Around the corner of every hallway in the church was a photograph or oil painting of Dr. and Mrs. Criswell. There was the Criswell Building, the Betty Criswell Library of the First Baptist Academy, the Criswell Bible in the pews, the Criswell College, the Criswell Foundation, and even the Criswell Kids Camp. The church radio station was allegedly going to have the call letters KWAC until, at the last minute before the application was filed, someone noted that the acronym read "quack." Still, despite all Criswell's honors, not even a plaque could go up without pricking his ego. I requested that this entire absurdity be dropped for the sake of common sense if not common decency. I had no desire to be in a "war of the plaques."

A similar thing happened with the pastoral portrait hung in the church's main dining area, Coleman Hall. On the wall of Coleman Hall hung three pictures. There was an oil painting of George Truett, a photograph of Criswell by a famous photographer, and an oil of Robert Coleman, Truett's beloved assistant for whom the hall was named. I personally had no thought of being installed with these legendary gentleman, considering that an honor for the distant future if I should last so long. Eugene Green, however, wanted to hang a life-sized heroic portrait. A prestigious photographer in Dallas shot me all over the church. I stood in front of stained glass windows, the pulpit, the railings, the pews and elsewhere. I was then told that none of these poses were what they wanted.

The church next flew in a famous Houston photographer who shot me in the Dallas studio. They finally captured the picture they wanted, whatever that was.

The church next flew in a famous Houston photographer who shot me in a Dallas studio. They finally captured the picture they wanted, whatever that was. He kept telling me to look strong and visionary, like a leader. I kept telling myself that if I did not already look like a leader I could hardly strike the appropriate pose. So I stared into the middle distance, trying to imagine how Napoleon felt reviewing his troops and other such leaderly thoughts. For six thousand dollars, they captured this ineffable image. Months later it suddenly showed up on the wall in Coleman Hall. But it did not stay where it was placed. Some soul had the temerity to hang it in the middle between Truett and Criswell, seeing how I was the present pastor. When I saw that, I told myself in the original Greek, "There ain't no way that will stay." Sure enough, when Mrs. C. got wind of it, the picture was moved to the far right. She considered Coleman Hall, where the chosen three hundred attended her Bible class, a sort of personal fiefdom. Perhaps she didn't want me peering down from that position on the gathering of her class.

ॐ

W. A. SETS THE AGENDA

SHORTLY AFTER ARRIVING I was summoned to the church office of Dr. Criswell. You always had to be told which of his offices. In a grandfatherly way he opened the calendar. He intoned, "Now, lad, let's look at the calendar for the year." In all concourse with me in private and small groups Dr. C. was never anything other than affectionate. It was only in larger group settings before the general staff or in the services that he would be patronizing or worse. He really had no stomach for personal confrontation whatever.

Dr. C. wanted to talk about the schedule for the year. Other than the meetings I have already described, he had a number to add to the agenda. The general staff met once a month. This meeting included virtually all of the full-time employees who were actually at the physical plant of the church. Everyone from the janitors to the pastor sat together for lunch on an upper floor of the youth building. I do not know why we met in the youth building. I once asked how many individual kitchens the church had. I was told "forty-seven." Over the years every group and constituency got its own kitchen. Many of these were considered veritably personal property of the group, kept under lock and key by that group. Why the general staff met in the youth kitchen two city blocks from where we worked was one of the imponderables I never questioned.

Dr. C. wanted to anchor these meetings on the calendar as a high priority. It was the only meeting of the church staff that he attended regularly. We would eat at the same table and then assume a position on a raised dais before the assembled staff. A microphone was placed at the table for both of us to address the staff. We were usually joined there by Mazzola or later by Hedquist, the administrator who came in August 1991. It turned out that in these meetings more than any other Criswell publicly undermined my ministry. Whether we would discuss the calendar, the budget, the staff organization, or the program, he would invariably launch into a soliloquy about the way things used to be or the way things ought to be.

With few exceptions, when I sought to change a tradition of his program at the church, he would openly question the change. For example, in his glory days every fall there was a "round up" that lasted all week, every night of the week. In the fifties and the sixties the whole church came downtown for this heavenly hootenanny. By the nineties this relic had no appeal to the church. It was a major triumph to get a few hundred people to come downtown in the September heat and eat a hotdog. They did it so as not to disappoint Dr. C. and the staff.

The author and W. A. Criswell appear to be having what could be described as a "pointed conversation." (Photo by Ron Jenkins, *Fort Worth Star-Telegram*)

When I sought to limit this hoary tradition to one merciful night, one would have thought I had eliminated Easter Sunday. Month by month I came to dread these meetings. The staff looked back and forth between the two of us as if to ask, "Who's really in charge?" The staff more loyal to me would get a morose, hang-dog look. I never once suggested anything other than respect to Dr. C. in this monthly second-guessing meeting. In front of the staff I tried to downplay his insinuations. On a few occasions, especially when he gave me a patronizing lecture about the budget in front of the staff I was supposed to lead, I was at the very edge of exploding into a confrontation. How would former Dallas Cowboys Coach Jimmy Johnson have felt if predecessor Tom Landry attended the team meetings and second-guessed Johnson's play calling? I later considered that it was little wonder Dr. C. wanted to get these meetings on the calendar.

Peering at his calendar, he then wanted to fix dates for the "three council meetings." Over the years Dr. C. had originated three monthly meetings that were unofficial and by invitation only. The first of these was the "pastor's council." This was a small group of male and female business executives and entrepreneurs in the church fellowship. The head of the gas company, the electric company, Mrs. H. L. Hunt, and other prominent members attended this luncheon. It was hosted in rotation by the members of the committee. It was always hosted in a tony venue, sometimes the private dining room of the executive.

The purpose of this pastor's meeting of the pastor's council seemed primarily to be the promotion of Criswell College. After the first few meetings, there always seemed to be a slight edge of tension in the meeting. The meeting had been styled "the pastor's council" for some years. I was now the pastor, but it was obvious that Criswell was convening the meetings and if not by title at least by tenure and presence still in charge of the show. These meetings were a convivial time of badinage among peers in the Dallas power elite. Toward the end of my tenure the outgoing chairman asked for an appointment. He recognized the situation in a fair-minded way and wished to know what I wanted to do with the group, since I was now the pastor. I could hardly dismiss them. I had no desire to snub the group. In fact, I rather enjoyed the meals and the fellowship, although I was never exactly sure of the rationale for the group.

As Criswell appraised the calendar that day, he next wanted to anchor the dates for the women's council meetings. There was a senior women's council and a younger women's council. Ostensibly these were advisory groups, sounding boards to provide the women's perspective on church life. But they had another, less obvious rationale.

First Baptist is run by a male oligarchy. That means at First not only the deacon body is male, but also every major committee is composed of male deacons. Only a few church committees with relatively innocuous tasks welcome female members. In the Baptist battle of left vs. right, First Baptist was adamantly against allowing women to be deacons or wield any significant power. Among other problems, this meant that Sherryn Cates, the director of the business office, was not even present when the deacons would debate for hours about church finances. I nearly caused a constitutional crisis when I insisted she be present at the meetings. After all, she knew more than anyone else knew about the finances of the church.

With these rare exceptions, First was run by men. The advisory councils of women were to some degree a nod toward recent

American cultural trends (recent meaning this century, since women have the vote and all, etc.). There were in the fellowship some women of enormous achievement, ability, and energy. These councils gave a very limited forum for the expression of that ability, but at least they gave something. Had I remained at the church, there would have been women represented on the major church committees in addition to the deacons. By 1991, the time had come.

The senior women's council met each month in a beautiful Dallas home. For the most part the women on the council were married to successful Dallas business executives. The homes where we met were gorgeous. The furniture, art, statuary, and table place settings revealed impeccable taste. These were occasions of grace and beauty, for the most part a respite from the month's pressures. Gentility, decorousness, and taste reigned. A gourmand would have delighted in the meals. I was treated like a king. The women fussed over Criswell and me. After the luncheon, we would retire to a great room where he and I would be seated before the assembled ladies. They would discuss their several concerns, usually oriented toward the mission ministry of the church or the celebration of its coming one hundred twenty-fifth anniversary. Then Criswell and I would make a statement.

In reflection this was the one meeting of the church in which I felt as if I were really the pastor. These mature women had raised their families in the church and many of their grandchildren were still in the fellowship. They seemed protective of me, as if to shield me against the invidious things that had happened to other would-be successors to Criswell. They were also the most outspoken group in dealing with W. A. Most of them had known him for decades. They would remonstrate with him as if he were an older brother. For some reason in this setting he seemed to be more deferential to me than in any other. He may have known intuitively that his usual condescension would not go down well with these ladies. Or he might have simply been caught up in the warmth of the occasion and the good food.

The young women's council met in the Sonshine Building at the church in a room with one of the forty-seven kitchens. This was a group of younger married women, mostly in their thirties, whose husbands were young businessmen and deacons in the church. I always had the feeling of being in a sort of sorority meeting. I was not as comfortable in this meeting as I was with the older women. In fact, in this one instance I appreciated W. A. coming to the meeting. His presence seemed to leaven the group with the wisdom of age, and also to cause the young women to direct toward him their criticisms of the church.

And criticize they did. The meeting became a monthly complaint session for what they found wrong with the church. Although the president of the group tried valiantly to move the agenda in a positive direction, it invariably mutated into a criticism of the church program. Most of the criticism was leveled at the children's programs. I would furiously take notes and try to remedy things shortly after the meetings. I would leave with promises and covenants that things would be better. Throw me to the lions, but please do not set me in a group of irate young churchwomen. I left the meetings feeling whipped. It was the one meeting which Criswell actually stopped attending. A few of the spitfires in the group did not mind laying some deficiencies at his feet. He found it best that I preside solo in this gathering.

Actually, I was not without sympathy for the young women's plight. Couples by the hundreds had abandoned the old downtown

church in the eighties. The north Dallas churches offered conve-
nience, modern programming, clean facilities, and a lifestyle familiar to the young Dallas elite. The only reason a couple would drive
miles to downtown, park in a multi-story garage, and send their
child to an ancient building had to be love for the church. The
young couples left at First when I arrived had some enduring reason to be there. Their family was there, they had grown up under
Libby Reynolds's excellent program and wanted the
same for their children, or they just liked the com- *Couples by the*
fortable tradition of a program that smacked more of *hundreds had*
the fifties than the nineties. After defying the traffic
on Central Expressway and running the gauntlet of *abandoned the old*
the parking garages, they felt they had a right to say *downtown church*
something about the church program.

in the eighties.
These three councils did, however, create some
jealousy in the church. Since admission was by
invitation, a few folks felt left out. The younger women's group
in particular was charged with elitism. It seemed some of those
outside wanted inside. In the myriad of insoluble problems at
First, I did not address who ought to be in these groups.

Before I left his office on that agenda-setting day, W. A. mentioned two more items: the weekly "television meeting" and the
"pre-Easter services." Late one afternoon each week a small ad
hoc group met to discuss the progress of the television ministry.
That meeting included Dr. Criswell, media minister Ron Harris,
a layman with promotional experience named Aaron Manley,
minister of music Fred McNabb, and Criswell's business partner
Jack Pogue.

The most powerful nonCatholic church in America had a
curious relationship with television. The church could have

owned the finest equipment in the world and have been on hundreds of stations, similar to Robert Schuller or Charles Stanley. Instead, the church had miserably outdated equipment and limped along raising money to stay on the major independent station in Dallas/Fort Worth, Channel 11. That outlet did beam its signal down to 397 cable systems which gave some national play to the ministry.

My view, to paraphrase the Pope, was, "Drink deep, or drink not at all from the TV thing." If you do not do church television well, you should not do it at all. First Baptist, which didn't do it well, found itself in a position of diminishing returns. We were paying one of the highest rates in the nation—twelve thousand dollars per week—for an hour of local television, yet we were using outdated cameras and equipment that projected an inferior product. When I was first shown the control room, I could not believe what I was seeing. It sat close to the attic of the century-old sanctuary, and above the balcony was a tiny crow's nest. In this antique room with its exposed nineteenth-century floorboards had been crammed some television switching equipment. The result was that some Sundays we had neither a color telecast nor a black and white, but something penumbral between the two.

Besides the inferior equipment, there were constant communication problems between the control room and the floor where the cameras sat. One Sunday a camera fell off its support platform, banged an elderly lady in the head, and created a commotion in the sanctuary. Travis Avenue, with 20 percent of FBC's budget, had provided a state-of-the-art television production system.

The weekly meeting studied the previous week's production. Criswell insisted on live television. Without question that does add a sense of immediacy, a certain atmosphere in the service as well as in the viewing audience. Yet it makes great production demands. It is far easier to edit a service with a one-week's delay. The timing is easier, the transitions smoother, and the product more professional. In live church television you cannot help but capture such scintillating shots as dozing men in the choir about to fall out of their chairs, women in the congregation digging through their purses for a tissue to wipe Junior's nose, and men on the platform fiddling with their cufflinks during the prayer (a transgression of my own).

The meeting primarily focused on raising money to stay on the air. The church was a minority partner in this venture. We depended upon money raised from the audience and designated gifts from church members to keep the thing afloat. To that end we interrupted the service with commercials pushing our books and begging people to join the "Investors in Eternity." The latter were anyone who would commit to give a small weekly amount to keep us on the air. Criswell had just published a ghost-written autobiography. That was offered on the air, along with the *Believer's Study Bible*, which was a new edition of the former Criswell Bible. The marketing arm of the Bible publisher involved had discovered that Bibles with a man's name on the spine just under "Holy Bible" did not do as well as generically named Bibles, seeing as how God is the author.

By the time I came to First I had written four books. Several of these were offered on the air. In generosity Criswell gave all of the proceeds from the sale of his books to pay for the television time. It was simply assumed that I would do the same. I was never asked. It was taken for granted that revenues from the pastor's books would pay for television time. Thus the church bought out every copy of my book from the publisher at a steep discount and used the margin for television. I watched this happen with something, of a jaundiced eye, seeing how there were several million bucks' difference between Criswell's personal balance sheet and mine.

Criswell and I would tape the promotional spots selling our books at various places in the church. The favorite was before a stained glass window in the sanctuary. Many members resented these commercials aired during the worship services. They felt it detracted from the dignity and reputation of First Baptist. The other hour-long church broadcast on Channel 11, the First United Methodist Church of Fort Worth, had no such commercial intrusions. I was approached in the church hallways, by letters, and in the council meetings about the embarrassment caused by the commercials. As in everything else, I had simply inherited this as a tradition of the church and was now supposed to fix it, and do so without ruffling W. A.'s feathers or making it appear that anything amiss had been done. I did shorten the commercials, but could not eliminate them without knocking us off the tube.

The final agenda item was the pre-Easter services. Starting with George Truett and continuing with Criswell, the church offered a series of services each day of Holy Week at noon. In Criswell's palmy days he preached the services in the old Palace Theater where three thousand downtown workers crammed the hall. In more recent years the church moved the services to the sanctuary. They were only a shadow of what they had been in the golden age of the church. A few hundred people came to sit in the lower floor while the academy students were forced to sit squirming in the balcony. I chose as a theme "Evidences that Demand A Resurrection." A decent crowd of downtown workers appeared promptly at noon. They were comfortably seated in the sanctuary, meaning that each of them could have laid down on a pew. As in everything else, I had inherited W. A.'s program and lived under the shadow of what used to be. With years of promotion these services could have been revived. There is a place for such an effort during Holy Week in downtown Dallas.

With the agenda thus set, Criswell and I clasped hands while I invoked the Lord to bless us in the days ahead. I did not know how much blessing I would need.

❧

THE OFFICE SITUATION

NO SPECIFIC PLANS HAD BEEN MADE for the new pastor's office. As an interim arrangement I was given an office that had recently belonged to the church administrators. It was down a long, narrow corridor on the northeast corner of the Criswell building. The outer office was a cubbyhole with no seating at all for visiting guests. The office had an inauspicious aura in the recent years. It had been the office of Jimmy Draper, Tom Melzoni, Denny Dawson, and Charles McLaughlin. Three of these four had left under unfavorable circumstances. The ill-omened atmosphere seemed to cling to the office walls.

While risking the tiresome repetition of inscrutable things at First Baptist, this outdid some of the other imponderables. Why would they search the nation twenty-seven months for a pastor and render him up without an office? It put me in the awkward position of having to make inquiries about my own office.

Ed Rawls, the architect and deacon who drew my home study, came to my aid. He drew up plans to modify the northeast corner of the second floor of the Criswell Building into a pastor's suite with a waiting room, secretary/receptionist's office, my office, an assistant's office, an assistant secretary's office, and a private conference room.

Ed, always kind and generous, had given his professional time and had worked with the building staff to see that the entire project would be done in-house, with our own carpentry crew. Still, the planned suite was more elaborate than I needed or expected. I was already aware of Criswell's four offices and knew that invidious comparisons would be made between the size of my office at the church and his office at the church. Some folk were already vigilant that I not be slighted and some vigilant that W. A. not be slighted.

It was a wearisome situation. Just to be safe, I told Ed that I did not want a personal office that was one centimeter larger than his. I asked him to measure Criswell's office to the inch and be sure I came up short.

The office question was made tougher by the money situation. I had been forced to cut the 1991 budget by $750,000. It would hardly have been appropriate to deficit-spend for an office under the circumstances. Luckily, an anonymous donor pledged the amount necessary to finish the office from non-budget, designated funds. By mid-summer of 1991, work was underway, supervised by Mart Cuttrell, the director of our physical plant; Ed Rawls; and Patsy Wallace of the pastor search committee. Patsy brought swatches of fabric, carpet samples, and works of art to be previewed. She was a lady of southern charm, graciousness, and ability. The finished product was an office of impeccable taste and durable usefulness.

The first rumblings I heard indirectly from Mrs. C. concerned the construction of the office. As a member told me,

"She has started her crusade." Mrs. C. was apparently trying to raise the hackles of church members over the provision of the office, which she allegedly characterized as too lavish. She did not get enough response to make a campaign out of it, but I was warned she would watch to see where I would be vulnerable in the future.

This episode put me in a state of vigilance in which every decision I made had to be measured not only by what it would do for the church but also by how Mrs. C. would react. Administrator Tim Hedquist and I would discuss decisions that in and of themselves should have been run-of-the-mill but had to be weighed as to how much trouble Mrs. C. would cause if we implemented the decision. This created gridlock in many cases where action was needed but it was deemed not worth the trouble it would cause.

The first rumblings I heard indirectly from Mrs. C. concerned the construction of the office.

In all of this we sought to be gracious and honoring to the Criswells, who tested our patience often. One of the most ludicrous events of my twenty-one months came just after the office incident. Most Texas Baptist churches have a Wednesday night service, First Baptist being no exception. On the Wednesday before Thanksgiving Day many active members leave for an extended weekend trip. Because of that exodus, the Wednesday evening service before Thanksgiving is historically one of the lowest in attendance for the year. To obviate that, many churches have elected to move the Wednesday service to Tuesday night of Thanksgiving week. The attendance is better and the people can leave for Grandma's on Wednesday evening.

When I proposed this for First Baptist, Criswell objected. Never in history, said he, had First Baptist Church of Dallas closed its doors on Wednesday evening. He would be there on Wednesday to meet with whoever showed up. This left me promoting a Tuesday night mid-week service and Criswell promoting a Wednesday night mid-week service. It was an unnecessary, gratuitous direct challenge to my leadership of the church. In support of Dr. C. the Wednesday night service was promoted in Mrs. C.'s class. In the public services of the church I promoted the Tuesday evening service and Criswell stated that he would be there on Wednesday for whoever showed up. The whole episode was absurd but also partook of the tragicomic. Here was a Christian world figure, needing to hold onto power so much that he would risk looking absurd to do so.

Expecting that he would be humiliated by the no-shows on Wednesday, I acted to head off a public or private breach between the Criswells and me. We invited the Criswells to our home for soup after the Wednesday evening "Criswell" service. Thus the farce took place. On Tuesday night a respectable mid-week crowd showed up for the "Gregory" service. On Wednesday evening ten people showed up in the cavernous old hall. Several of these were staff members related to the Criswell's interests in the church. Dr. C. got up and said a few things about Thanksgiving, I prayed, and we left. We then met at the Gregory home for after-service soup with the Criswells.

This scene demonstrates the unreality of the charade that took place at the church. Criswell had attempted a bald-faced power play by insisting on a Wednesday service. The whole episode had been a distracting, comical irrelevancy. Yet on the social level we all got together at the table for after-church fellowship. I wonder if Criswell saw that as an effort to keep the peace or as obsequious groveling. Personal energies that should have been devoted to leading the church were constantly being drained by these infightings.

❧

NUMBERS AND TV

NUMBERS HAD BEEN THE NAME of the game at First for years. It was an unwritten rule that numbers were always supposed to go up. Great efforts were made in counting both attendance and money in order to achieve that. But in church leadership accurate and meaningful numbers are the only basis of comparison from year to year. Did we grow in attendance? The only truthful answer comes from comparing numbers related to real people who show up at church on Sunday morning.

During my first year we continued counting as the church had been doing. After Tim Hedquist became administrator we launched an all-out program to get the straight skinny concerning the number of people actually showing up.

To choose a Sunday at random under the old system, this is the report for June 10-16, 1991:

Sunday School..7,178
Weekday Bible Studies:
Monday School 183
Tuesday School..134
Wednesday School 353
Thursday School..467
Friday School...110
Total Bible Studies..8,425

It was the big number at the bottom that stuck in peoples' minds. That was to them "how many people we had in Bible study," which to an indifferent observer meant Sunday school. Even before my first official day in office, concerned members bent my ear on "getting honest about the numbers." People who had been in the church for decades watched the attendance figures go up and up, but did not see it represented in live human bodies.

It took me almost my entire tenure, from January 1, 1991, until May 8, 1992, to find out for certain how many people were actually at First Baptist Church on Sunday mornings. It took the administrative genius of Tim Hedquist to ferret out the smoke and mirrors and find out how many folks were really there in Sunday school and church. For the first time in history, on May 8, 1992, we listed the attendance as it really was for April 26, 1992:

WORSHIP SERVICE ATTENDANCE
8:15 A.M. 1,241
9:30 A.M. 565
10:50 A.M. 1,370
TOTAL A.M. 3,176

6:30 P.M. 1,028

BIBLE STUDY ATTENDANCE
Preschool 656
Children 535
Youth 398
Single Adult 215

Adult 1,260
Bible Division 819
New Member Orientation 13
Special Education 92
General Officers 23
ON CAMPUS TOTAL 4,011

Primary Plus 405
Nursing Homes 254
Missions 2,505
TOTAL 7,175

To the casual reader this might appear a debate about how many Baptists can stand on the head of a pin. Actually, one of the great unanswered questions in Baptist life was, "How many people really are going downtown at First Baptist, Dallas?" We received immediate response from other mega-church pastors congratulating us for breaking out the actual figures. They were stunned that we would actually do it. Several of them had five thousand or more on their main campus Sunday school, yet in the annual comparisons with First Baptist, they were bested by our numbers.

Reaching this accurate total took some stern measures. Some folks were counting rest homes in a skewed way. That is, they were counting folks in rest homes who were not actually sitting in an extension Sunday school class at the rest home. Others had "radio members." It took the razor-sharp mind of Hedquist to press the staff to a totally accurate accounting.

Even more interesting was the response of the membership. Many told me, "We've needed to do that for years." It laid down a real base line for measuring achievement in growth. The hardest revelation on Criswell and me was the actual attendance in the sanctuary at worship services. Although a number of larger churches had counted that for years, First had never done so, and had certainly never published it. There was a great mythology about how many people could actually sit in our sanctuary. Tim had it measured on the basis of eighteen inches per person in every pew and seat. The verdict was a seating capacity of 2,020 people. Since even the narrowest Baptists occupy more than eighteen inches, that was a generous allowance. Some people had been under the general impression that there were four or five thousand people sitting in our services on Sunday. There were usually a little more or less than three thousand.

At the first general staff meeting after we started publishing this count, Criswell could not believe it. Incredulous, he asked Hedquist, "But what about the financial program of our church?" By that he meant: How can that few people give as much money as we collected? ("Few" being used in the relative sense of mega-churches.)

I felt genuinely sorry for the Old Man when he was confronted, perhaps for the first time ever, about the actual number of people sitting out there. It was a disappointment to me as well. After seventeen months we had shown no real forward movement in worship attendance. In every other city church I had served the attendance had exploded in the first two years. This was not the case at First. An obvious and self-serving rationale would be to claim I was preaching only half the time in each of the morning services and thus the growth was diluted by Criswell's continued presence. I really doubt, however, that was the case.

External factors had stopped the growth at First years earlier. An 80-percent factor caps the growth of any church. A sanctuary will not consistently hold more than 80 percent of its capacity. For example, when we had by actual count nineteen hundred people in the sanctuary, it appeared to be jammed. Sixteen hundred looked comfortably full. In my first few months during the honeymoon when I preached the 8:15 A.M. service only, the crowd skewed heavily toward that service. It was on some Sundays an embarrassment. Things increasingly leveled out after W. A. and I started rotating, which is another story.

When I became pastor it was agreed that in the mornings I would preach at 8:15 A.M. and Criswell at 10:50 A.M. "for a few months." In my lexicon, few meant "three." By any stretch it could not mean more than "four." But the 10:50 A.M. service was showtime for Criswell. They thundered out the call to worship until the boards in the old hall rattled with the volume. The television cameras came on. Criswell did not want to give this up. After several months he had made no mention again of giving it up. Still, there were several problems. First, the attendance had risen in the 8:15 A.M. service and fallen at 10:50 A.M. Many on the staff and among the members knew that it was only a matter of time until unflattering comparisons would be made, Mrs. C. would go on the warpath, and there would be another disaster like the Draper debacle.

A larger problem was the creation of two churches within the church. Prolonged leadership by a different pastor in each service divided the congregation into camps. By the third month that was already happening. There was hallway talk of "Gregory" people and "Criswell" people. This was obviously unhealthy and would lead to more problems.

Then there was the problem of manipulation in public decisions, or "walking the aisle." As noted earlier, the usual measure of success in a Baptist service is "how many walked the aisle." There was nothing left to chance at First about how many walked the aisle, and at which service. It was a very rare event that someone unexpected walked the aisle at the end of the service. The huge education staff was kept under pressure to produce open decisions in the services.

In that regard I was as big a transgressor as Criswell. The staff reported to me weekly on Friday afternoon by a written tally sheet how many people in each division were to walk the aisle and in which service. The existence of that sheet had preceded my coming, but I beefed it up. When the number of public decisions was low, I would gather the troops on Saturday and we would go out to shake the bushes. After several months there was open comparison of how many people were joining when I preached and how many when Criswell preached. It was at this time that I found evidence that the process was being manipulated. People who intended to walk the aisle when I preached were being shuffled to the other service. This outraged me, but there was nothing to be done about it. To flush it out would make me look terminally petty and cause a royal confrontation with the Criswells. So I just stifled my complaints and went on.

A further ruinous difficulty in the proposed system was my inability to lead the church from the pulpit. I needed the ear of all the people to challenge the old church to move forward. The pulpit promotion of the program was a necessity in the church. I could not establish leadership without access to the entire congregation. Additionally, I needed the television exposure to attract people downtown. Without the outreach provided by television, my ministry at the church was unknown to the masses in Dallas. That is not to say that Dr. C. was without television appeal. He reached a constituency with his kind of preaching, but there was also a group he definitely did not reach. For a comprehensive television appeal, we both needed to be there.

When March ended and there was no mention at his initiative about changing or rotating, I became vigilant. By the end of April I was ready to act. It would be the first test of power with Criswell, but I had to do it.

On the Friday of the last weekend of April 1991, I requested an appointment with Dr. C. in his office. After pleasantries, we got down to business. I did not give him all the reasons listed above. I did tell him that we were creating two congregations, that I could not lead the entire church without access to the entire church, and that I needed the exposure of television. Then I sweetened the pot. On coming to First Baptist, Dallas, I brought with me the Southern Baptist television "Baptist Hour." This was carried on the ACTS Network, the satellite to cable system of the denomination. ACTS was received by ten million homes. In addition, Southern Baptists had bought the Family Net network formerly operated by Jerry Falwell. This added another twelve million homes served by the former Family Net. For four months my morning or evening sermon had been carried on these two networks. I made the offer to W. A. that when he preached at 8:15 A.M. his message would be carried to this audience of potentially twenty-two million homes. When I preached at 10:50 A.M. I would be live on Channel 11. We would rotate

Without the outreach provided by television, my ministry at the church was unknown to the masses in Dallas.

the services between the two of us and between these local and national networks. I was under no obligation to do this, but I thought it would ease the transition for the Old Man.

He then gently remonstrated. First, he simply said that things were going so well, why should we change them? I reminded him that we had talked in terms of my preaching at 8:15 A.M. for "a few months." Waving that off, he then objected that we were both series preachers. We could sustain a series best if we were preaching it in the same service each week. If we rotated, the series would be interrupted. I countered that all of our services were carried on the church-related radio station. The people could listen to both morning services, as in fact most of them did. They would not lose the continuity. He then quietly said, "Things have just been going so well…" It was obvious that I was simply going to have to say I would do it. He finally said, "Whatever you think is best." I really regretted having to come into his office and force him to keep this earlier agreement. It was uncomfortable for us both. Yet not to do so placed us on a collision path of building two constituencies that would cause an ecclesiastical train wreck.

I made this appointment late Friday afternoon for a definite reason. I would announce the new scheme to the church on Sunday morning as a done deal. This would not allow the Criswellites time to orchestrate a disrupting response. It also allowed me to submit it in my "Pastor's Pen" column for the next week. In the first paragraph of my column I wrote concerning the former arrangement, "From the beginning Dr. Criswell and I understood this would be a temporary arrangement." I added, "And thus shall we continue until the dictates of providence and the direction of the spirit bids us otherwise." That rather unctuous statement was a deliberate appropriation of the

Criswellian syntax. One thing I learned from the Old Man was the value of the indefinite, the pragmatism of the vague, and the worth of a hedging statement.

To my surprise this coup went uncontested. Perhaps he thought I would come in, and was just waiting for me to take it away from him. At any rate, we began the rotation that would, with a few exceptions, characterize the remainder of my tenure at First Baptist. This leveled out the attendance in the two services. A few folks followed one or the other of us back and forth, some went to both services, but the net effect over a year was to bring about a draw.

∾

COUNTING MONEY

THE ACTUAL INCOME SITUATION at First Baptist took some time to grasp. The church adopted a budget for some years in the neighborhood of ten million dollars annually. The operating budget for 1992, which was adopted in 1991, was $9,598,928. The sources of income were varied. The undesignated contributions of people in the pews to the general operating budget of the church were slightly more than seven million dollars. The church leased parking spaces to downtown workers in the church-owned parking garages. These revenues were a whopping $1.2 million. This had originally been intended for capital improvements at the church. In the oil and real estate crunch days it was necessary to use these revenues for operations. The church received some other operational funds from income on endowments and other church-related enterprises.

The total income reported by the church of gifts for all purposes soared far beyond the operating income. One reason for this was a peculiar emphasis that Criswell made through the years on giving everything charitable through the church. This resulted in the First Baptist Church business office having to keep up with more than eight hundred designated accounts of giving through the church. These included not only every conceivable charity in Dallas, but also fraternal organizations, alumni organizations of universities, and a host of other causes for which people pumped money through the offices of First Baptist. One day Bill Grubbs, one of the distinguished deacons of the church and a Southern Baptist lay leader, took me to lunch to discuss identifying and limiting this enormous pool of designated giving. The custom was so entrenched that it seemed untouchable.

Criswell explained to me on numerous occasions that he started this practice "to get men used to giving through the church." In his own logic, W. A. said, "If a man will give to something through the church, if a man gets into the habit of giving at the church, he will give more to the church." He could point to the increase of gifts to First over forty-six years as the evidence of his theory's accuracy.

I never bought that argument. It attributed an effect to the wrong cause. The multiplication of designated giving through the church had diminished the giving to the operations of the church, not increased it. It did result in a huge year-end report of total gifts to First Baptist, Dallas.

When Bill Grubbs presided over the 1991 fall budget campaign we decided to bite the bullet and make a major change. The church pledge cards had for years had one line for the budget and another line of designated giving to other causes. By a joint decision we simply eliminated the designated line from the pledge card. For the first time there was one line and one line only on the card, gifts to the operating budget of First Baptist Church. That would result in an honest, clear, forthright statement of what the people were actually giving to the work of First Baptist. It would eliminate all inflation of numbers related to the budget.

Criswell put up a howl. He called me early in the morning at my home study when he had seen the card. "Lad, this will be a financial disaster for the church," he wailed. He pleaded and cajoled and caterwauled that we reprint the cards with the designated line on the card. It is very hard to stand up to such an appeal from the Old Man. I did so by using one of the very phrases I heard him use when he wanted to pass the buck. I said, "That man, that man, uh, ah, em, hem, ah…Grubbs!…do you know him?…that deacon Grubbs has made me do this and he just won't budge. That's just what the man wants to do. My hands are tied!"

In the aftermath of this skirmish, Mrs. C.'s class and others simply drew in a "designated gift" line on their pledge cards by hand. They would not follow the scheme to make their pledges to the budget of the church. The Criswells wanted support from the church to go to the Criswell College. Without the presence of the line for special, designated gifts on the pledge card, there was little opportunity for people to so direct their gifts. For me the church was the priority, not the college. We needed every dime we could attract. The business office had to do interfund borrowing weekly in order to pay the bills due. We were making some vendors wait for months before paying. The church needed to emphasize its operating budget.

CARLOS MCLEOD DIES

IT IS LONELY AT THE TOP. I felt an increased sense of isolation in the position. One friend was always there to cheer me, Dr. Carlos Ray McLeod. On April 2, just three months into my tenure, Carlos suddenly died. I wrote of him, "Dr. McLeod was a friend, encourager, evangelist, motivator, planner, loyal husband, and beloved father. He was a dear, beloved confidante to Dr. Criswell and to me. I shall miss him greatly.

"He loved this church, Mrs. Criswell's class, and his pastors. He served on the pastor search committee, and through that experience he and I shared some of life's deepest moments. Heaven is the richer and we are the poorer in this loss."

To my surprise, the family asked me to preach his funeral with Dr. Criswell assisting. He loved us both and we were both honored to participate. In an intuitive way I feel that things would have been different for me at First if God had left Carlos there. I cannot say how, but he seemed to make a difference in the situation. I never felt a loss of a brother in the work more keenly than that of Carlos.

I would need friends beside me. There was no one there when I came with whom I had worked. It would help when I talked some friends into joining me on the staff. It would hurt when I had to leave them there.

Chapter Seven

❧

The Politics of Faith

I went to be the pastor. I arrived to be the mediator of a dispute. As the Criswell College drained the energies of First Baptist for the duration of my short tenure, I often asked myself: Why was there a Criswell College to begin with?

Southern Baptists were born at Augusta, Georgia, in 1845. In the pre-Civil War rancor that divided every major denomination the question of slavery took center stage. A southern missionary wished to take his slaves with him to the mission field. The northern Baptists, abolitionist in sentiment, refused. Added to all the other regional issues, that became the flashpoint for the organization of the Southern Baptist Convention. Baptists in the South had one seminary, the Southern Baptist Theological Seminary. It moved from Greenville to Louisville where it is today, the mother seminary of Baptists. Its founders, led by John Broadus, were southern gentleman-scholars. By world standards of nineteenth-century theology, they were conservative, orthodox theologians. Among Baptists in the South there was no debate about the nature of scripture or the cardinal doctrines of orthodox Christianity. The Bible was a perfect book, and the orthodoxy of historic Christianity was never even questioned. There was a grand consensus. From the Piedmont of the Carolinas to the High Plains of Texas, Jesus was born of a virgin, lived a sinless life, died a vicarious death of redemption for the world's sins, was buried, physically rose from the tomb, was witnessed by the apostles for forty days as risen Savior, and bodily ascended into heaven from whence He would return triumphantly in His second Advent. These truths were precious to millions of Southern Baptists. From those who grew tobacco in the Carolinas or chopped cotton in Mississippi, to those who raised cattle on the plains of Texas, there was one great *unam sanctum*, one faith. (For those who might think that I am now a cynic—let me state clearly that these truths are my faith, more precious to me than life. No experience with corruption in a local church has changed that for me. I believe the historic Christian faith.)

Southern Baptists entered the twentieth century with these truths intact. They would found five more seminaries to train their clergy: Southwestern in Fort Worth, New Orleans, Midwestern in Kansas City, Southeastern in North Carolina, and Golden Gate in Marin County, California. Nothing in American denominational history could approach the Southern Baptist system for educating its ministry. Nearly forty thousand churches pooled their resources for these six schools to educate their clergy. The students themselves attended virtually tuition-free. All one had to do was show up with a college diploma and an endorsement from his "home church" indicating that the folks back home thought he was "called to the ministry." Churches entrusted their preacher-boys to the faculties of the seminaries expecting that they would return home to propagate the biblical faith that represented the congregations of the South.

This grand consensus continued with very few exceptions until after World War II. Following that war there were two developments in theological education that would ultimately destroy the consensus of America's largest nonCatholic denomination.

First, a German layperson named Rudolph Bultmann at the University of Marburg spearheaded a school of biblical criticism called "form criticism." Bultmann considered the twentieth century church member unable to accept a miraculous Christianity. Scientific human beings could not accept the New Testament record as it stood with healings, exorcisms, and resurrections. So he set about to recover the core of the gospel message that had been papered over with legends, myths, and inventions by the early Christians. They had attributed statements to Jesus that He had never spoken and miracles that had never taken place.

For Bultmann, the role of the church was to recover this irreducible minimum of the *ipsissima verba*, the actual words Jesus Christ spoke. This process was like peeling back the layers of an onion. As if sediments had deposited in layers of soil, the New Testament had to be excavated to find out what Jesus actually said. For the disciples of Bultmann, there was no question of a perfect Bible. It was a hodgepodge of rumor, myth, legend, and invention which obscured the real words of Jesus.

Bultmann's theory saturated the universities of the continent and much of Great Britain. From those venerated shrines of learning, it leaped the Atlantic to the prestigious divinity schools of the northeastern United States. The Southern Baptists were insulated from all of this until after World War II.

Then the most promising faculty and students of Baptist seminaries began to venture to Harvard Divinity, Union Theological in New York, or to the continental centers of learning. There they were swept off their feet by the erudition of the form critics. A southern boy sitting in a seminar at Harvard or Oxford met a very different face of Christianity than he had ever known. Instead of a well-meaning but semi-literate, pulpit-pounding home pastor, he met urbane, credentialed, cosmopolitan theologians. Smug, multi-degreed, and confident liberals, they intimidated him from the very beginning. He saw no midpoint between the faith of his home church and the scholarly consensus of form criticism. As a matter of intellectual pride, he became ashamed of sitting in the pews of a clapboard wooden church in southern Alabama singing "Are You Washed in the Blood of the Lamb?" If he were going to join the world fraternity of leading scholars, he could no longer embrace the simple biblicism of his Southern roots.

Then he got appointed to the faculty of a Baptist seminary. Almost no one in the pews had even heard of the form criticism that was now his biblical hermeneutic. The fresh-faced kids who showed up in his seminary classes only wanted to learn more about Jesus and how to build churches like the ones in which they grew up. So he modified his form criticism, covertly raising enough questions about the biblical narrative that some of those kids had doubts of their own about Jesus walking on the water or raising Lazarus. The brighter among these were then shipped off to the same theological finishing schools and came back as the next generation of Southern Baptist professors.

This scenario did not describe every professor in all of the schools. It did typify enough of them that a major conflict developed between the biblical faith represented in the Southern pews and the form criticism in the seminaries. The two camps were on a collision course that would rock the denomination. By the sixties, Baptist pastors awakened to the invasion of their seminaries by liberals. The denominational establishment, including its executives in Nashville and its presidents elected annually, simply wanted it all to go away for the sake of "missions and evange-lism." They wanted millions of Baptists to pre-tend that a consensus continued that was really no longer there, at least in the seminaries.

By the sixties, Baptist pastors awakened to the invasion of their seminaries by liberals.

Enter Criswell. By the sixties, W. A. had with typical intuition sniffed out this whole shift. He possesses an unquestioned perspicacity. As a lonely voice he became the defender of the faith. I have no question that Criswell is deeply devoted to the historic fundamentals of the Christian religion. In that I grant him a consistency and genuineness that I cannot grant him in his relationship with me. In the face of an entrenched denomi-national establishment he became a voice crying in the wilder-ness, decrying any change in the Southern Baptist Zion. His defense of the faith reached a boiling point during his presiden-cy of the Southern Baptist Convention with his publication of the volume *Why I Believe the Bible Is Literally True*. This book contained his impassioned defense of a perfect Bible as the basis of the Christian faith.

Dissatisfied with the status quo and desiring to perpetuate his unique blend of pulpit passion, church-growth methodology, and biblical conservatism, he founded the Criswell Bible Institute in 1970. At first it appeared to be an institute for the advanced training of laity at the church as well as ministers. Criswell employed a former seminary president to head it up. Housed in the church facilities, the school, the faculty and the church were intertwined.

Then Dr. Paige Patterson became President of Criswell College. He was a Baptist blue-blood. His father T. A. "Pat" Patterson had been the chief executive for the Baptists of Texas, the juggernaut of the Southern Baptist Convention. Paige was graduated from Hardin-Simmons University in Abilene, a more conservative school than Baylor. He chose New Orleans Seminary where he eventually earned the doctor of theology degree, then moved through the ranks of churches until he became pastor of First Baptist, Fayetteville, Arkansas. From there the natural-born polemicist, admiring Criswell and raring to lead a school, came to Dallas. With Paige, the Criswell College had a driving force and a mentor.

ℜ

PATTERSON-PRESSLER COALITION

BY 1979, PATTERSON HAD JOINED with Houston judge Paul Pressler to forge a coalition that would return the SBC to its conservative roots. Crisscrossing the South, Patterson and Pressler warned the pastors of the denominational defection to the left. Baptists were called to converge on the Astrodome in Houston to recapture Zion. In June 1979, they did just that with the election of Adrian Rogers as president of the Southern Baptist Convention. This shot began the most heralded denominational war in U.S. history. After fifteen years it shows few signs of abatement. The denominational establishment quickly seized the high ground by calling themselves moderates and branding the right with the term fundamentalists. At this time in American cultural history fundamentalists were identified with the white-clad followers of the Ayatollah, not to mention other folks in the South who wore sheets.

To the astonishment of the establishment, the "Patterson-Pressler" coalition won the election in Houston. The denominationalists considered this a one-year aberration that would be quickly corrected when the "right folks" showed up at the next annual meeting. When the right wing won every election through 1984, the establishment sounded the alarm. They must be stopped at Dallas in June 1985. The uproar before and after the Dallas convention cannot be compared with anything else. The left wing ran Dr. Winfred Moore, the venerable pastor of First Baptist, Amarillo, who insisted that he had never met a liberal in the SBC and the whole thing was a power play by the right wing, who ran Dr. Charles Stanley, pastor of the First Baptist Church of Atlanta and "America's pastor." Forty-five thousand messengers showed up at Dallas.

I had sat out the controversy. From 1979 until 1982, I pastored the seminary church in Fort Worth, Gambrell Street Baptist Church. At the same time I was trying to finish writing a Ph.D. dissertation and hardly had time to sleep, much less engage in controversy. From 1982 until 1985 I served as assistant professor of preaching at Southwestern Seminary. As a denominational employee I was expected to keep my nose out of the controversy. The seminary president Russell H. Dilday, Jr., had little open involvement with the controversy until 1985, when he jumped in with both feet. I left the seminary to become pastor of Travis Avenue Baptist Church in Fort Worth.

Welcome to the war. In leaving Southwestern Seminary after three years, I did not desire to reflect on Russell Dilday. I had been his pastor from 1978 until 1982, when he installed me on the faculty. In my farewell conversation with Russell he informed me that I could leave with his good wishes if I would nominate Dr. Winfred Moore for the convention presidency. Since addressing the SBC five times in Pittsburgh in 1983, I had built up some cache with the "nonaligned" pastors who not had fallen off the fence to the left or the right. Since the margin of victory for six years had been a cat's whisker, it was felt that whoever captured the middle in Dallas would win. I hedged in responding to my recent boss. Then in quick succession I was called by Dr. Jimmy Allen, president of the Southern Baptist Radio and Television Commission and the outgoing interim pastor of Travis Avenue. He likewise leaned on me to nominate Winfred Moore. When I caught my breath, I received a call from Dr. Keith Parks, president of the foreign mission board of the Southern Baptist Convention, imploring me to nominate Dr. Moore. Then a call came from my alma mater, Baylor, asking me to nominate Dr. Moore. I had never known such pressure in my life.

For all of them I had a simple answer. I had been asked to speak that week in Glorieta, New Mexico, to two thousand Baptist laypersons meeting in the mountain retreat outside Santa Fe. To break that commitment was unthinkable; it was a desired platform and an honor to be invited. I could not be in Dallas that June day.

Then the pressure came from the other side. Dr. Richard Land, Dean of the Criswell College and a D.Phil. of Oxford University, asked to meet with me. We met in the dining room of the Fort Worth Club. He represented the right wing of the SBC and was asking me on their behalf to nominate Dr. Stanley. I had just become pastor of a church divided down the middle over the controversy. To have nominated the right-wing candidate would have created a furor in the fellowship. My sentiment was with the conservatives, but my reality was to pastor a local church.

Then another call came from the Baylor crowd. They would send the Baylor jet to Santa Fe to fetch me in the midday. I could fly to Dallas, nominate Moore, and be back in New Mexico for my evening engagement. That struck me as ironic. The left wing had bashed the fundamentalists for busing people into the annual meetings to pad their vote. The left wing did not bother with buses; they had jets! I declined to nominate either candidate, offended both men, raised suspicion about my true inclination on both sides, and breathed a long sigh when the meeting was over. Stanley won.

Throughout the eighties I held intermittent conversations with Paige. When I was guest preacher at First in 1984, he showed me where the mines were buried. From time to time I was invited to speak at the college or for the School of the Prophets, the annual church/college open house for preachers from around the world to show them how to do it. Just before the 1985 showdown I hosted a clandestine meeting between Patterson and Dilday in Patterson's office on a rainy night. My intent was to see if there was any hope for a rapprochement before a terminal schism. In a prolonged dialogue that night in Dallas it became obvious there would be no peace.

Paige recognized in the eighties that I would jeopardize my leadership at Travis Avenue to align overtly with the right wing. The influence of Southwestern Seminary on the church preclud-ed an open alliance. We talked many times of my responsibility in the denominational war and the right use of personal influence. I told Paige, "I will fire my shot when it will count."

I did and it cost me. It looked as if all the marbles were on the table when Dr. Morris Chapman of First Baptist, Wichita Falls, Texas, would be the candidate against Dr. Daniel Vestal, then of the Dunwoody Church in Atlanta. Scurrilous rumors were circulated about Chapman's mental health and alleged difficulties with his own congregation. Chapman came out with an appeal that it was time to "enlarge the tent," meaning to include those conservative Baptists who had been shut out by the right-wing political movement. Along with Dr. John Bisagno of First Baptist, Houston, I publicly endorsed Morris Chapman under his "enlarge the tent" platform.

The reaction was swift and hot. The *Fort Worth Star-Telegram* carried my endorsement on the front page of the Saturday morning edition. I wrote my rationale in the Travis church paper. Russell Dilday called asking to meet with me. I warned him that I had already taken action and did not want a confrontation with him. He pleaded to meet with me. I requested that we meet at the Men's Grill of the Fort Worth Club. He was agitated with me. I had been his pastor, he had been my boss, and we had been friends. I had dreaded this moment for years but knew that it would eventually come. With tears in his eyes he told me that he felt betrayed by my endorsement of Chapman. He took it very personally. How could I align myself with the fundamentalists? I responded that he knew of my personal conservative convictions. The denomination was in terminal gridlock. Morris had promised to enlarge the tent, but I believed it was time to put most of the people under one tent and ask the others to stay or go. Russell bought none of this; I did not expect that he would. We parted, never to have the same relationship again. For years I had been invited to preach or to guest-lecture at Southwestern. I was never asked back again.

At Travis there was a tangible tension in the air on Sunday morning. I announced that I would not politicize the pulpit, but would hold a pastor's forum at 5:00 P.M. that afternoon. A thousand people showed up in the massive sanctuary. An assortment of seminary professors, laymen who did not like Morris Chapman, the wife of a prominent denominational leader and others all confronted me before the gathered throng. They blasted Chapman, the conservatives, and questioned my "dragging Travis Avenue" into the battle. All of this was actually melodramatic and a bit overdone. I took my lickin', acted diplomatically, and dismissed the crowd for Sunday evening worship. But things were never exactly the same at Travis after this endorsement. Although hundreds of members openly supported the right wing, the big guns in the church did not want me involved in the political process.

In the midst of this public pressure, Paige called me in a jocular tone. He cajoled me, "You really sat down on a Bunsen burner, didn't you? Now you know what I've lived with for years." I had felt ill at ease for years that men on both sides had put their ministerial careers on the line, undergone traumatic personal attack, and withstood pressure within their own churches while I sat it out. Whatever the price, I did not feel I could do that any longer. In a sense I felt that I had undergone a baptism by fire, a sort of rite of passage into the bloodied warriors of the conservative camp. Paige welcomed me into the arena. Although he and I had endured some harsh personal differences in denominational politics, I always found him on the personal level to be forgiving and embracing.

During the twenty-seven months of pastoral search Paige and I talked a dozen times. Paige often insinuated that Mrs. C. wanted him out, but he had trustees standing between him and her. I took that to be the case when I accepted the call of the church. I had no idea that he had spent the last year in a pitched battle with the trustees over his own stewardship of the school. I have already written of my first office visit with Bo Sexton concerning "the problem at the college." It was news to me.

LIVING WITH THE COLLEGE PROBLEM

I CAME TO DREAD THE GATHERING of the Criswell College trustees. Before each meeting of the group there was a firestorm of speculation that Patterson would be fired. The professors issued statements. The students protested. The campus was in an uproar. My phone rang. My mailbox was full.

Dr. Patterson had once taught a large, nongraded Sunday school class for adults. It was now named "The Patterson Class." A young firebrand professor, Danny Akin, taught the class. The class became a beachhead for agitation in the church in favor of Patterson. I was threatened with a mass exodus of both people and money if I did not save Patterson. Akin, who suffered from aggravated epistolary compulsion, fired off hotheaded letters to trustee leaders. In one scorching letter he accused me of cowardice for not taking a Martin Luther-like "Here I stand" posture to save Patterson, do or die. Danny was young, inexperienced, and loyal to his friend. I dismissed his insinuations.

But I could not dismiss the appeals of more seasoned veterans in the church leadership. Nor could I ignore the phone calls from national Baptist leaders—former presidents of the SBC—imploring me to hold off the wolves until Paige could find suitable employment. My first effort of amelioration came early in the fray. With the threat underway that Patterson would be immediately dismissed, I attempted a sort of compromise between Criswell, Sexton, and Patterson. Paige constantly traveled the nation and the world for the conservative Baptist cause. I suggested that he become a distinguished emeritus, a sort of super-professor-at-large with full salary, office, credentials, and portfolio to travel the earth on behalf of conservative Baptist needs and whatever else he needed to represent. He would retain the title of associate pastor at the church. The school would simply get another president. Paige would move over but not out. Paige heard me carefully and asked for time to consider the proposal. I hoped it would work and the issue would be solved.

Paige called later to say he could not accept the offer. To do so would be to admit implicitly the validity of the charges against him. He felt that his integrity was at stake in maintaining the presidency. I had no real answer for this argument; that is a personal judgment beyond another's intervention. Breathing a sigh and anticipating a battle ahead, I wished him well.

Not to beg the question, but I was never sure what the issues were, who was in the right, or what should be done. Sexton, most of the vice-presidents and the trustees accused Patterson of negligence in administration. They charged him with excessive absenteeism, fiscal mismanagement, the failure to raise capital funds, and various other mortal and venial administrative faults. The whole thing was accompanied with a great deal of the "I-really-like-him-personally-but…" kind of rhetoric.

Criswell, the namesake of the school, wanted Paige out but wanted nothing to do with the ouster directly. I listened to Criswell undermine Paige in numerous settings. Something about this never set well with me. Paige Patterson had been Criswell's anointed spear-carrier in the battle for the Bible. Without Paige Patterson's efforts Criswell's vision for the Southern Baptist Convention would never have materialized. Criswell could never stand the personal confrontations necessary to pull it off. As Paige became increasingly embroiled in the controversy, however, Criswell distanced himself from Paige. Under pressure from denominationalists in the church, W. A. even attempted to muzzle Paige in the eighties.

I did respect the business judgment of Bo Sexton. If Sexton said there were financial and administrative problems at the school, I had to grant Bo credibility. In every other context I found Bo to be a straight-shooter. What I did not ever know was the extent to which Bo's judgment on Paige was shaped by the Criswells and the extent to which it was independent. They were all there before I joined the wagon train.

Paige responded that he had been misused. He pointed to the growth of the school under his leadership. There were three hundred students, twenty faculty members, a highly respected theological journal, a new facility, and thirty million dollars in wills targeted at the school. He argued that no new Bible college in the country could point to such illustrious achievement in such a short time. In fact, for most Southern Baptists the school was more identified with Paige than with the name it bore. His detractors had another agenda according to Paige. Just what that agenda was, however, I never could augur. Individuals and delegations of lay people came into my office arguing the merits of both sides of the question. Concerned churchmen with furrowed brows hoped that it "would not blow the church up." Those in the Patterson camp threatened that First Baptist would only be a shadow of itself when his devotees abandoned the old ship. The longer the battle lasted the less inclined I was to believe that there would be a mass exodus from First. By 1991, just about everyone had gone who would go. For folks who loved the kind of melodrama represented in the Patterson conflict, First was the only show in town. The other big churches in town had nothing like the continuous sideshows that intrigued the members at First.

THE GREAT AIRPORT MEETING

AT THE ZENITH OF THE CONFLICT came the great airport meeting. I doubt it will stand in church history alongside the Diet of Worms or the Council of Chalcedon, but those who were there will remember it. It appeared that the noose was around Paige's neck. I had learned to live with the college problem as a dull ache, a dripping faucet in the bathroom of church administration. What I had not yet lived with was a fired Paige Patterson. Given the options, I thought it best to forestall any precipitous actions. So I called one of the wiser denominational heads, Dr. Adrian Rogers, three-time president of the SBC and pastor of behemoth Bellvue Baptist in Memphis. Tall, Hollywood-handsome, with a voice like the bass register of a rumbling pipe organ, and possessed of a lightning-fast, intuitive mind, Rogers is the man you want in a problem. He knew the struggle that the Patterson problem was within the church and had empathy for me. His church was related to the Mid-America Seminary.

We came to the conclusion that it would be good to have a summit of Baptist conservative leadership meet the trustees available, Criswell, and me.

There resulted a gathering of men who otherwise would not have been present on such short notice. Adrian Rogers, Jerry Vines, co-pastor of the gigantic First Baptist in Jacksonville, Florida, Charles Stanley, Jack Graham of Prestonwood Baptist in Dallas, Tom Elliff of Del City First Baptist in Oklahoma, several trustees, Sexton, Criswell, and me. Rogers, Vines, and Stanley were former presidents of the Southern Baptist Convention. Stanley is a recluse who hardly ever leaves his home study. The fact that men of this stature would drop everything and fly to Dallas/Fort Worth Airport to support Paige was an elegant tribute to his place in their lives. Each of the former presidents recognized that they owed their positions humanly to the efforts of Paige Patterson. Along with Paul Pressler, Paige had gotten out the vote for the conservative presidents at the annual meeting of the SBC.

We sat around a square of skirted tables in a basement conference room of the airport hotel. The meeting lasted nine hours. At the head of the table I sat with Bo Sexton. Criswell occupied an unaccustomed inconspicuous place at a back corner of the table. He knew where the power seats were in any meeting, and in this one he tried to fade into the wallpaper. He knew what was coming.

After opening the meeting I let the visiting dignitaries have their say. And have it they did. These pastors were not in the habit of interference from laymen in their churches. They ruled like kings. They proceeded to lecture the trustees at length concerning the person and value of Paige Patterson. Jerry Vines and Charles Stanley were clearly hot. Stanley recounted his own battles at First Baptist, Atlanta. On his accession to the pastorate, an oligarchy of laypersons opposed him. He then spelled out to Bo Sexton and the trustees the horrible things that had happened to the families of those who opposed him: disease, death, divorce, etc. The implication was clear: if you touch Paige Patterson, God will get you. I was sitting next to Bo and thought he would explode.

As usual, Rogers was the class act. Deliberate, calming, respectful, and sage, he moved the meeting toward some pacific conclusion. Through the hours Criswell had not said one word. I doubt in Criswellian history he had sat so quietly for so long. Finally Stanley nailed him. He wanted a word from Criswell. His name was on the college. He could not sit this one out. What did he want to do with Patterson? This was a moment of highest drama. The heirs of Criswell's vision for the SBC, the men who brought it to pass, the closest thing to peers he had in the world, all stared at the silent W. A. If this had been in the Cotton Bowl and if people had known that this moment would come, I could have sold tickets and filled the thing up.

Criswell stood up. His taut face paled, his skin looked like parchment, and his eyes filled with tears. He then uttered the words we had awaited for nine hours: "Let's just wait on God."

That was it. Bo Sexton looked as if someone had pulled a cork out from the bottom of his foot. The blood drained from his face, he picked up his notes with agitation, and said he was leaving. Criswell had just pulled the rug out from under Bo. From Sexton's viewpoint I could understand his anger. He had led the trustees to do the very thing W. A. wanted, and then the Old Man put it all on hold.

Of course, "Let's just wait on God," meant nothing definite. It was a typical display of Criswellian ambiguity. W. A. did not want to be held responsible by the pastors assembled in that room for putting Paige Patterson out on the street. When it came to being judged by his peers or supporting his own layman, he chose his peers. This stung Bo so much that he told me he was quitting the church and leaving organized Christianity. Late that night, exhausted after the meeting, I drove to Bo's house in Highland Park and talked him out of resigning his positions at the church. He was due to be elected as chairman of the deacons. He stood tall among the lay leaders and did not need to surrender.

Criswell's statement left Patterson in no-man's land, a twilight zone where he would sit for months until something else, God only knew what, happened. The implication seemed to be that the powerful men in that room would go to work and find Patterson another job. When we left the room, the media waiting outside wanted to know what had happened. When given the explanation that we were "waiting on God," they wanted to know the status of Patterson. Paige was hung out to dry, in a job and not in a job at the same time. It was clear that everybody had better get to work while we "waited on God."

I stayed in contact with Edwin Young, pastor of Second Baptist, Houston, and president of the SBC. Ed asked me to hold off the wolves for three months. He was working with the trustees of his alma mater Southeastern Seminary as they sought a new president. Sure enough, as if by clockwork, in May 1992, Patterson left for his appointment as president of Southeastern Seminary. The troops had come through for their old warrior. I thought that Paige deserved a reception at the church for his

W. A. Criswell and Paige Patterson, during his tenure as Criswell College president, participate in a press conference. (Photo by David Woo, *Dallas Morning News*)

years at the school and the church, but he declined the reception. He had seen too many staff members muscled out and then given a reception as if everything were aboveboard and loving. I wrote a brief tribute to Paige in my column and he was gone.

Several abiding lessons lodged in my mind from the Patterson battle. The first was a historical irony. Patterson led the conservative revolution in the SBC on the platform that trustees of our seminaries should be proactive. Then in turn when his own trustees became proactive, they tried to fire him. I further saw that one could serve W. A. and the church for years and then be shown the door ignominiously. As one prominent former ministerial staff member reflected, "There is one thing you must understand—Criswell has no personal loyalties."

I took a profound personal lesson from this experience. In a contest with the Criswells, the architect of the conservative resurgence in the SBC, the president of the college that bore Criswell's name, the associate pastor of First, and a man with powerful friends in and out of First Baptist lost and was shown the door without even so much as a decent farewell. I had no question that I could be dispatched to the ministerial boneyard even faster.

❧

CRISWELL AND THE COLLEGE

EVEN BEFORE I ARRIVED AT FIRST BAPTIST, I was told that Criswell would move to the college where he would be the "CEO." This is an unusual nomenclature for an academic institution, but FBC, Inc., being the business it is, I never questioned the term. I was handed a letter from W. A. Criswell to

Ray Hunt, who wanted some assurance that the Old Man would actually move to the college if the Hunts provided the gift for the acquisition of new property:

To my beloved son in the work of the Lord, Ray Hunt:

Before the end of this year of 1989, I shall be eighty years of age. This is a tremendous milestone in my life.

For several years I have felt that when, under the leadership of the Holy Spirit, I turned aside from the pastoral ministry of our dear First Baptist Church here in Dallas, that I was called of God thereafter to pour the remainder of my life into our Criswell College. That time has come, and I hereby represent to you that if the Gaston Avenue Baptist Church property is acquired that I will assume the responsibilities of chief executive officer of the college as soon as possible.

Under the leadership of the Holy Spirit we are persuaded and believing that within the next few months our search committee will be led to the man God has ordained to come here to be pastor of the church. Dear Mrs. Ruth Ray Hunt (a member of the search committee) can keep us abreast and fully aware of this development. This certainly means that when this servant of Christ comes as pastor, my life and energy will immediately be transferred to the committee, and through them the church, that the present pastor is turning to the college, and we must therein and thereby do something under God to bring another pastor immediately. Under these circumstances, I will assume the full-time responsibilities of the chief executive officer of the college no later than January 2, 1990.

This means that the First Baptist Church in Dallas must call another pastor, and it also means that I will pour the strength of my life into the college. I shall still love the church and serve the congregation in any way that I can, but my first and primary assignment will be to the vast ministries that await our great school. I would love to share my life with those men and women who will be leading our churches and building the kingdom of Christ throughout these coming generations.

Pray with me in this dedication, and may God be pleased with our mutual commitment to exalt the name of our Savior in the earth.

Faithfully and devotedly,
Your old pastor,
W. A. Criswell

This letter clarifies Criswell's dealings both with Paige Patterson and myself. In order to consummate the Hunt family's generous offer to buy a new campus for the Criswell College, he had to promise that he would become the chief executive officer. There were several reasons for this. Mrs. H. L. (Ruth Ray) Hunt had been in the flock for four decades. A devoted and prayerful woman of refinement and grace, she well knew Criswell's temperament. She knew that he would have Herculean difficulty in bringing himself to quit the church. This insistence quietly but firmly put his feet to the fire to move on with getting out so another man could have a chance.

Standing in the driveway of Mount Vernon, her beautiful home overlooking White Rock Lake, Ruth Ray Hunt reflected on Criswell and the college. She felt that the college had no future unless Criswell poured his own life into the school. She had made a major bequest to buy the new campus with the anticipation that its namesake would move there and use his formidable influence to endow, direct, recruit, and energize the school. She now faced the sad fact that he had no intention to do so. The consecrated Christian philanthropist who had given so much to the church and school was not mad, just sad.

From another perspective, this promise left Paige in limbo. He had served as president of Criswell College and presumably its CEO. What would happen to him with Criswell literally installed in one end of the building and Paige in the other was anyone's guess. For his own part, Paige was pleased that the Old Man had not moved out there. I was just as eager that he not be down the hall from me. Neither of us wanted him down the hall from the other of us.

The existence of this letter, added to verbal assurances from Criswell and search committee members, had further given me confidence that I would really be able to lead as pastor. This assurance was weighed against the fact, however, that by my arrival in January 1991, W. A. was already one year overdue to arrive behind his desk as CEO of the college. I did not wait with bated breath.

Late in my tenure the Hunts wanted a meeting with W. A. and the trustees to inquire why he had not kept his commitment to the college. So we gathered around the conference table in the fabulously decorated board room of the Criswell College. Patsy Wallace had appointed it with her usual understated elegance. The afternoon sun reflected through the stained glass windows left from the Gaston Avenue Baptist Church. The rich wood color of the room shimmered in the purplish hues of the old glass.

At the head of the table sat Ray Hunt, beside him his sister June, and his mother Ruth Ray Hunt. Ray had become a Methodist, heavily involved in the affairs of Southern Methodist University. A sage man of business acumen, he had long since become wary of W. A. June Hunt remained in the church with her mother. June is an accomplished radio personality with her own nationally syndicated program, "Hope for the Heart." She had at one time served on the staff at First Baptist and entertained definite opinions about the chicanery that took place under the guise of God's kingdom.

He was nailed to the wall with the question, "Why have you not kept your word?"

In that meeting W. A. was confronted with the literal copy of his 1989 letter. He was nailed to the wall with the question, "Why have you not kept your word?" I sat across the massive horseshoe table from the Old Man. His parchment skin appeared more pale than usual. He seemed to shrink. I swear, it looked as if he could make himself appear old and pitiful. He then launched into what I called his "poor old man" routine: "I am just an old man and I have such a short time left."

He insisted that the church needed him there just "to keep things going." By 1992, that line both irritated and insulted me. If I were not capable of "keeping things going" I had no business there. Mrs. Hunt looked as if she would weep. I had the feeling that Ray and June wanted this confrontation more than she.

The meeting more or less dissolved with nothing else being decided, although Ray Hunt did say that not another dime of money would come from the Hunts to the college. Given the circumstances of the default, that was about as gentle a response as could be made.

As we walked out of the board room into the awesome contrast of Gaston Avenue poverty and need, I knew that absolutely nothing would move W. A. out of the church. If he would default on a promise to powerful benefactors like the Hunt family, there was no one else in the fellowship who could make him get out of the way so I could lead.

Criswell had another problem at the college. He was not welcomed at the college that bore his name. The students had staged various protests about the threatened dismissal of Patterson. One of them had actually insulted W. A. to his face in the school named for him. Another professor of theology had openly threatened Criswell with a certain anatomical feat that is quite untheological. The atmosphere at the college was not exactly warm and welcoming.

I did feel sorry for the Old Man in that regard. He felt he was losing his grip the longer I stayed at the church, but because he had engineered Paige's dismissal he was not welcomed at the school. Yet the whole thing was his own doing. If he wanted to remain pastor of the church he should have called a young associate. If he wanted to lead the school, he should have moved out there, dealt with Paige, and gotten on with it. Instead, we all lived in limbo.

ॐ

A THIRD SERVICE

MEANWHILE BACK AT THE CHURCH, I needed to do something to attract younger couples back downtown. There was a lot of gray sitting out there. On paper we were out of business in a generation. It took a major recruiting job to attract a young couple from the suburbs. While we attracted some couples from the eastern suburbs of Garland and Mesquite, the North Dallas yuppies had flown north. Although the century-old sanctuary and the thunderous music still appealed to the churched young couples, it had no appeal to the unchurched.

With the dilemma my eye turned to the north, the far north, yea, even to Chicago. In the suburb of South Barrington, Illinois had exploded the largest attendance of any congregation in America, the Willow Creek Community Church. In 1975, a twenty-three-year-old youth minister, Bill Hybels, organized the church with some buddies who were tired of the lifelessness of mainline efforts. He started the church by selling tomatoes to rent a movie theater. Within three years the church had exploded into three thousand. Now eighteen thousand attend the weekend services and seven thousand attend the midweek Bible studies. They are under the roof of a 352,000-square-foot building on a 120-acre campus in an upscale suburb. Three times a year, five hundred pastors make a pilgrimage to find out what has happened at Willow Creek.

For one thing, the church does not look like a church. It targets the unchurched with its "seeker's services." These combine a dramatic centerpiece with contemporary music and a related sermon. There is no aisle-walking invitation. Willow Creek has turned traditional church upside down on its head.

Thus I projected a "seeker's service" at 9:30 A.M. in the sanctuary of First Baptist, Dallas. There was no need to duplicate the two existing services. The house was not full for either of those. We had no future trying to seduce members away from other congregations. Eighty percent of Dallas went to no one's church, and they were the people who needed to be reached.

Southern Baptists did not know what to do with Hybel's Willow Creek model. We could not swallow it whole, but we could tweak it in a way that would work in the confines of a staid old downtown church. I would keep the existing two services exactly as they were. No one would be forced to attend a contemporary service with a saxophone wailing out pop music, but the unchurched crowd that filled Reunion Arena to the rafters to hear Kenny G might just come to a service that had his kind of music.

This discussion began in February 1991. We did not inaugurate the seeker's service until March 29, 1992. No end of planning intervened. Strategic issues challenged us at every front. First, Zig Ziglar's magnetic class met in the sanctuary at 9:30 A.M. We would need Zig's cooperation in making a move to another part of the building. He was more than accommodating, but with the passage of time decided to take a "sabbatical" from teaching his class because of his international travel schedule. When Zig took this sabbatical, I began to teach the auditorium class, hoping to hold the group together and lure them into the projected seeker's service. I taught the class for months, in addition to preaching on Sunday morning, Sunday evening, and Wednesday.

We further had to provide Bible study for those who came to the 9:30 A.M. service. This required the provision of a Sunday school at both 8:15 A.M. and 10:50 A.M. These logistical challenges took months for the staff to address. It was a revolution in the way of doing things.

Because each of the services was built around a topic presented in a drama, they had to be planned months in advance.

Fred McNabb engaged a dramatist from out of town to write the scripts. He also put together a stage band with a contemporary sound and a group of praise singers. There would be no hymnals. The words for praise choruses were projected onto a screen so the congregation could worship without use of any other aids. The first seeker's service was planned around the theme "Whatever Happened to Me?" (Mark 5:1-20). As a set piece we used the Statler Brothers song "The Class of '57 Had Its Dreams." This southern ballad addressed the expectations and outcomes for the class of 1957. We used a high-speed slide change to show pictures illustrating the hapless people in the song.

To do this required a quick change in the old platform. George Truett's pulpit was moved off the stage, as well as the pulpit furniture. I took off my coat from the early service and preached in my suit pants, shirt, tie, and braces—sans any dress coat. This was to accommodate the unchurched crowd who supposedly would find my presence less intimidating. I stood without a pulpit wearing a wireless lavaliere microphone. At the conclusion of the service seekers were told that my "friends" would be standing by the doors of the sanctuary in case any of them had questions. We used the seeker-friendly term "friends" because nonchurch folk think the word "counselor" means you think they are psycho.

With great fanfare the seeker's service was launched. Attendance at the service immediately ran between five and six hundred. Most of this was shift from the other two services, but some folks brought their unchurched friends. Criswell did absolutely nothing to help me. The only thing he ever said was, "I hear you are preaching in suspenders." I presume he heard I also had on other clothes as well. After being begged to visit one of the services, he came and sat in the balcony, looking over the railing as if he were watching an unsightly surgical operation. He scarcely concealed his dislike.

This service showed more promise than anything I tried in my twenty-one months. Other than personal relationships with the staff and members, it was the thing I most regretted leaving. Had we continued the service for several years, I believe we would have filled up the old hall with seekers.

At First Baptist we had a golden moment to have the best of both worlds. With two traditional services that were very churchly in the Baptist sense, we addressed the needs of those who wanted the time-honored approach. With the seeker's service sandwiched between them we had the opportunity to reach those who would never attend the other services. By September 30, 1992, this was all gone with the wind. No sadder words of tongue or pen than the words, "it might have been."

This raises the philosophical question of continued innovation within the Christian church. My friend Frank Cooke, president of the British Baptist Union, once observed that Americans were making the same mistake that British Christians made fifty years ago. They changed the message but refused to change the methods. They should never have changed the message, Frank said, but should have changed any method necessary to reach the nation.

First Baptist represented a church that had changed neither. It was good to preserve the essential Christian message. But Criswell seemed unaware that America then would never again be the same after the sixties, Vietnam, and the collapse of the cultural consensus. He himself had been a brilliant innovator from the forties to the sixties, but First Baptist had essentially frozen its program at that time. I found many of the people, even the senior members, willing to innovate again. The church had been on the edge of risk before, and that had made it great. Now the church found itself at the point of risk once again. That opportunity for risk, however, was truncated by the events of the coming months.

Chapter Eight

∾

Of Camps, Conferences, and Controversy

*S*ummertime among Baptists brings an annual round of activities that form the landscape of life for several million people, and the First Baptist Church of Dallas did its share to fill every moment. First Baptist fielded one of the great camping programs in the nation with separate camps for younger children, older children, and youth. It was expected that the pastor would speak at each of these gatherings.

In addition to the off-campus summer camps, the church organized one of the largest vacation Bible schools in the nation. With an attendance of nearly two thousand per day, the church was alive with the voices of little children. They were picked up at various points around the metropolitan area and driven to First on chartered buses. These buses surrounded the entire plant of the church like a cavalcade of aluminum cracker boxes. In the midst of the burdens of leadership, these summer Bible schools and camps were a pleasure.

With the youngest children I gave a tender appeal concerning their need to make a "step toward God." Criswell had in a sense rewritten the soteriology of Baptists. He made a decision in mid-career that he would no longer baptize children beneath the age of nine. Before that time, they would make a "step toward God" whenever and as many times as they wished. This would place them in a Baptist catechetical program leading up to a profession of faith and baptism at the age of nine or thereabouts. I stood in agreement with this program, having witnessed pressure applied to young children to make a premature confession of faith. To the older children I gave a more explicit appeal to Christian discipleship and to the youth an outright challenge concerning the claims of Christ.

It had been Criswell's practice to interview each child in his office before the child made a public profession of faith. Under the guiding eye of Libby Reynolds, these little children would come to my office with their parents for a final discussion before their baptism. Nothing in the life of First Baptist was more affecting than these conversations. Some of the parents had made the same trips to see Dr. Criswell twenty and thirty years before. One comes to appreciate the roots of life in a great church fellowship when he sees the multiple generations of families that make up its life. These interviews with little children were the brightest spots of the week.

Then, every June, the Southern Baptist Convention meets. There was a special recognition for the Criswells at the Atlanta meeting in June 1991. The *Atlanta Constitution* honored the Criswells with a major article in its Sunday, June 2, 1991 edition, paying tribute to Dr. Criswell as the "soul and inspiration of what he likes to call the 'conservative resurgence' in the fifteen-million-member Southern Baptist Convention." The article was accompanied by a beautiful color picture of Dr. Criswell preaching in a recent service at First.

On Monday evening, June 3, he spoke to twenty thousand in the concluding meeting of the Southern Baptist Pastor's Conference, an annual preaching marathon preceding the convention. Introduced by President Richard Lee as Southern Baptist's greatest leader, Dr. Criswell was greeted with a standing ovation, thunderous applause, and shouts of loving affirmation. Upon returning I wrote all the above in the First Baptist Church paper, ending with the accolade: "He thereafter preached one of the greatest messages ever heard by that conference, ending with thousands of pastors on their knees rededicating life and ministry to the Lord Jesus Christ. All of us thank God for the ongoing leadership of our venerable patriarch. His very presence was an uplift to thousands of pastors at this meeting." At the same meeting I spoke to the convention on the occasion of the fiftieth anniversary of the "Baptist Hour" radio broadcast, for which I was the "permanent" speaker.

Until a few months before my resignation, everything I wrote about Dr. C. was glowing and glorious.

Until a few months before my resignation, everything I wrote about Dr. C. was glowing and glorious. I never wanted the church to accuse me of neglecting to honor him or pay tribute to him. As it turned out, I praised him so much that it left the people confused when I suddenly resigned. Some asked why I had praised him if I disagreed with his continuing tenure, but there was really no choice. We could not duke it out on the platform in the best three out of four falls. I worked under the misapprehension that treating him with honor and tribute would ease his transition out of office. It only encouraged him to stay in office.

It was at the Atlanta convention that I learned of Mrs. C.'s troublemaking over my allegedly "lavish" office. At that moment I knew I needed help. So I met with Tim Hedquist, assistant pastor in administration for Dr. Adrian Rogers, pastor of the Bellvue Baptist Church in Memphis. Before that Tim had served for thirteen years as vice-president of the executive board of the Southern Baptist Convention. In that capacity he was responsible for the day-to-day operations of our entire denomination's executive committee.

I appealed to Hedquist for help. The church had no administrator. I had been meeting weekly with the administrative leadership of the church, but no one can both pastor the church and meet its huge business, plant, and personnel challenges. Tim consented to come and joined us in late summer. In addition, I engaged a friend since high school to come in a part-time capacity. Dr. Gary Waller taught at Southwestern Seminary, had earned both the Ed.D. and the Ph.D., and was a seasoned churchman. I gave him the title of assistant pastor in strategic planning and evangelism to help me with a broad range of projects. I needed someone I knew and trusted to keep an eye on things for me. With Tim's expertise and Gary's long-term friendship, I could breathe a little easier and not have to spend every hour watching my flanks.

With this help in place, I prepared to depart on a round-the-world trip to Bangalore, India, to dedicate a wing of the Bangalore Baptist hospital built by First Baptist. The famous missionary surgeon Dr. Rebekah Naylor was a member of First Baptist, and she had requested that I come to dedicate the wing. A generous family in First Baptist paid for all four of our family to fly by way of London and Rome to Bangalore. While in India we not only dedicated the hospital but went with extension workers into the bush where we visited remote Hindu villages cared for by the Baptist Hospital. This grueling trip was actually a respite from the constant pressures of the church. I could see why both Criswell and Truett had spent long chunks of time away from the church, in Truett's instance as much as six months at a time. In the same way that U.S. presidents will take a foreign junket to get away from the ceaseless pressures of domestic problems, the pastors of FBC have fled the country to escape the constant problems of administration.

ॐ

THE BAYLOR CONTROVERSY

WHEN I ARRIVED BACK IN DALLAS, I faced another problem that I needed like the plague. I had to decide whether or not to take a public stand on the defection of Baylor University from its historic relationship with the Baptist General Convention of Texas.

Baylor University was chartered in 1845 by the Republic of Texas and is the oldest institution of higher learning in the state. That Baylor was chartered by Texas Baptists and for Texas Baptists is indisputable from its charter, heritage, and constituency. In September 1990, when a majority of trustees voted unilaterally to remove Baylor from its historic relationship with the Baptist General Convention of Texas, that clearly violated the constitution of the state denomination of Baptists.

The backdrop of this defection was the larger Southern Baptist denominational war. Baylor University provided a primary center of the left wing in Baptist life. John Baugh, a Houston millionaire and benefactor of Baylor, had joined forces with Dr. Herbert Reynolds, the president of Baylor, adding his significant financial backing to the ongoing effort to oust the right wing from control of the national denomination. In the larger context of Southern Baptist life, Baylor had aligned itself with the left wing, or self-styled moderate camp. Although to some folks "left-wing Baptist" is an oxymoron, to Baptists it makes sense within our context.

Reynolds rightly assumed that the national conservative movement would ultimately filter down to the state Baptist institutions, especially the largest Baptist university in the world, Baylor. During the eighties, Reynolds warned repeatedly of the unwashed multitudes of narrow fundamentalists that would invade the Waco campus and drive the university into the dark ages of fundamentalism. Having spent eight years at Baylor working on a B.A. and Ph.D., I was on to Herbert's game. Fundamentalists had about as much chance as a snowball in hell to influence Baylor University. The school had named its own trustees for years, simply sending the list to the state denominational meeting to have them rubber-stamped. Baylor University for all practical purposes owned the state denomination.

Reynolds's dramatic end run in September 1990 was a winner-take-all risk. With the trustees behind closed doors and uninformed of the agenda, they were presented with the request that they declare themselves self-perpetuating regents. This would put them outside accountability of the more than two million Texas Baptists who had been under the hitherto mistaken assumption that Baylor had belonged to them. On one breathtaking vote the trustees asserted their sole proprietorship of a major university, Baylor Hospital in Dallas, and its related enterprises. Then they stood back and dared the state denomination to sue them to get it back.

They walked off with $750 million in assets and 145 years of Baptist history.

From the moment of the vote I felt both inward compulsion and outward pressure to do something about it. For one thing, there was my own long history with Baylor stretching back to January 1966, when I arrived as a seventeen-year old freshman, so eager to get there that I would forgo the spring of my senior year in high school. Like thousands of others, I fell in love with the old school on the Brazos. Half its current size, there were six thousand students, most of them Baptists. I would earn a B.A. summa cum laude with a double major in religion and Greek.

Yet I also discovered something else at Baylor—a kind of Baptist I had not encountered. They would stand before fresh-faced kids just out of their last Baptist youth camp the summer before and declare that Moses did not write the first five books of the Bible, that there were two Isaiahs, and that the gospels were a collection of sayings, not all of which came from Jesus. It would be one thing to spout this to graduate students or even university seniors, but to indoctrinate kids the first week of university with a system that blew away all the moorings of their life was another thing. I had a sense that not all the folks back home knew this was going on at Baylor. It had not been going on for that many years, and the old alums wanted to remember Baylor the way it was in the forties and fifties.

I did not know it at the time, but what I discovered was the Waco branch of another stream in southern Baptist life that had grown up in post-War America. As a freshman, I felt that something was out of joint with what I had always heard from the pulpit and the Sunday school room. I was intellectually infantile, culturally circumscribed, and had no frame of reference to evaluate what I heard. I had been warned by my home pastor to "watch out for liberalism at Baylor," and I was vigilant.

Over the four years of undergraduate work, I became more aware of what was happening. The students at Baylor were being presented a history-of-religions approach to the Old Testament similar to that found at Duke, Vanderbilt, Emory, and across the old South. That would not even have been so discomforting if a rational, conservative alternative had been presented as well. Instead, the kind of faith that nurtured most Baylor students until they went to university was openly lampooned. The professors in the department of religion, whom I consider friends to this day, considered it their calling to abolish the juvenile faith of Baptist teenagers and replace it with a more durable model born at the university. We were often told that the professionals in the churches we might some day pastor would barrage us with questions concerning the multiple authorship of the Pentateuch, the existence of the document "Q" as a source for the synoptic gospels, and the non-Pauline authorship of the pastoral epistles. In later years I reflected that not a single young doctor, lawyer, or accountant ever one time asked me those promised questions. In fact, the yuppies at Travis and First were the most hidebound fundamentalists in the church. The young professionals went to Bible study fellowship, listened to radio Bible teachers, and believed in fiat creation. I was loaded for bear to answer questions that were not asked.

Though I have my criticisms of the Baylor liberals, I must pay tribute to Baylor for giving me a splendid liberal arts education in a (sort of) Baptist environment. I sat in front of Dr. Richard Cutter for four years learning the grammar and syntax of the Greek New Testament until I could read it like the newspaper.

Professor Robert Reid was a mesmerizing thespian in the history class who made Greece and Rome live. To my chagrin, in the Baylor controversy of 1990-91, Herbert Reynolds accused me of biting the hand that fed me, of being disloyal to my alma mater. Baylor wants to be loved uncritically. There is no room for the loyal opposition.

After earning a master of divinity degree at Southwestern Seminary in Fort Worth, I returned to Baylor for a Ph.D. Although that put my education in a rather narrow circle, it was the affordable and desirable thing to do at the time. The theology of Baylor did not concern me so much as a doctoral student. The Ph.D. program was a pluralistic environment with a score of denominations represented. The doctoral students were far into the formation of their own personal theologies. The same profs I had met as an undergraduate seemed less militant about reforming Baptist opinions at the doctoral level. With Lutherans, Presbyterians, Church of Christ, and even Episcopalians in the doctoral program, a more cosmopolitan atmosphere prevailed. Because of pastoring throughout doctoral work and writing a dissertation, it took me nine years to finish the degree. I finally walked out of Baylor in 1983 as a thirty-five-year-old with a Ph.D.

In 1985, I was surprised to receive an invitation from Dr. Herbert Reynolds, who asked that I meet with him to discuss a proposed relationship with the Baylor administration. He wanted me to join the administration and report to him as a sort of denominational liaison/traveling preacher for Baylor. We sat in the skybox of Baylor Stadium watching the Bears war on the gridiron while we ate steaks in the presidential suite. It was a rather heady ambiance for an assistant professor at the seminary where I had taught for three years. Although the job had some attraction, I had an intuition that something would happen at Baylor that I could not support and I would be in a compromised position with Reynolds. (The denominational war would ultimately cause Baylor to make a move that I could not support. There was an unwillingness to give a firm definition of the left on the part of the moderate camp. I did not feel I could give carte blanche to anything an institution might do.) I had felt just enough of that in Dilday's flirtations with the moderates while at Southwestern that I never, ever wanted again to work for a president whose Baptist political connections created a strain in friendship. With that in view I accepted the call of Travis Avenue Baptist Church. I really wanted to get back to the pastorate anyway.

By 1988 I was elected president of the Baptist General Convention of Texas. With its 2.2 million members and five thousand churches/missions, being president was more than an avocation. I also landed in office amidst a growing controversy about the direction of Baylor University. Reynolds had been making unmistakably independent growlings as the Head Bear. There had been a controversy concerning the artistic showing of skin flicks on campus, and the Baptist natives were restless as we moved toward the annual gathering in Austin. It looked like there would be a showdown on the floor of the convention which anticipated four thousand in attendance. The denominational crowd and the Baylor establishment wanted to ignore it, stonewall, and send the troops home. I knew better. The right wing of Texas Baptist life was ready to go to war over Baylor in 1988. I thought the statesmanlike thing to do as president was to address the issue as harmoniously as possible.

The night before giving this message I invited Reynolds and Dr. Winfred Moore to the presidential suite in the hotel. I had a lawyer friend from Travis who was also the parliamentarian sit in the meeting. In an act of courtesy I read my next-day's address to the two Baylor leaders. I thought they would appreciate my diffusing a floor fight that was inevitable. Instead they asserted their absolute, categorical opposition to my address. They said I should not even mention the Baylor problem. If I did not bring it up, it would go away. Don't hit them when they are down. It would only cause more trouble, etc. I told them goodnight and went to bed.

They said I should not even mention the Baylor problem. If I did not bring it up, it would go away.

In my presidential address I spoke to the "caring custodians of Baylor." I referred to a "long list" of things that were right with Baylor and a "short list" of things that needed to be addressed. I enumerated the "long list" item by item and did not even specify the short list. The response was a standing ovation from the crowd which included hundreds of Baylor supporters. The rank-and-file Baptists present knew that I had addressed the question on everyone's mind. Reynolds was infuriated. I was later told that he wanted to call a news conference on the spot to denounce me, but was restrained from doing so by Presnall Wood, editor of the *Baptist Standard*, and Dewey Presley, a prominent Dallas layman and longtime Baylor trustee.

Subsequently Reynolds did take a shot at me in the Baylor alumni magazine. The possibility of a war between the president of the denomination and the president of its university concerned the executive director of the state denomination, so Dr. William Pinson arranged a private luncheon between

Reynolds and me at a Dallas hotel. There Reynolds and I talked for several hours about our disparate views concerning Baylor, while Pinson more or less presided. It was something of a rapprochement between Reynolds and me. He indicated that his invitation three years earlier to join the Baylor administration had been portentous of something bigger. He was disappointed that I had become a critic of my alma mater. We buried that hatchet and I even dropped him off at his next appointment.

Nothing prepared anyone for the Baylor coup of September 1990. It was a premeditated coup of incredible gall. It caught everyone by surprise, including Bill Pinson, the denominational executive who professed to know nothing of it. They co-opted the school and dared the denomination to sue them in order to get it back. Since Baylor people had hand-picked virtually everyone on every major board of the denomination, it was a safe bet they could get away with it.

At first the Texas Baptist establishment professed opposition to the move. The powerful *Baptist Standard* editorialized against it—for one week. Under the crunching power of the Baylor machine, all denominational opposition was quickly silenced. The constitution of the state denomination had without question been breached. Baylor argued that her trustees held their trust for the benefit of the institution, not as stewards of the denomination—a novel interpretation of trustee which no Texas Baptists had heard before. To calm the waters a special ad hoc committee was appointed with the venerable statesman Robert E. Naylor, a predecessor at Travis, as the chairman. It was stacked with Baylor people and in spite of Dr. Naylor's independent leadership could not make the Baylor Bears leave their new den.

When the final report was given to the executive board of the Texas Baptist denomination, I could not even get recognized as a former president or pastor of the state's largest church. The official action of the denomination allowed Baylor to elect 75 percent of its own trustees as self-perpetuating regents while the state denomination would elect 25 percent, an obviously ineffective minority. Since the state denomination was owned and operated by Baylor already, this gave the Baylor Bears a 100–percent hegemony over their new empire. They would be accountable to no one except themselves for all time.

❧

SPEAKING OUT

WHY THE FUSS? Why did the vote matter? Historical research by James Tunstead Burtchaell of Notre Dame indicated that not a single denominational college or university in America that had severed its organic ties to its denomination had remained distinctively Christian, no less denominational. If Baylor continued as a Baptist institution, it would be an unprecedented exception in the history of American higher education. Added to this was the fact that Texas Baptists had given hundreds of millions of dollars in the capital and operating needs of Baylor for 145 years.

There were other reasons I felt compelled to speak out. First Baptist had hundreds if not thousands of Baylor graduates. Dr. George W. Truett had used his natural eloquence to save the school from bankruptcy in the late nineteenth century. Criswell was graduated from Baylor with distinction and received the honorary doctorate. I had two degrees from Baylor. Baylor had been part of the landscape of life for the leadership and membership of First Baptist.

If anyone were to speak to the issue, it needed to be a megachurch pastor, and no other such pastor in Texas had Baylor ties. Letters and calls poured in that I speak up as a last-ditch effort to save the old school, the crown jewel of Texas Baptist life. I felt it impossible, irresponsible, and wrong to remain silent. I also knew from the first that it would be a losing cause. It would be a protest in the face of a historic inevitability. As part of the grand scheme of Baylor, the annual meeting of the state denomination that would approve the deal was meeting on the campus of Baylor. As they say in West Texas, it was already "saucered and blowed." I also knew that a public statement would infuriate Reynolds and estrange me forever from my alma mater. Yet I was the person to say something in the face of the hijacking of a major university from the denomination that loved it.

So on Sunday morning, September 27, 1991, at 10:50 A.M., on live television and radio, I delivered the message "Texas Baptists and Baylor." It was a stinging indictment of Reynolds and the trustees who voted to remove the school from its historic ties. I called on Texas Baptists to rise up, descend on Waco in November, and challenge the Baylor coup. The sanctuary was packed to the rafters and deadly quiet. The sermon had been announced on the marquees outside the church for six days before and the title published in the paper. Paige Patterson estimated that 75 percent of the church members supported my stand. The rest knew well enough to remain quiet, given the pervasive deep feelings in the church concerning the issue. The deacons moved immediately to have the message printed in pamphlet form and to send it along with an audio tape to every Baptist church in Texas. Retired missionary Perry Ellis and Texas evangelist Freddy Gage were called in to organize a phone bank effort to get out the vote.

The Baylor response was quick, even during the sermon. We printed a call-in number on television for folks to respond to the message. Old Bears started calling and cussing me during the sermon. On Monday morning a livid Herbert Reynolds called a press conference in Waco. He called me a liar, a hypocrite, and an "immature sycophant." The latter term sent several members to the dictionary, seeing how they thought it had to do with some other kind of personal aberration. Herb was never one to mess with the issues. His forte was argument ad hominem. As the lawyers say, if the law and the facts are not on your side, attack the witness.

I spent the next six weeks immersed in the Baylor controversy. Everything was put on hold in the battle for the old school. I had to cheer the troops on while I knew in my heart it was a losing battle. There were daily conference calls, meetings, planning sessions, and reports from the hinterlands concerning how many votes we could count on in the showdown on the Brazos in November. Some of the finest legal minds in Texas advised our organization. We could not undo the vote of the trustees, who were a separate legal entity, but we could move that the state convention sue Baylor over the coup. We also knew that would never pass a vote on the floor. Edwin Young of Houston proposed another approach. We would make a motion that the Rev. Dr. Billy Graham be asked to appoint an impartial arbitration group to rule on the question. This was supposed to be a surprise motion that would catch the convention off guard and carry the day.

On November 11, more than ten thousand Baptists packed the new basketball arena on Baylor's campus. The streets were lined with signs prepared by bright-eyed Baylor students urging the Baptists to save the school from the fundamentalists. We flew in the Southern Baptist Convention parliamentarian to assist us with the floor effort, not knowing what the Baylor crew would do. The young denominational president Phil Lineberger left the platform and spoke for Baylor himself, an anomaly I thought for a former University of Arkansas football player. Since I had been riding on point from the first, it was thought best that I take a less visible role lest the whole thing be seen as my fight against Baylor. After Edwin Young made his Billy Graham motion, I spoke to it from the floor. The moment I said, "This is not a fundamentalist-moderate issue," a rousing chorus of boos swept over the arena. This was an unprecedented insult in a Texas Baptist meeting. The Baylor crowd was out for blood.

We lost the substitute motion to retain Baylor for the state denomination by a 5,967-4,714 vote. At the announcement of the vote the Baylor crowd whooped, hollered, cat-called and put on an outlandish celebration against their defeated Texas Baptist brothers and sisters—all in the spirit of Jesus, of course. Our 4,714 were more people than usually attended the convention. The convention looked like a geriatric society. Baylor had bused in old folks from all over Central Texas, taking a leaf from the strategy book of the right wing. Retired school teachers by the scores poured out of Clifton, Chilton, Corsicana, and dozens of other Central Texas hamlets "to save Baylor." They may have been fuzzy on just what they were saving the school from, but save it they did.

The enduring loss of the Baylor defection has nothing to do with the fundamentalists failing to capture Baylor. They could never have done that anyway, and would not have known what to do with it if they had it. The sadness is that Baylor will drift away from Baptists in Texas as they really are, a great-hearted, reverent, conservative, biblical people. For a few years Baylor will try to look more Baptist than ever. Then the inevitable distancing will occur because of the natural forces in academia. The academy looks askance at schools with strong confessional ties, especially those related to sectarian movements. The custodians of Baylor wish it to be competitive with Duke and Vanderbilt in the South. You can hardly find anyone today who even remembers that Vanderbilt was begun as a bastion of Methodism. Baylor could have been the Notre Dame of Baptists. Unless it is an exception in the extreme to the historical forces that have shaped every other institution that departed its denominational heritage, it will become another private university with a friendly nod toward Christianity, treating the faith like an old beau from decades before with whom things did not quite work out.

~

CRISWELL'S FORTY-SEVENTH

NINE MONTHS INTO MY FLEDGLING TENURE AS PASTOR, it was time to celebrate the forty-seventh anniversary of Criswell's pastorate. There had been speculation for years that he would announce his retirement when he equaled Truett's longevity. Truett served 1897-1944, and Criswell would arrive at 1991 with forty-seven years complete. I felt that we could have a huge celebration and help the Old Man gracefully leave the church, move to the college, and let me get on with it.

In speaking with the lay leaders to plan the event, I proposed that we send Dr. and Mrs. Criswell around the world for three months on a cruise. If that did not work I suggested we send them somewhere, anywhere. So I called W. A. to my office with the proposal that he accept a global cruise. He saw through that in a flash.

"Lad," he intoned, "I have been everywhere and have seen everything. I want to stay right here in Dallas. And Betty will not go anywhere but London, year after year." I continued to dilate on the wonders of modern cruise ships, as if he would be delighted to play shuffleboard across the Atlantic. There was nothing doing.

So I called W. A. to my office with the proposal that he accept a global cruise. He saw through that in a flash.

So I retrenched to consider other appropriate gestures that might in some sense hasten his decision to depart, and yet give him due recognition. There was a picture of Criswell around every corner of the five square blocks, so why not a statue? When I mentioned this to Jack Pogue, he thought it would be fine and volunteered to cooperate in the financing of the project. Through a Dallas art dealer we were given the portfolio of Blair Buswell, the sculptor for the National Football League Hall of Fame. Looking at his likenesses of Tom Landry and former Cowboys general manager Tex Schramm, we supposed that he could do a reasonable job for Criswell. We arranged to fly him in for the anniversary service. In addition, I arranged for the fifty volumes of Criswell's writings to be bound in genuine leather as a presentation set.

In the church paper before Criswell's anniversary I printed the most laudatory paean ever penned about a Baptist preacher. I had two motives. I did think the Old Man was worthy of a laudation, a sort of panegyric in his own style of prose. I also hoped that an over-the-top accolade would somehow let him know that there was nothing else to be said and he would see his way clear to step out of the picture. So I penned my hosannas in the *Reminder*:

This Sunday the First Baptist Church of Dallas will celebrate a monumental event. That event represents a rarity so seldom seen in Christian history that we should all pause with wonder. Our congregation will celebrate the forty-seventh anniversary of the ministry of Dr. and Mrs. W. A. Criswell. In the annals of Baptist history, in the sweep of Christian history or, for that matter in the whole story of human leadership of any kind, the extended tenure of our senior pastor towers above human example (that this hyperbole vaulted Criswell over Alexander the Great, Charlemagne, and Churchill did not matter; overstatement at First never surprised anybody). An influence so pervasive, a presence so extended, and a personality so venerated for so long beggars the imagination.

It was on October 6, 1944 that Dr. Criswell preached after having been called as pastor on Wednesday evening, September 27, 1944. After the moving service, the revered Bob Coleman told the new undershepherd, "Young pastor, when you come, and I have no doubt that you will come for God has called you to come, always let the first Sunday in October be your anniversary Sunday rather than the date you move to Dallas. I have never before seen such a service!" Who could have imagined that in a world inestimably different from that of 1944, the young pastor who followed the mighty titan of Baptist life would in 1991 not only equal but exceed the tenure of his predecessor.

For many of you the presence of Dr. Criswell must be like that of Mt. Everest to those who live in its shadow. The mountain is always there—timeless, certain, the landscape of life. Yet those who live in the shadow of that mountain must sometimes stand back in awe even in the midst of such familiarity. Likewise, it is time on this occasion for those most familiar with our senior pastor as well as those newest to the fellowship to stand back in confession, "To God be the glory, great things He hath done."

Consider his preaching ministry. From this pulpit and in a thousand others at conventions, conferences, encampments, and mission fields, his voice of pathos has resounded around this planet. If he had done nothing else, the towering achievement of preaching through the Bible over seventeen years would stand as a singular standard in American preaching history.

Reckon with his written word. In fifty volumes his pen has reduced to writing what his mind has conceived in constant discipline of study. To author one book is an effort known only to those who do so. To write fifty books and contemplate yet more stands in Christian history alongside the contributions of Luther, Calvin, and Spurgeon. On thousands of shelves in thousands of libraries for the untold years to come his volumes will illuminate the mind of scholars and the hearts of preachers.

Meditate on the building of this church. There have been great preachers in Christian history whose preaching was unmixed blessing to their generation. Yet the pulpit was the center and circumference of their influence. They built no Sunday school, enlarged no organization, projected no vision, and at the end of their stay left only the empty shell of a once-filled sanctuary. Not so has been the mighty ministry of Dr. Criswell. While thrilling the Christian world with his preaching, he at the same time masterminded the building of the mightiest church of his generation. He was literally decades ahead of other church growth strategists. The vision of his mind became the action of his hands. He pioneered the church staff used by all large churches today. He foresaw the need for educational space, parking buildings, recreational facilities, a great music program, a church saturating the city with mission chapels, a camp program and a thousand other details before others could even imagine the need of such things. As a student of preaching and church growth I can say with confidence that not since Spurgeon and the Metropolitan Tabernacle of London has one man so combined pulpit mastery with building a magnificent church program.

Evaluate his denominational influence. Long before others detected the drift, Dr. Criswell's voice was that of one crying in the wilderness of the Southern Baptist Zion. He thundered and pleaded for years that our denomination was drifting from its early commitment to an inerrant Bible. When it was unpopular, when he stood alone like a Churchill warning against Germany in the 1930s, Dr. Criswell in this pulpit and across the country sounded the warning that we must return to the book or perish. His warning words reached an unforgettable crescendo at the 1985 Southern Baptist Pastor's Conference in Dallas. Asking our pastors, "Shall We Live or Shall We Die?" he brought a message that will be studied a century from now as the great turning point in the historic controversy of our generation. He has lived so long as to see his warning heeded, his denomination reclaimed, and his position vindicated. Even the mighty Spurgeon whose preaching shook the earth and whose church towered over its times was unable to retrieve the British Baptist Union from its awful downgrade into liberal infidelity. By any measure in that regard, our senior pastor's influence stands unique in Baptist history.

Would these accomplishments not have been enough? Added to these is Dr. Criswell's record as an educator. For years he pleaded with the church to begin an academy. Now the nine hundred students on two campuses are a tribute to that persevering vision. Out of that same drive to educate was born what is now the Criswell College. Its beautiful facilities, its phenomenal growth, and its promising future will write unknown chapters into the legacy book of Dr. Criswell. That bequest to Christian education cannot be measured until its last graduate before the trumpet's sound and the Lord's return. Until that moment may our college train legions of ministers to sound the inerrant word.

Alongside our senior pastor across these years has been Mrs. Criswell. In every way she has been involved in his ministry and advancing the cause of Christ in her own right. Her Sunday school class reaches more than three hundred each Sunday plus a vast radio audience. By every

man of God there is a helpmate of the years, and
Dr. Criswell is no exception. We salute her as we salute him.

So ended the eulogium. In my heart I meant it. I had admired
the Old Man since boyhood. But I wanted him to quit. In some
way I supposed that if we could stage an event of recognition big
enough, he would discern that nothing more could be done and
would go out gracefully. So it was on October 6, 1991, Blair
Buswell the sculptor was flown from Provo to the platform of
First Baptist to be commissioned for the larger-than-life statue.
That Sunday evening I preached another tribute to Dr. C. and
there was a reception in his honor. But he did not quit. He did
not even make a gesture about leaving. We all then began to
suppose that he would stay until his forty-eighth anniversary and
thus exceed Truett's tenure by one year. I went home that
evening with the weighty feeling that we might be in for a much
longer haul than I ever imagined.

The statue became a thing of public amusement. In order to
pay the sculptor's commission, we further asked for a number of
smaller replicas cast in bronze to be sold to admirers. Later the
idea of little Criswell statues was too much for the press to
resist. Baptists had often made snide remarks about the
Catholic practice of dashboard statues in their car, but those
were nothing compared to fifteen-hundred-dollar statuettes of
Criswell. To set the record straight, however, Dr. C. did not
commission the statue or the diminutive replicas. I envisioned
the statue being placed in the Kadane Plaza between the sanctuary and the education buildings. Criswell, however, wished it
to be installed under the dome inside the Criswell College. In
that connection there were some rather humorous observations

made about the fate of Lord Nelson bombarded by pigeons high over Trafalgar. We figured W. A. wanted the statue inside lest he suffer such a fate.

I never saw the finished product. In the firestorm surrounding my resignation the statue project simply disappeared. It has, I am told, been placed under the dome of the college. I did have the responsibility of dedicating the dome which was provided in gold leaf by Criswell's business partner Jack Pogue. I traced the domes of history and their significance, including the Pantheon in Rome. Now W. A. stands in bronze holding aloft a Bible under the gold dome of the Criswell College.

∾

CHRISTMAS AND OTHER PARTIES

THE SOCIAL ROUND at First Baptist never ended. To the Old Man's credit he was more available to the people than any other megachurch pastor in the country. It was the custom for W. A. to be at Sunday school class parties, awards ceremonies in the church for every group, private dinners, departmental retreats, recreational events, and numberless meetings with small groups and individuals in and out of the office. That meant constant breakfast, lunch, and dinner appointments. A typical week would include breakfasts with the deacon officers one day and individual members needing a word with the pastor on the others. Lunch would be with a committee chairman. Dinner would be a banquet for one of the hundreds of sub-groups in the church, a private meal hosted by an extended family in the church, or a visit to one of the ethnic missions of the church for dinner and a program.

W. A. Criswell and Joel Gregory seated together in front of the
First Baptist, Dallas choir during a church service, although
their thoughts appear to be elsewhere. (Photo by David Leeson,
Dallas Morning News)

A week chosen at random from my calendar shows Monday preaching the closing message of the Florida evangelism conference in Jacksonville, Tuesday evening eating with and presenting a plaque to the Junior Board of Deacons leadership, Wednesday eating with the chairman of the personnel committee, Thursday dinner at a steak house with an extended family of the church, Friday eating with W. A. and Jack Pogue along with their guests, Saturday a surprise birthday party for a deacon's wife, and Sunday lunch at the Park City Club with a distinguished deacon. Unless I excluded them in advance every breakfast, lunch, and dinner was booked with church-related meals. Some weeks I was certain I would die with a fork in my hand.

Most days W. A. and I were together at the table somewhere. His culinary habits were always an amazement to me. First, he devoured glasses of whole milk poured over ice with his meals. When I came as pastor the kitchen staff likewise began to bring me glasses of milk on ice with every meal. I did not particularly dislike milk, but neither had I imbibed it with meals. At first I let them bring me the milk because I did not want to embarrass them. I supposed they thought that all pastors drank milk poured over ice cubes with every meal. After some weeks of this, however, I was cornered. If I told them that I did not want the milk, it would reflect on what they had done for weeks and embarrass the kitchen staff. It was one of those situations where the longer it went, the more difficult it would be to call it off. So I drank milk.

When W. A. was served a baked potato, he would peel back the foil, take the milk or cream from the table, pour it into the potato and make a sort of potato soup. As in all things he was utterly uninhibited at the table. I never saw anyone enjoy eating as much as he did. Nor did I ever see anyone make it such a communal experience. If he did not want what was on his plate, he would give it away to me or someone else. If he liked what was on my plate and I did not eat it, he would sometimes ask for it. The kitchen staff was wonderful to prepare for me and for him what we wanted to eat, regardless of what was being served at the church. I did not want to eat red meat so the staff always prepared a chicken or fish dish for me. The huge church kitchen was open house for the pastor. At any time I needed something to eat, they prepared it and would even bring it to the office.

Criswell loved to eat oranges. One day he told me of his orange-eating routine. He would get into the bath, fill the tub with water, set a basket of oranges by the tub, peel them and eat them right there. He said in his famous vibrato, "The juice runs down my chin and down my arms, but I just splash the water on me and am never sticky." He was a fastidious dresser and I can imagine the relief he felt from any orange juice spotting his garments.

From Thanksgiving to Christmas at First was one continuous Christmas party. Every division and department and class and group had its own gathering, and all wanted the pastor to be present. The pastor was not expected to stay the entire time at any party but would hop from one to another making brief stops. I planned these routes like a military invasion in order not to disappoint any of the classes. One evening we went to seven parties in a row in order to fulfill the invitations. The children's departments would hold some of their parties at the church. Dr. C. and I would visit floor after floor of children's Sunday school departments during their parties. We would go into one of the scores of children's departments divided by months into age groups, talk with the little children, let them hug us, and move on to the next.

On a cold night before Christmas we were racing up and down the stairs of the old Truett Building trying to stop at all the children's groups. Dr. C. had some type of respiratory ailment and went into spasms of coughing as he and I went up and down the stairs (he did not like to take the elevators for the sake of exercise). After several hours of climbing steps and coughing, I suggested that he go home and rest. He insisted that he could go on. Finally, in a great fit of coughing he consented to leave for the evening.

At times like that I both admired and resented the Old Man. For forty-seven years he had been visiting the children's seasonal parties. He would rather risk aggravated respiratory infection than miss the children's parties. I would sometimes reflect on what it must have been like to see five decades of children grow up in the church. He wanted to be there. Yet on the other hand I felt keenly that he could not let go and trust me to assume responsibilities that an eighty-one-year-old man should not have to shoulder. My experience with him through that first year demonstrated conclusively that he simply could not and would not yield to my being the pastor of the church. When awards ceremonies were planned for the children's division, we would both stand there for several hours taking turns hanging medals around the children's necks. Every platform, meeting, party, group, and council had to be delicately balanced so that both of us had parity.

Consider a medical analogy: A distinguished coronary surgeon might take in a younger partner on the promise that he would retire from the practice shortly and render the practice to the younger surgeon. Yet in every office examination, in every scrub room, in the operating room, and the recovery room, the older doctor might insist on being present, equally. The office staff for the two doctors would understand that everything had to be balanced: appointments, days off, sharing calls. While operating on a patient, every instrument handed to one had to be handed to the other. When the operation was finished both of them must exit the operating room together to give the waiting family the news. Not one of them could visit the recovery room without the other one being present.

This recognition of the senior surgeon by the younger would not be out of bounds for awhile. But suppose there was a crisis after open-heart surgery. What if both doctors had to be summoned, had to stand in just the right place, be handed the instruments in precisely the same order, be recognized and fawned over by their attendants and congratulated equally by the family? Would it not be appropriate for someone to ask, "Where is the patient in all of this? Do not his interests count more than the continued balancing of accolades and recognition for the two doctors?" Suppose further that the senior physician began to question openly before the hospital staff the technique and effectiveness of his younger colleague. What if he stood in the hallways of the hospital and asked anxious families, "Do you think that the young doctor is operating correctly? I may just have to step back in, open grandpa's heart up again, and correct what he has done."

When I arrived the patient—the old church—needed immediate attention. Quality staff members had to be added, programs updated, buildings improved, finances revolutionized, and marginal members re-enlisted. The patient needed immediate attention. In the face of a challenge which would have called for enormous insight and tireless labor to recover the momentum in the old church, I was faced daily with this balancing act with Criswell. It consumed the energy and attention of the staff and the lay leadership. The loser was not Criswell or Gregory but the good people of the church who were caught up in this delicate balancing act. They were on the table and needed the vigilant attention and action necessary. When it became obvious that the other doctor was questioning me in front of the patients, it was too much.

ENJOYING THE DRIVE

AFTER THE CEASELESS ROUND of Christmas parties, we were invited both years to the wonderful old Crested Butte home of a kindly deacon, Bill Hunt. In the rat race of our schedule, one of the few activities our family could enjoy together was that of snow skiing. We could have flown to Colorado, but I enjoyed the drive in our Suburban. There was something about driving away from Dallas into the prairie and then the high plains of Texas that connected me with a larger, earthy reality. The endless miles of barbed-wire fence on rotting posts touched something deeper in my psyche than I could explain. Driving through the Texas towns named Chilicothe and Quanah, Dumas, and Dalhart, I would look for the steeple of the First Baptist Church and remember what it was like in earlier days when I served village churches. Pastors in those towns faced a different set of challenges than I had. They had no college, no academy, no senior pastor with whom to contend. On those drives I longed for earlier, simpler days when I would play dominoes with humble folk after Sunday night church, sit on a front porch and crank home-made ice cream with a deacon, or crawl around in the attic of the church trying to fix the air conditioning. There was another Baptist way of life that I could have taken.

The Baptist world and families from which I had come were in a different world from the one in which I now lived. My grandparents were people of the soil. On my father's side, Albert Gregory homesteaded at the turn of the century in an arid, mesquite-infested corner of Jack County, Texas. My father was born in a log cabin on that homestead. My maternal grandfather Henry Newton Selby was a cotton farmer seventy miles north of Dallas. Both were devout Baptist laymen. My parents were the only ones of their siblings to leave the farm or small towns and venture to a city.

Steinbeck wrote with his stark prose of that something about the soil that rubbed up against a person's soul. Driving through the flat, lonely landscape of the Texas Panhandle touches some-thing inside of me that is inter-generational, a call back to some-thing I cannot describe and may not even any longer be there. I remember looking at the white frame farm houses embraced by their cedar tree windbreaks and wondering what it would be like to live there. Who were the folks that loved, laughed, raised families, ate dinner, slept, got old and died in those houses? A hundred miles from Dallas life could be so utterly different that it could have been on another planet.

On the way to Colorado we drove through Texline, the ham-let of four hundred near where Criswell was born. His father tried farming and then became a barber. I actually peered out into the arid flatlands of the Texas-New Mexico border town as if I could discover some secret about the soul of Criswell, the wellspring that had given him the outsized persona, the iron will, the flinty determination to go on and on for decades. Is there something about parents, environment, the need for approval, the search for meaning or some other mystery that marks one man to endure, bound for destiny, and another to walk away from it voluntarily? The moonscape of the land with its barren scrub brush and patches of late December snow gave back no answer.

Those drives in December 1991 and 1992 were about the only time I could slow down enough even to ask what had happened to me. I could never get away from being Dr. Gregory. In the lift lines at Crested Butte, riding up the lifts, sitting in the warming houses, or walking down the streets of the town, Baptists hailed me. The combination of my own gifts and ambition, providence or dumb luck, circumstances or the will of God had put me into a place of notoriety. I wondered what it was like to live in those white frame houses on the horizon of the Panhandle farms.

Chapter Nine

~

A Super Church to the Super Stars

*I*t has sometimes been said of Baptist programming that if there is an empty hour we will invent something to fill it. Or as Will Rogers said of Oklahoma, "The state builds the roads and the Baptists wear them out going to meetings." In both Decembers during my tenure at First Baptist, I hastened back from the ski slopes to preside over the traditional midnight Lord's Supper on December 31. This watchnight service was dear to a few hundred members and a pain to the staff required to be there. Like the Roundup and a dozen other things, this was a relic of the previous generation. In Criswell's salad days the old house would fill to the rafters to hear him preach on New Year's Eve. In one marathon evening he preached for hours through the entire Bible. Times had changed and Dallas Baptists sought other forms of diversion on the eve of the New Year.

On January 5, 1992, the church recognized our first anniversary. Normally there had been a lavish gift and a reception following the evening service, but a decision had been made by the deacon leadership that the church would cease the annual emphasis on anniversaries that had characterized Criswell's tenure. Bo Sexton and I discussed the necessity of ending this if for no other reason than the financial example it would set for the church.

So we were presented with a tasteful G. Harvey signed print of a Russian church, timely in light of events in the former Soviet Union. A number of the people were shocked with this understated recognition of our first year. Instead, we placed a spiritual emphasis upon the deacons' commitment to the Sunday evening services of the church. I was in total agreement with the downsizing of recognitions. If we did not do so, every significant anniversary would become an exercise in one-upmanship.

The New Year also sent another signal that the expected transition would not take place. Criswell continued his announced series from Ecclesiastes. In May 1992, he would announce a series of sermons through Romans, a lengthy doctrinal endeavor. With these two announcements of series, it became clear that he had no intention of stepping aside in anything like the time frame we had discussed in my coming. This began to be an object of increasing discussion in the church. It also began to project a definite lethargy and loss of momentum over the situation. This loss of momentum touched the entire congregation. The first few months had been a time of excited expectation about things to come. It was supposed to be a new day. Instead, the same thing continued with no sign of ending. I could see the whole thing start to slow down, like on old, wind-up clock.

With the announcement of these lengthy sermon series, something like a dull drumroll began in the back of my head. I knew that we were headed toward some as yet unknown denouement, a terminus at some hitherto undated omega point. Others began to feel this as well. An indefinable but real sense of new tension characterized meetings of the staff and lay people. No one ever spoke of it; it was the great unspoken. The congregation knew that this was not the deal we had all expected, but they did not know exactly what the deal was.

In January, the Dallas Baptist University awarded me with an honorary doctorate, a doctor of divinity diploma. Criswell was invited and sat on the front row with my family. I appreciated his coming and told him so. It was a shock to see him seated in the audience as I received recognition. There were times in these months when I hoped against hope that he was reaching out toward some type of amicable conclusion to our present arrangement. When we were together alone in his office he would always ask me to pray at the end of our meeting. We would join hands like an older father and his middle-aged son. There were times when I simply wanted to ask him how we would work it out. Why was he second-guessing me to the members, holding on to the pastorate when both of us knew it could not work with the two of us there? Those words were on the tip of my tongue several times. But until one week before my resignation I was unwilling to broach what when once spoken could never be taken back.

In January 1992, we also set aside a day to recognize our most prominent member, Zig Ziglar. He had taught the auditorium class for ten years and was asking for a "sabbatical." What I did not know was that Zig was on the way out. He had earlier made his dramatic appeal that I take a three-month leave of absence and let the church deal with Criswell. He was totally disgusted with the treatment given Paige Patterson. For some reason I could never fathom, other prominent leaders of the church seemed to lack appreciation for what he had done in the auditorium class.

Over the following months Zig was in the worship services less and less, until one day I received a kindly letter from him informing me that he had joined the Prestonwood Baptist Church. This was a blow to me and a blow to the First Baptist Church. Although Zig expressed personal appreciation for me and did not connect his leaving with my pastorate, he nevertheless left under my watch. However much one may attempt to rationalize, it was big news that Zig joined the other big church in town. When he left, so did scores of his devotees. Although lay leaders attempted to put a good construction on it all, I knew it was a loss of the one person who attracted more unchurched people to First than anyone else. Zig's leaving, coupled with Criswell's announcement of a long series of sermons, made it clear to me that we were moving toward some day of decision. Defections from the church were like the enormous debt; they would not be laid at the feet of Old Teflon but sooner or later be attached to me. I would be lamed and then be damned for limping.

During my first year I did not do much to toot my own horn; I was always tooting W. A.'s. By January 1992, I realized I had better tout my leadership or it would never be recognized. Although Criswell would bleat unctuous generalizations about me in the services ("our gifted pastor," etc.) he would not commend any specific steps or programs I had taken in leading the church. For the first time I penned a definite and deliberate comparison between his leadership and mine (it appeared in the *First Baptist Reminder*):

The year 1991 witnessed a difficult economic climate in our city and region, yet you were found faithful in your support of Christ's work through First Baptist. Our people gave $7,204,804 in undesignated tithes and offerings toward our budgeted amount of $7,050,000. You also met our steward-ship enrichment building fund goal of $750,000 by giving over $758,000.

We received total revenues of $9,444,031 with paid expenses of $9,692,940. This ended 1991 with an operating fund deficit of $185,909 representing two percent of our operating budget. This figure compares to an operating fund deficit of over $1,040,000 in the year 1990.

I thank God for your faithfulness to his work through First Baptist. I commend and appreciate our staff for mak-ing adjustments throughout the year in order to approach our goal. This included reducing our expenses by $1,250,000 in March 1991.

It is our goal and desire under the pastor's supervision and the management of Tom Hedquist along with Sherryn Cates to field and fully fund our program in 1992.

I heard through the grapevine that this was not appreciated on Swiss Avenue. That mattered not to me. The time had come to assert leadership and to see what the consequences might be.

∾

PROMINENT GUESTS

FIRST BAPTIST HAD ALWAYS SHOWCASED celebrity guests. A school of church-growth leadership in the seventies emphasized the need for exciting outside personalities to punch up attendance intermittently. I had experimented with that enough to learn a hard lesson: What it takes to get people to church is what it takes to keep people at church. Over the years I had depended on consistent pulpit delivery, strong musical worship, and consistent educational programs to build the church on a foundation of weekly, predictable, and repeatable strengths. A line of celebrities becomes a matter of diminishing returns when the congregation comes to expect that the next "hot" visitor will be bigger than the last.

As in most things, First Baptist was not the typical church in this regard. The church had presented so many famous guests for so many years that it was in a sense part of the regular order of worship. Not to have a high-profile guest regularly would have been as noted as skipping the opening prayer.

Many of these celebrities were Republican politicians such as Governor John Ashcroft of Missouri, chairman of the Republican Governors Association and chair of the Republican Platform Committee in President Bush's losing attempt at re-election. In typical Criswellian fashion, W. A. predicted from the platform that the governor would one day be a candidate for the presidency of the United States. This was the first of several Republican guests we would have at First Baptist.

Texas Senator Phil Gramm was also our guest on another day. Gramm, an Episcopalian, is a favorite among conservative evangelicals in Texas and elsewhere. At the request of Republicans at Travis, I had also hosted him on that platform. Gramm knows Baptists better than most Baptists. He knows precisely how to ring the changes in a Baptist pulpit. His reception at First, like that of all Republicans, was effusive.

To say that First Baptist had a high identity with the Republican Party is to say that fish have a high identity with the ocean. If there were Democrats in the church, they could have gathered in a janitor's closet. Since the Reagan era, the right wing of American evangelicalism had identified with the Republican Party. The Democrats' inclusion of pro-abortion planks in their platform cemented right-wing religious folks to the Republican Party, which at least on paper opposed abortion on demand. The Republicans further made appropriate noises about prayer in public schools and other value-related issues. It seemed to sail right over the head of most evangelicals that twelve years of Reagan and Bush did not produce a single substantive change in national policy concerning abortion or prayer in public schools. This was, of course, laid at the feet of the intransigent and godless Democrats. When Nancy Reagan was found to consult an astrologer this seemed to be only a blip on the screen.

To say that First Baptist had a high identity with the Republican Party is to say that fish have a high identity with the ocean.

The identification of conservative evangelicals with the Republican Party always made me nervous. To graft a secular political agenda onto the kingdom of God never felt comfortable. Not to make a comparison but to make a point, the rise of Hitler and Nazism in Germany was at first embraced by the state church in Germany. The emphasis upon discipline, order, and commitment among the Hitler youth appealed to the post-Weimar cultural chaos in Deutschland. Only lonely voices such as those of Martin Neimoller and Dietrich Bonhoeffer sounded a warning against identifying a secular political regime with the church and the kingdom of God.

This is by no means to compare the Republican Party to Hitler's Reich; I vote Republican myself. It is to state that the

Church had best not hitch its wagon to any political party. The prophet Daniel was a Hebrew with amazing influence on the pagan empire of Babylon. He was not, however, on the committee to re-elect Nebuchadnezzar. He stood outside the political structure and spoke a word to it from the outside where he maintained his independence. It is easy to be co-opted and hard to stand with independence.

First Baptist also welcomed a variety of sports figures to its pulpit. Evangelicals in general and Baptists in particular like the endorsement of Christianity by prominent athletes. Sports figures do draw in unchurched folks on the Sunday they are there. We hosted pitcher Dave Dravecky of the Giants. After he lost his arm, his subsequent Christian testimony established him as a major force among Christian athletes. Dravecky was a wholesome and unpretentious figure who remained with us far longer than he was expected to, answering the questions of our youth for several hours.

A regular guest at First over the years was Dallas Cowboys Coach Tom Landry. For those of us who grew up in North Texas and knew nothing else but Landry for three decades, he is up there with the president, Billy Graham, and the pope. He is already a figure of mythological proportions. He had not been back to First since the Jimmy Johnson/Jerry Jones era. So we hosted the Cowboy for a Christian testimony. Landry in retirement is still a striking, erect, and imposing figure. As we sat down in the minister's room before the service, his quiet dignity, presence, and persona was one of the few that seemed even to impress W. A. I saw to it that Landry sat next to me on the platform.

Landry is also very perceptive. By coincidence he and I used the same barber in North Dallas, and after my resignation the barber related to me a conversation with Landry after the coach's appearance at First Baptist. According to the barber, Landry could tell that something was not right in the relationship between Criswell and me as we sat in the minister's room. That led me to wonder how many other prominent guests had sat in the room and felt the same tension. I expect that Landry had sat with so many men in so many circumstances that he could evaluate leadership situations in a moment with a subliminal analysis refined over decades. I used to say that there were only two men in Dallas who were ultimately secure, Landry and Criswell. Now there is one.

The biggest visitor of them all attended First Baptist five weeks before my resignation, President George Bush and the first lady. From time to time Dallas hosted the national affairs briefing at the Dallas Convention Center. In 1992, it met August 21 and 22. The concluding keynote speaker on Saturday night was President Bush, wrapping up a program of other right-wing figures featuring Ollie North, Phyllis Schlafly, and Pat Buchanan. First Baptist deacon Ed Drake was chairman of the local committee for the event. Months before, I had been asked to speak. As the situation developed I was demoted several times until I was finally asked only to say a prayer. I had the distinct impression that some behind-the-scenes maneuvering had taken place.

On Saturday night the platform party assembled for the final session of the rally at the Dallas Convention Center. Of course at center stage was Dr. Criswell. I was given a seat at the end of the platform and very rudely told by an officious platform officer to "stay in my seat." Criswell marched down to a position one seat away from the president and began an animated conversation

285

W. A. Criswell leans in to listen to President George Bush before Bush spoke to the national affairs briefing at the Dallas Convention Center in 1992. Bush also visited First Baptist during his trip to Dallas. (Photo by Bill Janscha, *Fort Worth Star-Telegram*)

with the commander-in-chief. After my resignation, Jim Jones of the *Fort Worth Star-Telegram* wrote a very perceptive analysis of my tenure at the church titled "Being the Wind Beneath W. A. Criswell's Wings." He wrote:

> It was Criswell who got the attention when President Bush recently attended First Baptist as news commentators pointed out that Criswell had been friends with former Presidents Gerald Ford and Ronald Reagan. During the same visit to Dallas by Bush, Criswell and Gregory both were on stage when the president spoke at the national affairs briefing, a conservative political rally. But Criswell sat near the president while Gregory was at the end of the table. At one point, Criswell leaned across another person to carry on an animated conversation with Bush."[4]

The situation between Criswell and I had come to the point that even secular journalists were beginning to note that no real transition had taken place. While I was told by some self-important functionary to sit in my seat alone for thirty minutes at the end of row, Criswell cavorted with the president, underscoring that things were not right. W. A. was introduced to welcome folks to Dallas and received with whoops and hollers. I quietly led the assigned prayer and sat down.

By this time I was so weary of this constant public juxtaposition with Criswell that I did not care. After twenty months it was obvious that in the eyes of Dallas and everyone else W. A. Criswell was still the pastor of First Baptist Church. No laudatory column, reception, statue, confrontation, or pleading would

4 Fort Worth Star-Telegram, Saturday, October 10, 1992, Section F, page 5

change that fact. I sat on the platform that night with a certain numbness about the situation. A hazy, vaguely formed intuition had come over me that I could stand this for only a short time longer. As "Hail to the Chief" sounded I stood with the remainder of the platform to honor our president. Bush spoke, shook hands with those of us on the platform, and made his exit.

Feeling like a fifth wheel, I walked down the metal stairs on platform left. At the bottom of the steps a very young lady respectfully detained me for a moment. She told me discreetly that President and Mrs. Bush wished to attend First Baptist as worshippers at the 8:15 A.M. service the next morning. They did not wish to be recognized or to speak from the platform. She asked that I say nothing about this for security reasons.

I was suddenly very alert. I was preaching at the 8:15 A.M. service. Hurrying home, I called Tim Hedquist late that night to inform him of the necessary arrangements. He and others were up most of the night working with the White House advance team to prepare for the visit. At midnight I sat alone in my home study pondering on the evening's events. One moment I sat in a melancholy reflection on my inability to be the pastor and the next I was jolted with the news that I would preach to the president. There was really not much time to weigh the vagaries of personal fortune. I had to review what I would preach. Faced with the responsibility to preach to the president and leader of the free world, what should you say? I had already announced as usual the topic for the Sunday morning sermon. I was preaching a series called "Encounters with the Christ." The announced subject was "One Out of the Dark" (John 9:1-12). It is the story of the man born blind who was given sight by Jesus. I weighed the implication of preaching to the president on the subject "One Out of the Dark." What kind of implication might that have when the one visitor most conspicuous in that service was the president of the United States? Yet my subject had already been printed on the marquees, in the church paper, and in the printed program for worshippers' use on Sunday. I decided to stick with the subject and the message as it was. In recognition of the "light/dark" motif in the passage, I made one passing reference to the president's famous "thousand points of light" statement about private goodness in American life. A slight smile passed over his face when I touched on that theme.

Early the next morning the advance team for a presidential visit took over First Baptist. The SWAT teams were placed on the roofs of nearby buildings with their weapons. Secret Service brought dogs into the sanctuary to sniff for bombs. Metal detectors were placed at each door. Arriving worshippers had no idea that the president was coming, but caught on quickly as they were passed through the detectors. I had arranged for the president and first lady to be seated next to my family. A few moments after the service started, the youth orchestra rang out "Hail to the Chief" and before the excited congregation George Herbert Walker Bush and the first lady entered and were seated.

That I was preaching at the service and not W. A. presented a challenge. Criswell could certainly not be ignored during a presidential visit. At my invitation I asked the Old Man to introduce the president. Hedquist and I both told Criswell that the president did not want to speak or even to stand up. Criswell simply could not hear that. He insisted that Bush come to the platform. We reminded him that the Secret Service had distinctly said they did not want Bush to stand.

Criswell continued to insist and I let it drop. I was caught between the will of Criswell and the Secret Service, and that was a place I did not desire to stand in for long. When W. A. welcomed Bush in the service he did not try to make him come to the platform. He did want the president to stand. Secret Service men all over the house winced, but the entire house stood at the same time, I suppose lowering the security risk.

I was caught between the will of Criswell and the Secret Service, and that was a place I did not desire to stand in for long.

With the nervousness appropriate for such a situation I stood to preach and then gave the appeal. Several responded to the invitation for church membership and Christian profession.

As he left, the president walked over to shake the hand of a little girl who had professed faith in Christ. She was thrilled. He looked tired. We walked out. At the entrance of the church the Criswells, Bushes, and Gregorys spoke for a few minutes. The *Dallas Morning News* snapped a picture of my sons talking with the president that landed on the front page. Then he was gone to the airport. I received a hand-written note of appreciation on stationery imprinted "Aboard Air Force One."

The situation is an ironic lesson in how reality compares with perception. Anyone watching would have seen a forty-four-year-old minister at the most influential church of the times having just preached to the president. How could anyone know that in just one month I would be gone and in four so would he?

❧

INDIANAPOLIS

FROM JUNE 9-11, 1992, I was out of Dallas for the Southern
Baptist Convention in Indianapolis. On Monday afternoon I
brought the closing message at the huge Southern Baptist pastor's conference in the Hoosierdome. In front of me sat a sea of
faces, hazed over by the glaring spotlights aimed at the platform.
As fate would have it and unknown to me, this was the last time
I would ever address a mass of Baptists at such a meeting. For a
decade I had spoken to as many or more such sessions as any
Baptist in the nation. I had grown used to the curious dynamics
of speaking to twenty thousand people in a large hall or domed
stadium. The sound system blares your words back into your
own face with a split-second of delay caused by the recalcitrant
speed of sound. Until one grows used to the boomerang of his
own words, it is a disquieting phenomenon. The lights on the
platform penetrate with such intensity that the audience sits in
a surrealistic aurora. I have compared the experience to standing
in the mouth of a massive cave with a spotlight shining back at
you from its depths. Of course, W. A. was on the platform
behind me, as always.

On Tuesday I was to nominate Dr. Edwin Young for the presidency of the Southern Baptist Convention. Each year a cabal of
the former leaders of the conservative resurgence would by some
series of conversations arrive at a consensus candidate to
continue the cause. This year a new twist made the election less
than sure and created more drama than the several previous
years where things were more cut and dried. One of the conservatives' own captains, Dr. Nelson Price of Marietta, Georgia, had

broken ranks with the consensus and was running an independent campaign. In addition, the comedian and Baptist layperson Jerry Clower from Yazoo City, Mississippi, would nominate popular Californian Dr. Jess Moody, an innovator from the Shepherd of the Hills Church. This led to some nervousness.

Thus came time for The Meeting. Each year on Monday night of the Southern Baptist Convention there was The Meeting. Attendance was by invitation only. It was usually hosted in the presidential suite of the sitting president. Security was tight with the meeting often taking place on an elevator-keyed floor. This was the strategy meeting for the next day's election. The heroes of the conservative resurgence led the meeting. Adrian Rogers by force of personality usually became the unofficial chair. Around the room sat the major voices of the conservative wing of the Southern Baptist Convention. With three candidates seeking to lead the sixteen-million-member denomination amidst a thirteen-year-long war for control, certainty was not a guest at this gathering.

I was seated on a couch in the middle of thirty or so conservative powers, most of them friends of the years. I read to them my thoughts of a nominating speech for Ed Young the next day. It was not well-received. Paige Patterson, Paul Pressler, Adrian Rogers, Bailey Smith, Jerry Vines, and Charles Stanley all began to submit their ideas for a better direction of thought in the speech. Then the second rank of younger leaders around the periphery of the room added their opinions. As I took notes on my lap-top, it began to look like a speech by committee. Since Ed was perceived by some as an elitist, some wanted to emphasize his populist roots in Mississippi. Others wanted to underscore his astonishing achievement at Second, Houston. Some said this, some that, and some something else. Finally, Adrian made the suggestion that since they had asked me to do it, they must have thought I had sense enough to write the speech. As usual, his wisdom carried the day. Dr. Charles Stanley of First Baptist, Atlanta, approached me as the meeting broke up. With his gaunt presence and basset-hound eyes he laid his hand on my shoulder to say, "Joel, this may well be the most important speech of your life."

I was not sure if this was an affirmation or a warning. This was the second of three times in as many years that Charles would say something like that to me. During the Paige Patterson airport meeting described earlier, Charles told me something of the same ilk concerning my stand to save Paige's job. A year later and months after my resignation from the church, I presented the new candidate for the presidency of the Foreign Mission Board. Again, Charles informed me of the uniqueness of the moment.

For thirteen years the anointed candidate of the conservatives had won. No one, but no one, wanted to be the nominee or the nominator who lost that election. The stakes were sky-high. If there was ever one conservative loss, the left wing of the denomination could gain momentum again. There was a domino theory that the whole Baptist civil war could reverse itself. Whether or not that was true, no one knew, and no one wanted to find out.

I awoke early Tuesday morning to write and rewrite my speech. Edwin called and wanted to meet with me. He seemed to be nervous about my speech as well. We went over the speech and he tweaked it in a place or two. We prayed and I left to the room again to commit the thing to memory. At the moment for the nomination I ascended the platform and waited with the other nominators. Jerry Clower clowned around with me, putting me in a headlock and giving a mock-threat. He and I had spoken on platforms before and joshed one another in nervousness before our respective speeches. The theme of my speech was from the Apostle Paul's question, "If the trumpet gives an uncertain sound, who shall prepare himself to the battle?" I rang the changes on Ed's past, pastorates, perspective, and passion. I ended the speech with the cry, "He is a kingdom man for a kingdom hour. He possesses the leadership that ignites us and the vision that unites us. Let the trumpet sound a certain sound—Ed Young." There was a moment of silence and then the Hoosierdome exploded into a wild, foot-stomping, amen-shouting, hand-clapping demonstration. When the vote was counted, Ed won by 60 percent, the largest margin of victory during the resurgence.

I was glad it was over.

∾

BARCELONA

AFTER RETURNING HOME I led a group of seventy-three members to Glorieta, New Mexico, where I spoke every day to two thousand laypersons gathered in the mountain camp outside Santa Fe. Our family had gone to Glorieta every summer for many years, where I had spoken to similar groups. There was an element of sadness with the recognition that the boys were about grown and this would be the last such trip for them. We flew to Albuquerque, rented a Lincoln, and drove to the camp. I enticed the boys for this one last trip with the promise they could take the Lincoln into Santa Fe and haunt the art galleries.

The last big deal before events leading to my resignation was the chapel choir and orchestra tour to the 1992 Olympic Games in Barcelona. The youth choir of First had often taken such grand tours, although in recent years there had been debate in the church concerning the value of such investments. A year before I had made the decision that we would go, and I had given the minister of music, Fred McNabb, the green light. Rather than pay commercial air rates, we made the decision to charter our own 757. With one landing at Ganders, Newfoundland, we could make Barcelona the same day. These efforts were a combination of church-provided funds and those raised by the youth. The church sponsored "the world's largest garage sale" in an empty grocery store. Hundreds of church members submitted their junk for sale and then dutifully bought the junk of their fellow church members. Teenagers hired themselves out as workers to church members in order to raise their portion of the cash necessary for the trip.

In the twenty-one months of anomalies, lunacies, and inanities, this provided one of the most ridiculous. The charter company for the airline had set up a periodic payment schedule in which we made incremental payments on the chartered airplane. Several months before the trip the kids had fallen behind in making their advance payments for the trip. If we lost the plane, we lost the entire trip and the deposit with it. The trip had already been extensively publicized in the Dallas media and of course at the church. It was unthinkable to cancel the trip.

The only way to float the money on an interim basis within the church was to call a deacons' meeting. That was the last thing I wanted to do about this trip. Over the years choir trips

had run up a deficit paid for by the church as a whole. The deacons were watch-dog vigilant about such expenses on choir
trips. As it would later turn out, the Barcelona trip was the straw
that broke the camel's back; after our return in a heated meeting
the deacons demanded prior approval of all such trips and budgets. But before the trip I took the attitude that forgiveness was
easier to get than permission. I nixed the idea of any such deacons' meeting.

The only other alternative at the moment was the Criswell
Foundation. With their having thirteen million dollars, I rea-
soned they would not mind lending us a hundred thousand or so
to pay for a chartered airplane until the kids came up with their
part. I called Jack Pogue. Jack was very sympathetic, but
informed me that the legal charter of the Foundation prohibited
it from loaning money without collateral. Any money loaned
from the restricted funds had to be secured. A young layman in
the church, Tom Pulley, had been an advocate of the trip from
the beginning. With his help several of us put up private collateral to the Criswell Foundation in order to secure the money to
save the plane. I pledged my four-thousand-volume theological
library to the Criswell Foundation in case of default. This must
surely have been the zaniest episode of my tenure. That the present pastor of the church would have to hock his library to the
foundation of the former pastor of the church in order to keep a
jet chartered for the youth choir trip must rank as one of the
unique pieces of conjuring in local ecclesiastical history. Yet by
this stage I had no desire to face the alternative, a meeting of
furious deacons once again confronted with a deficit for a choir
trip. To add insult to injury, after my resignation the Morning
News ran a story indicating that at one point I had to hock my

library. There was no explanation of the fact; for all the reader may have known I used it to speculate on the market!

On Monday, July 27, 1992, more than 180 of us departed on our now-secured charter jet for Barcelona. The local TV media covered the departure "live at ten" from D/FW International. Once at Barcelona our group alternated between singing concerts, witnessing for Christ, and attending Olympic events. The presence of 180 Baptists from Texas was a big event for Baptists in Spain where our work had struggled for years. Great crowds gathered at every venue on the concert tour to hear the Texas youth sing. Our presence drew national media attention in Spain. The group sang and I spoke at the Protestant Chapel in the Olympic Village. By any measurement it was a great trip for the kids and may have helped Baptist work in Spain. If I had known what awaited me when I returned, I might well have stayed in Catalonia.

ॐ

CRISWELL DROPS THE BOMB

I SUPPOSE IT WAS AN APPROPRIATE SETTING for the announcement that would shortly lead to my sudden resignation. The Criswell College had provided more than its share of difficulties during my stay; it was ironically appropriate that its board room would witness the one statement that pushed me over the edge. With the departure of Paige Patterson in May 1992, there was a breathless effort to find a new president by the fall semester. Criswell and I sat as ex officio members of the presidential search committee. By August 1992, the search had narrowed to one candidate. We met in the board room of

Criswell College to discuss his candidacy and the future of the college. But that discussion suddenly diminished in importance compared to a throw-away line by Criswell during the meeting.

David Wicker was vice-chairman of the deacons, would be chairman next, and was sitting on the search committee. At a point in the conversation Criswell looked at Wicker and said, "David, you will be chairman of the deacons on my fiftieth anniversary." The remark at the moment was actually apropos of nothing. Wicker and I looked at one another. Whatever David thought, I could not believe what I had just heard. In August 1992, Criswell had just made the off-handed remark that he intended to stay in his current position two more years.

This was a vintage Criswellian ploy. He had never said one word to me in private concerning his intention to prolong the "transition" to a four-year period.

This was a vintage Criswellian ploy. He had never said one word to me in private concerning his intention to prolong the "transition" to a four-year period. His fiftieth anniversary would not occur until October 1994. Everything implicitly assumed and explicitly agreed about the transition had intended a matter of "a few months." Now in a group setting he dropped this bomb. It was totally manipulative. If I remained silent, it would be assumed that I consented to what he had just said. The group would assume an earlier agreement between Criswell and me. If I spoke up at the moment, it would appear to be a precipitous lack of respect. I sat at the table stunned that the Old Man would have the gall to make such a statement absent any discussion with me whatsoever. I felt dizzy with shock.

Shortly after the meeting I spoke with Wicker on the phone. He wanted to know if I had taken note of what W. A. said about the fiftieth anniversary. I was glad Wicker brought it up rather than me. I had grown so habituated to doing nothing to reflect on Criswell that even at this point, I was throttled by a reluctance to address the ultimate issue—when he would leave. Wicker reflected with me on W. A.'s style. He had observed the Old Man for decades. Criswell, David rationalized, would often make such public statements as trial balloons to see what kind of response would be forthcoming. We might well be quiet and see if he retreated after no affirmation.

I did not have to wait for long. On Friday evening, August 21, Criswell and I were scheduled to make a joint appearance at the leadership retreat of the church's strongest Sunday school division. Leaving at 5:00 P.M., we rode a chartered bus from First Baptist to Kaleo Lodge in East Texas. I was already tired. I had spent the first three days of the week in Richmond, Virginia, at the trustees' meeting of the Foreign Mission Board and chairing the presidential search committee, a draining responsibility that became a second vocation. Flying back from Richmond Wednesday afternoon, I had to speak at the midweek service Wednesday night, meet with the financial advisory committee at 8:00 P.M., and attend the rehearsal of the seeker's service at 9:00 P.M. Thursday had been jammed with catch-up responsibilities because of my out-of-town trip. Thursday night was a prolonged meeting of the finance committee. The national affairs briefing began Friday and I hosted an extended lunch at the Petroleum Club for Jerry Falwell and his wife, along with other dignitaries, and my deacon Aaron Manley, a trustee of Falwell's university. By departure time (5:00 P.M.) on Friday I was so exhausted I could hardly sit up. The meridian director had arranged the drive to East Texas so that I could have fifteen minutes with each of the departmental directors in her division while we traveled on the bus. They took turns sitting next to us in the front of the bus. I needed to be alert to speak with the lay leaders of the many departments in the strongest division of the church. It took all of my energy to focus on the conversations with the folks on the bus at the end of the exhausting week.

When we arrived there was a buffet dinner in the comfortable lodge situated on a picturesque private lake. After our staff member challenged the departmental directors, Criswell and I (as always) were both to say a word. When we finished challenging the sixty-something leaders, we were driven back to Dallas by the minister of education Jody Mazzola. It was in the near-midnight darkness of that return drive when Criswell chose to fire his second shot. Mazzola was driving and W. A. was in the front seat beside him. My wife and I were riding in the back seat. Once again, suddenly, germane to nothing in the conversation during the dark, sleepy drive back to Dallas, he said it. Placing his hand on my knee in the back seat, W. A. intoned, "Wouldn't it be wonderful for the church, lad, if I had a fiftieth anniversary?" It was the same manipulative scenario as a week before. He had never said a word to me in our almost daily private conversations concerning any such extension of his tenure. Now with the minister of education and my wife in the car he again raised the subject. I considered his approach more coy this time than before. "Wouldn't it be wonderful for the church..." He couched it in terms of the good of the church. Whether I had a day, a week, or a month to weigh it, the benefits of continuing a charade in which Criswell and his wife were undermining me, failing to support me, and tenaciously holding on for dear life to their positions were benefits that eluded me. The momentum from my first year had decreased, the people constantly speculated about the state of the transition, the staff shuffled uneasily between giving attention to me and to Criswell, and the whole situation was not what anyone expected. It escaped me how two more years of that—four years in all—would be wonderful for the church.

In a moment of decision, I could not and would not acquiesce in the Old Man's deliberately manipulative ploy to put me on record in front of another staff member. I gave him back his own medicine. In an echo of ambiguous Criswellian rhetoric that I had begun to master, I responded, "That would be a matter of providence." It was a deliberate non-answer, a hedge, an evasion. I was once again so stunned that he would casually introduce a matter of such weighty importance in such an inopportune setting that I felt dizzy. That nonresponse ended the conversation. We rode on in the darkness of the Texas midnight as the farmers slept in their quiet homes east of Dallas. Jody Mazzola dropped us off at our home first, and then took Criswell around to the Swiss Avenue mansion. I dropped into an exhausted but troubled sleep after the week. The next night I would be told that the president of the United States would be in our services on Sunday. The excitement of such an occasion was muted by the inevitable confrontation I now saw coming. I did not have to deliberate about my willingness to endure this situation for two more years. There was never a moment when I would even consider it. There was no decision to make.

The next day I openly discussed Criswell's comment with Jody Mazzola. He clued me in on the conversation after we were dropped off at our house. In the short ride from our home to Criswells, W. A. had remarked to Jody, "He did not answer me about the fiftieth anniversary, did he?"

ॐ

RESPONSE

RECOGNIZING THAT WHATEVER CAME NEXT would determine so much else for me, the Criswells, and thousands in the church, I kept my own counsel for several days. I spoke with Hedquist about the two exchanges. Unknown to me, he would warn the lay leadership that if they did not do something, they would lose me. In quiet conversation with lay leaders of various persuasions, degrees of loyalty to Criswell, and positions in the church, I made some preliminary soundings.

I was suddenly surprised when a small delegation of deacons asked to meet me at our home. They were headed by some men who had been unmistakable loyalists to the pastor as pastor, whether Criswell or me. One of them had been baited by Criswell for a negative response to me and had then heard W. A. say that he must take the church back over. One had been a member of the pastor search committee. This group offered to me their full support if I wished to take Criswell on publicly and force the issue of his resignation. They assured me that it would be bloody, but I had enough support in the pews to win. The men were honest, earnest, and committed to my support. As they talked, however, I could see the future of raucous business meetings, headlines in the Morning News after votes of confidence, private and public insults to the Criswells and the Gregorys, and a general spectacle of disintegration in the church. Had I won such a war I would have inherited a burned-out shell, the ruins of a bombed city. We would have staggered around for years, recovered somewhat, and then left the rebuilding to another generation. I expressed my appreciation to those men with the assurance that I would take up the matter with the official leaders of the congregation shortly.

That led to the power breakfast at the Lakewood Country Club described in chapter one and the various "solutions"—all of them unsatisfactory—for confronting Criswell. The power breakfast led to the meeting with Jack Pogue also described in that initial chapter. As the alter ego of Criswell he was the best sounding board for any action I would take. My discussion with Jack was critical in the decision process that led to resignation. Across the coming days a series of sub-groups quietly met with me to discuss the alternatives in private. These conversations all ended with the same sentiment: You talk with Dr. C. and we are behind you all the way. I already knew that I would have about as much success chiseling Washington's face off Mount Rushmore as I would deposing Dr. C.

Tuesday, September 22, 1992, Bo Sexton, David Wicker, and Doug Brady met with me in the traditional pre-deacons' meeting discussion with the pastor. We sat down in my office at 5:00 P.M. The conversation soon turned to the issue of the hour; what would we do about the stalled transition. They wished to know when I intended to talk with W. A. By Criswell's own initiative that would come the following evening. I recognized that an honest discussion with W. A. would touch on incendiary issues. Even to say the things that had to be said would open a Pandora's box that would never be closed. In that light, I wanted to know from these three men explicitly that they would stand behind the severance agreement I had signed with the church in coming. We might be entering into months of public controversy in the church that would end with my resignation or being forced out.

The three men readily said they would stand behind the agreement. Doug Brady, the young lawyer/secretary of the deacons, had not seen the agreement and wished to examine it. Upon seeing the simple agreement noted earlier, he informed me that it might well not be legal or binding. At his initiative that earlier simpler document was expanded into a more elaborate version. I was given that several days later and it was signed by the corporate officers of the church. Later after the resignation some of the rabid Criswellites and a few deacons would act as if I had hijacked the church with a gun to their head for six month's severance pay. Bo, David, and Doug knew better than that. Before confronting Criswell personally, I wanted some assurance that our family would not be out on the street. At Brady's initiative he tightened up that document and returned it to me with the proper signatures. I was now ready to talk with W. A. I would not have to wait long.

∾

LAST THINGS AT FIRST

CRISWELL CALLED and requested to meet with me. After forty-eight years he had developed an intuition for conversations going on around the church. What he did not know by intuition he must have been told by Pogue or someone. We agreed to meet after the mid-week service September 30, 1992. After I spoke that Wednesday evening, we retreated to my office on the second floor of the Criswell Building. In front of my desk were two wing chairs arranged at either end of a couch and facing one another. He sat in one and I sat in the other, peering at one another over the oriental rug.

W. A. was animated, almost feisty. He began by saying, "They tell me you are down. We don't want you down, we want you up!" He spoke as if the problem were a slight case of indigestion or an evanescent bout of depression that would lift after a good night's sleep and some fresh air. For once I was not going to be taken in by his rhetoric. I told him that we had some serious problems and that I had been meeting with the lay leadership of the church. He responded by leaning forward and earnestly saying, "Well, what are they, lad? Let's talk."

Out of deference to his age and station I began the conversation with a quote of Paul's famous admonition to Timothy, "Rebuke not an elder." Even at this extreme stage of frustration, I recognized who W. A. Criswell was and who I was. I told him that I was reluctant to tell him the situation but must do so respectfully. There were four things, I told him, that I wished to speak about.

First, I told him of the oft-repeated reports of Mrs. Criswell's criticism. I asked him how long he thought I would last in the church if Mrs. Gregory were criticizing him? I told him that it was a ridiculous situation to be in my position and be criticized by the incumbent's wife.

He did not deny her criticism. Rather with full force he retorted, "That will stop. I promise you that will stop." Warming to the situation, I asked him how he proposed to stop something that had never been stopped before. He snorted, "That will stop." I was somewhat taken aback by the directness of his reply and the immediate unvarnished confession that Mrs. C. was indeed blasting me.

I next confronted him with his own criticism. Relying on the report from a deacon who had traveled with Criswell, I relayed the report of his baiting criticisms of me. He had asked the deacon, "How do you think things are going at the church?" The deacon had sensed it was a fishing expedition and gave no direct answer. Criswell had replied that he did not think things were going well. To this accusation Criswell shocked me by roaring, "Those deacons are pathological liars. I never said such a thing. You have no greater friend than I." I was faced with breaching a confidence and giving him the deacon's name, or simply letting it go. I told him that my source was certain and the report was sure. With more agitation he denied again that he had made critical statements about me to church leaders. I did not believe him. After circling this subject for awhile, I went on to my third concern.

I told him of my objection that he had not left his office at the church and moved to the college as he had promised the Hunts and as I had been told would happen. He began by telling me, "I know it is hard. Remember that I followed Dr. Truett." I replied by telling him that Dr. Truett was dead when Criswell arrived—not alive, down the hall in an office competing with Criswell. Criswell laughed at that statement and nodded his head in agreement. He then reverted to the ambiguous Criswell syntax: "I will move. It will not be today or tomorrow, but I will move. On a day I will be gone."

I had heard that kind of ethereal comment from him many times. It was the same kind of vague non-statement that had gotten me into the situation at the beginning when I had been told, "It will only be a few months." He further protested that the church paid his secretary's salary and that if he moved to the college she might lose her job. That was so lame I did not even respond. People would have stood in line to pay her salary if he had kept his promise to move to the college.

It was clear that he would not be pinned down about leaving the office. I did not even address his giving up the title senior pastor. The deacons at the power breakfast had made it clear they preferred that he keep that title until his fiftieth anniversary. They wanted to work on an approach that would leave him with his title, but get him out of the church and let me have the pulpit. It was obvious that if Criswell would not leave his office, he would not give up his title. No one who knew the situation expected that he would give up his title on the fiftieth anniversary anyway. In the aftermath of my resignation a longtime deacon told me that Criswell had tested the waters with him for an even longer stay by saying, "Wouldn't it be wonderful if Dr. Truett and I were here for one hundred years together?" meaning that Criswell intended to stay until his fifty-third anniversary, or five more years, a full seven years into the proposed time of "transition."

In the aftermath of my resignation a longtime deacon told me that Criswell had tested the waters with him for an even longer stay.

My fourth concern was the preaching schedule. By his presence on the platform and his preaching to half the congregation every Sunday morning in the current rotation, I could not establish my program or my leadership as pastor. He listened to this carefully and then replied that he would do whatever I told him to do.

I knew that this was a trap. The first whisper that I had taken the pulpit away from him would create mutiny among the Criswellites. I told him that. He replied that it would not be so.

What he did not do was voluntarily step aside from the present schedule. I would have to describe it, define it, and take it away from him. The moment the word was out in the church that I had leaned on him to step down from the pulpit, there would be a furious response from the minority of diehards that came up to him after every service and told him how great the message was.

The proof of this was the response in the church after I did in fact leave. Even in my absence there was an immediate backlash on the part of a minority in support of Criswell. They created front-page headlines in their attacks on the deacon officers, Hedquist, and the other staff I had brought, as well as a general furor in the church for months after my resignation, all in support of W. A. Had I stayed there, the very catalyst of their anger would have been perched in the pulpit before them every Sunday.

The ultimate vindication of my unilateral decision to resign was the future reaction of Criswell himself. He could have calmed the entire situation after my resignation by doing what he had promised to do two years before, simply resigning his office and moving to the college. He did nothing of the sort. When the church gathered in shock on Sunday, October 4, 1992, he could have resigned, not put on the charade of a semi-non-resignation only to have Bo Sexton explain that night that W. A. had not really resigned at all in the morning service.

After more than an hour of this dialogue with Criswell, I had had enough. It was obvious that he would not give me a specific date when he would leave his office. It was further clear that I would have to take the pulpit away from him; he would surrender nothing out of gracious acceptance of my leadership in the church. We ended the conversation with an agreement that I would "think about the preaching schedule and tell him later what I wanted." This was as good a way to end a pointless conversation as any. He left my office after nine o'clock that Wednesday night. In my heart I knew it was over. I really had not expected him to give anything up. The conversation had been a sort of due process or due diligence to keep faith with what the deacon leadership had asked me to attempt.

The only solution to the problem would have been a spontaneous act of resignation on Criswell's part in which he had given up his office and the preaching schedule, acknowledged my leadership of the church and relocated his office to the Criswell College. The conversation we had should never have been required. In the reality of the situation, however, at the late date we confronted the festering issues, it was already too late even for a unilateral, gracious withdrawal by Criswell. The passage of twenty-one months had lulled the people into a soporific acceptance of the status quo. Any change at that late date would have only upset the precarious equilibrium under which we had lived. If Criswell had kept his original promise and been gone "after a few months" the situation might have worked. When everyone acquiesced in the situation beyond those "few months," the situation had already become impossible and the stage was set for conflict.

The schedule printed on a calendar has an animus of its own. It takes life by the throat and pushes one forward, even when the activities seem pointless. On Thursday I had committed to a lunch with Bill Hunt and June Hunt (no relationship; Bill was my deacon friend who took our family skiing and June was Mrs. Ruth Ray Hunt's daughter.) We met at the Petroleum Club and discussed the situation in the church. They had some proposal for a solution, but time has obliterated that from my memory. Evidently, there was enough conversation about the impasse that subgroups were meeting to strategize. I appreciated their kindness, interest, and sentiment, but for me the problem was beyond repair. I met with a reporter for the Dallas Observer, kept my administrative appointment with Tim, met with a child about to be baptized, and kept a dinner engagement with a senior deacon and his missionary friends. On Friday and Saturday I convened the presidential search committee of the Foreign Mission Board meeting in a hotel near the D/FW airport. Sunday witnessed the kickoff for the 125th anniversary celebration of the church. Late Sunday afternoon the new singles minister came to my office and told me that he was resigning to go to another church. The vagaries of the situation were too much for him. Ordinarily this would have been devastating news, but knowing that the die was cast for me to leave, I let it go. After the evening service, we hosted a new members' reception at our home with a large group of new members and staff.

All of these activities had an aura of unreality. I felt as if I were standing outside myself watching myself going through the final steps of a familiar routine that would shortly end. Although I had not set the time of my resignation, everything pointed to the next Wednesday night.

I would later be accused of a deliberate attempt to disrupt W. A.'s forty-eighth anniversary celebration which was scheduled for the next Sunday. Actually, had I gone through the motions of commending Criswell for the anniversary and preached the expected eulogium the next Sunday evening, I would have looked even more ridiculous resigning a few days later. The people would certainly wonder why I had praised

Criswell to the high heavens and then quit the next Wednesday because he would not leave.

On Monday and Tuesday I went through the regularly calendared activities and appointments. On Wednesday, September 23, 1992, I did not go to the church. There was a luncheon scheduled with Ken Stohner, Jr., the young deacon who was secretary of the search committee. I did not want to see anyone. I canceled that appointment. I sat in my study at home. I wrote out my resignation. I asked my wife and sons to sit down and hear it. I drove to the church before the service. I walked across the street. I sat through the song service. I stood up and read the resignation. I walked out of First Baptist, Dallas.

Chapter Ten

❧

Inherit the Empire

irst Baptist was the first such church in recent history to attempt a transition between the founder/patriarch/visionary leader of the first generation and a new pastor attempting to inherit the empire and lead it forward. There was literally no manual for what I was trying to do with Criswell. This book might well stand as a warning for what will not work.

In writing this book, I of course wanted to make sense of my stormy, confusing twenty-one months as almost-pastor of First Baptist. But I also wanted to shed light on the problems that are common to other megachurches, not just First Baptist. Many megachurches of America will face a crisis of pastoral transition in the next decade. I hope that others will learn valuable lessons about the pastorate of big churches and the pastoral succession of power from my experience in Dallas.

To put this in an appropriate historical perspective, consider Jesus Christ's foundational proclamation: "Upon this rock I will build my church, and the gates of hell shall not prevail against it."

So said Jesus Christ in the uplands of Galilee six months before His crucifixion and resurrection. He stated His intention to build an "ecclesia." The word itself means "an assembly of people who are called out to meet." Its etymological roots are in the polis, the Greek city-state that had its own governing assembly or ecclesia. They were called out of the marketplace, the baths, and their homes whenever a civic problem needed to be solved. Jesus promised to build what he called "my ecclesia," a group of people called out in a distinctive assembly. The actual building was something that He Himself would do. Although there would be human instrumentality, He would be the guiding force through the ages in the construction of the church.

In our own time, the periodical *Church Growth Today* specializes in compiling records of the largest churches in the world. In its 1990 list of the twenty-seven largest churches in the world, only one of those churches is in North America, the First Baptist Church of Hammond, Indiana, with a claimed attendance in worship of twenty thousand. The largest church in the world is the Yoido Full Gospel Church in Seoul, Korea, with a worship attendance of 180,000. Korea dominates the list of the world's largest churches. This has often been attributed to the Korean penchant for yielding to authority, thus enabling single-minded church growth pastors to build such megachurches.

By what canons of judgment does one assess the legitimacy of huge churches? This question involves the most basic identification of what a church is. If it is simply how many people can be gathered under the roof to hear one preacher, the limit would be the size building(s) in which people might be housed. Few people would accept such a facile definition of church. The church growth specialists have emphasized counting church members in terms of responsible church attendance, that is, the people who actually show up. That is the most visible assessment. This has led to endless debate about "quantity" vs. "quality" in church growth. The left wing of American Christianity has emphasized quality and the right-wing quantity. Still other see this as a false antithesis.

∽

CHURCH GROWTH

"GOD DID NOT MAKE anything bigger than a whale," said Dr. Adrian Rogers about the upper limits of church growth. In physical creation, of course, there was a limit to size. Dinosaurs might have been bigger than whales, but they did not live to tell about it. Despite this natural wisdom, the church-growth movement seems to project endlessly burgeoning churches. Is there a decent or theological upper end to the size of a church?

If so, the Bible does not give us the numbers. In fact, early church history is filled with examples of gigantic—and presumably successful—churches. The Acts of the Apostles records the eruption of a huge church in Jerusalem following Peter's Pentecostal sermon fifty days after the resurrection. There were three thousand, five thousand, and then more. The early St. Peter's may have accommodated forty thousand people and St. John Lateran, also in Rome, twenty thousand. John Chrysostom, the golden-mouthed orator of Syrian Antioch, stated that the largest church in that city had one hundred thousand members about A.D. 323. It's clear that the early Christian movement consisted of both larger and smaller churches.

According to the periodical *Church Growth Today*, the largest church in North America is the First Baptist Church of Hammond, Indiana, with a claimed attendance in worship of twenty thousand. The Willow Creek Community Church in South Barrington, Illinois, discussed earlier, claims an attendance of eighteen thousand in its Saturday and Sunday seeker's services. Three Southern Baptist churches on the list exceed First Baptist, Dallas, in attendance: Second Baptist, Houston (11,514), North Phoenix (9,500), and First Baptist, Jacksonville, Florida (7,800).

First Baptist, Dallas, claims an attendance of 7,625 in worship. While my experience at First makes me suspicious of all these numbers, suffice it to say that the movement of large churches is well documented. Church growth experts feel that the decade ahead will witness the growth of more larger churches in North America than ever before. Is this development to be welcomed or feared?

∾

SIZE AND THE CHURCH:
THE DANGERS OF BIGNESS

IN MY OBSERVATION you cannot say a big church is "bad" and a little church is "good" anymore than you can say fat people are "bad" and skinny people are "good." There is more to it than that.

In Luke 17:20, Jesus stated that "the Kingdom of God comes without observation." He meant by that there are qualities in the reign of God through His church that cannot be measured. The real danger of our addiction to bigness is that we will forget this vital warning and give way to triumphalism, believing our own press notices about being "the greatest church in the world." Then we are prey to institutional hubris.

First, Dallas, stands as a striking illustration of this process. I never met any finer individuals than the Christians at First. The fathers, mothers, and children were model followers of Jesus Christ in the 1990s. The single adults stood out as strong witnesses to the redemptive power of Christ. Yet collectively, the people of First Dallas had created an icon in Criswell, a man whom many venerated to the point of worship. This shot the entire church through with a spiritual vertigo. Everything collective was a little off balance because of this negative synergism.

In the same way there were many good, Christian Germans in the rallies at Nuremberg. Not everyone standing in those crowds before Hitler was a demon. There were loving husbands, faithful wives, and devoted children, many of the members of the Evangelische Kirche Deutschland. Yet in the collective the whole became more than the sum of its parts. To me this is a fundamental warning to the church that would become big. Beware of a triumphalism that contradicts the very message.

Jesus made it clear that the greatest Christian would be the servant of them all. He further stated that Christians should live without self-consciousness of their own standing ("Do not let your left hand know what the right is doing"). Criswell would sometimes say before the television audience, "We are all going to heaven from here (meaning FBC)," causing more sensitive members to wince. Although he would disclaim the statement as humorous hyperbole, people listening on television would take that kind of triumphalism literally and wonder just who we thought we were. To me, size and servanthood are linked together in the life of a church. When a church becomes so large that it is master rather than servant, it has become too large.

Further, size must not rule out simplicity. The larger organizations become, the more complex they become. At First I found myself acting more like a mayor or governor than a pastor, and I know that is not what Jesus came to found.

Look at His life. It is a supreme statement of simplicity. He had twelve followers that slept beside Him under the stars of that far-away Syrian sky. The group itself seemed to have an inner circle, but there was no complex organization. When the disciples tended toward organizational self-importance, Jesus sat a little child down in the midst of them and told them greatness in His kingdom resonated with the simplicity of childlikeness. He had few personal possessions and was buried in a borrowed tomb.

This simplicity means that wherever the church of Jesus is to be found it should reflect that simple structure. Simple does not have to mean small, but simple does mean understandable, workable, and responsive. When church structures become so complex that they no longer work, cannot be understood, and do not respond, they have ceased to be what Jesus founded. He as Lord of the church may still elect to do something through them, but that is because He can hit some good licks with crooked sticks.

Further, size should not enable individual believers to hide within the anonymity of large, impersonal structures. The most effective megachurches have combined a large celebration service with small groups that number no more than ten. The ideal is a church large enough to meet a person's needs but small enough to miss that person when he or she is not there. Jesus' parable of the lost sheep (Luke 15) tells of a shepherd who left the ninety-nine sheep who were safely in the fold to find one that had strayed away. Gigantic churches have accepted a huge back door. It becomes a boastful numbers game unless there is a small group structure that misses the hundredth sheep.

❧

THE PASTOR AS MASTER

ONE OF THE CARDINAL PRINCIPLES in all the manuals for church growth is "strong pastoral leadership." There is a difference between leading and driving. I have done both in churches. I have driven churches at some times and led churches at others. There is a real difference in the response of the people and in the way I felt about myself as a pastor. Sheep can be led; they cannot be driven.

One of the ironies in church history is the development of a papal respect for pastors in large free churches that have nothing to do with the Roman tradition. Criswell would bellow, "A committee-run church is a dead church." He expected the pastor to be master. This may work so long as the pastor himself is subject to another Master. When ego, competition, recognition, and manipulation invade, the pastor as master no longer works for the cause of Christ.

One wholesome model for pastoral ministry today is the pastor as a fellow elder among other elders, primus inter pares. As a first among equals his voice is heard with greatest weight, but he is balanced and corrected by the other elders. Unfortunately, Southern Baptist life tends to solve the problem of too much pastoral authority by setting up a board of deacons with absolute control over the pastor and the church. Neither extreme reflects health in the church.

Small churches and megachurches alike should follow several principles to help control the pastor as master. First, the larger the church the stricter the accountability of the pastor to the board. Most free churches turn this upside down. In a small neighborhood church a young pastor is often under the tyranny of a board that has run off many a young man like him. They eat preachers for lunch. Yet in a smaller church everything a pastor does is open for scrutiny by the entire congregation. In a large church the pastor often controls vast resources, has enormous personal freedom, reports to no one, spends his time as he will, travels where he wants, makes deals in the name of the church without authorization, and uses church resources for his own personal needs. The pastor of a larger church has the opportunity to affect far more people with the abuse of his freedom than the pastor of the smaller church. Hence, pastors of lesser-sized churches should be extended more freedom while the pastors of larger churches should be held to a stricter accountability.

No congregation should bring in a younger man to work alongside an older, tenured senior pastor in order to inherit the church. If an older pastor requests this, the church should ask him why. Does he not think the laity have enough sense to find another leader in his absence? Criswell told me explicitly on a number of occasions that he feared the lay leadership of the church would select someone who would destroy what he gave his life building.

Ironically, just the opposite happened. When he insisted on remaining as a pedagogue to his successor, First was weakened and nearly destroyed. It would have been better for the church for Criswell to retire and then, after a prolonged interim, another man come on the scene. If a tenured pastor cannot trust God and the congregation to find the next leader, that is a depressing comment about the kind of church he has built.

That means the megachurch should have a definite policy of succession initiated by, planned by, and adopted by the congregation. The megachurch's tenured pastor should publicly sign off on that policy before a succession starts. Under no circumstances should the tenured pastor be allowed an ambiguous relationship with a younger man brought in to follow him. No cabal or oligarchy of leaders should cut a private deal orally communicated with a young potential successor. The enormous public pain endured by thousands of good members at First, Dallas, could have been avoided by such congregational action. Although I thought the trauma through which they passed would have taught them so, it seems that they have once again set up a similar situation. Only time will tell.

Megachurches need interim periods between pastors more than smaller churches. This once again turns commonplace wisdom on its head. Criswell wanted someone to follow him immediately lest people leave First by the thousands. Ironically, in the debacle that took place in my leaving the church lost more people than it would have lost with a strong interim, which would have provided a kind of psychological safety valve.

After decades of strong leadership, there is an inevitable repression of the view of the laity. I sensed this repression from the very beginning at Dallas. Under the enormous sway of the legendary Criswell persona, the laity had stifled themselves for years. They simply could not stand up and cross him in an open meeting. An interim period allows these silenced members to blow off steam and make their views known. When I left First they called an interim pastor and limited Criswell's time in the pulpit. They would have done better to let Criswell retire fully, get him out of the church, out of his office and off the scene before any new personality came into the church. They would have done better to have had an interim before I came. In one sense, I served as that interim during that twenty-one months to clear the decks for the next pastor. Megachurches are an extension of the persona of a strong pastor/leader. That image needs to fade before another personality comes on the scene. No one can compete with a god.

In the aftermath of my experience, I advocate that any pastor should have a written, contractual relationship with the church he serves. Business should not be spiritualized. The call, compensation, housing, and procedure for termination and severance should be spelled out openly for the entire church to see. There was an explosion at Dallas after my leaving just because there was no such explicit, open, congregationally approved agreement.

Further, discretionary funds for pastoral use should be prohibited. This guards the pastor from both temptation and accusation. In large churches pastors may control huge discretionary funds. They can solicit gifts for these funds rather than for the operation of the church budget. After my departure, a rumor circulated nationwide that I had left with millions of dollars in severance pay. I suppose that is why I became a door-to-door funeral salesman after leaving! Such gossip shows a suspicion of the pastor's control of money in the church.

My experience in leaving First Baptist caused a reversal of my opinion concerning the non-disclosure of pastoral compensation. I followed the national trend of hiding the pastor's compensation from the congregation under the guise that "the average member would not understand it." After I left, everything about my compensation and perks was questioned—in my absence and without my response. The salary of super-church pastors should be openly published before the entire congregation for annual approval. It is patronizing in the extreme to contend that the average congregant cannot understand a pastor's salary. I was paid $165,000 annually as pastor of First. The people who sat in the pews paid my salary. In a Baptist church every member is a member of the board of directors. No corporate board should be kept in the dark concerning the compensation of its CEO. I expect I wanted nondisclosure, because I knew the people in the pew would understand what I was being paid. A whole lot of common, hard-working tithers have a pretty good idea what it might be like to struggle by on $13,700 per month, plus country club, city club, and other perks.

I know the choking fear that pastors feel when it is time for the annual, congregational budget discussion. We all feared that the hottest-headed, reddest-necked malcontent in the church would take the floor in open conference and raise Cain about our compensation. But on further reflection, why feel so insecure? If a small cadre of naysayers can knock you out of the saddle, you are not in the saddle and you might as well find that out before the old horse bucks you off. In my reformed view of church compensation, I believe there is far more to be gained by open disclosure of pastoral salaries than there is to be lost. If my salary is so big that I want to hide it from the people who are paying it, maybe something is wrong. Frankly, one hundred sixty-five grand per year can in no way compensate for the pressure, stress, confrontations, loss of sleep, deprivation of privacy, and a host of other things you endure at First Baptist. The folks there and elsewhere should just be told openly and honestly what the pastor makes. If a few of them don't like it, they can go someplace where they starve the preacher and be happier. It is sure enough important when a pastor leaves under unexpected circumstances and extremists want to tar him with every conceivable accusation that everybody know beforehand what he actually made. Experience is a teacher.

☙

THE CHURCH OF GOD AND HUMANKIND

AM I A CYNIC about the church after my experience? No, but as never before I am realistic about what the church at its best is on this earth. It is an institution divine in its original foundation but tethered to this celestial ball by every frailty to which humans are subject. Covetousness, littleness, jealousy, lust for power, ego, sacrilege, and a hundred other demons all lurk within the hallways. Not only members as individuals but the church as an institution needs constant repentance and redemption. The downdrag of our humanity with its zoo of obsessions and compulsions always pulls the church down like spiritual gravity. No church should be given the seriousness that belongs to God alone.

The church on earth at its best is a crippled institution that God may elect to use for His purposes. The divinization of the church in an egotistic triumphalism denigrates the very purpose for which it is founded. After all, its founder died on the cross between two felons. Out of His weakness came strength and out of His death came life. Humanity does not consider Jesus Christ its centerpiece because he behaved like the CEO of a gigantic ecclesiastical corporation. He washed the feet of others; He did not trample them under His own in the name of God.

Jesus Christ came to announce the advent of "the kingdom of God." Interestingly, that was His main subject all the time. His parables were parables of the kingdom; His miracles were miracles of the kingdom; and His preaching was about the kingdom. Evangelicals talk a lot more about being saved and about the local church than they do about Jesus' favorite subject, the kingdom of God. In the Aramaic language used by Jesus, this phrase is better understood as "the reign of God" or "the kingship of God." The weight rests not on a particular location (the local church) but a world-wide, intergenerational, age-abiding reality of God's sovereign reign. Jesus said that in His first Advent He began the reign of God in the world and that in His second Advent He would return to consummate that reign. Nothing, absolutely nothing, could prevent the victory of His kingdom.

Further, His kingdom was announced as a gift of God. There is not even a hint that human effort, planning, triumphalism, money, or credentials could buy or build that kingdom. God does it. It is a gift for needy humans. There has been a lot of bad theology and hymnody at that point:

"Rise up O men of God/the kingdom tarries long/bring in the day of brotherhood/and end the night of wrong..." as if by our own main strength we ourselves could bring in the reign of God. God gives His reign to us as a gift, not as a human achievement in which we crow about our buildings, budgets, and baptisms.

The local church is never, ever to be identified with or taken with the same seriousness as the kingdom of God. Frankly, some local churches are little more than a joke. The pastor might be an ambitious egotist and the lay leaders pugnacious infighters who vent every frustration in their life at the monthly church conference. Other churches are led by devout, godly men and concerned lay leaders. But no church is to be granted the ultimate seriousness reserved for the kingdom of God. That kingdom will triumph. Some local churches should wither and die; they are a travesty. Even the greatest local churches in western civilization have seen their halcyon days and then declined, but God's work has continued. Spurgeon's Metropolitan Tabernacle in London's Victorian era was an astonishing local church with five thousand in attendance for four decades and sixty ancillary organizations. Spurgeon died in 1892, and the church was shortly after that all but dead. Few would argue that it was not a great outpost of the kingdom of God, but it had its day and was gone. The First Baptist Church of Dallas or any other huge church may or may not thrive into the next century. That is not of ultimate seriousness. The kingdom of God will thrive.

God Himself seems to have a preference for doing a new thing. The gospel moved its center from the old world to the new world. Its greatest gains by far are now in the third world. The center of gravity in the Christian movement has shifted from the Roman Church to the Reformation to the free churches to the evangelical and then to the charismatics.

Within this worldwide phenomenon, the pastor should have his appropriate place, which is not the place of an ecclesiastical superstar. I wore that crown long enough to know that it is very heavy and no mere human head can support it. The only crown in Christianity belongs on the head of Jesus Christ, who earned it by wearing another kind of crown. One of the interesting metaphors for the pastor in the New Testament was employed by Paul in the Greek word huperetes, which literally means "under-rower." It referred to the slave pulling at the oars on the lowest, hardest level of the Roman trireme. Those who prefer the New Testament word episkopos, or "overseer," might at least balance it with the concept of "under-rower." If an overseeing under-rower seems a contradiction, one must realize that the truths of Christianity are often dialectical. We worship a servant/Lord who is a wounded/healer and a dying/life-giver. Christians find life by losing it, receive by giving, wear a yoke that lifts them up, and save their lives by losing them. The pastor as superstar loses that dialectical tension.

The church that refuses to divinize the pastor also confesses that the local church is not inviolable. In the days of Jeremiah, the prophet of Jerusalem, the ecclesiastical crowd considered Solomon's temple to be inviolable. They divinized the temple and proclaimed that it could never, ever be destroyed. They gave to the organization the worship that belonged only to God Himself. The same misplaced reverence can be attached to a local church. No such church is inviolable, not even FBC, Inc. As beloved as it is, the day will come when those five blocks of Dallas real estate will be folded up like an old parchment in the final denouement of history with the triumphant return of the Lord of the Church.

Yet with all that said, the most amazing phenomenon in the world is the church of Jesus Christ. Two thousand years ago, He proclaimed in a backwater of the Roman Empire that He was founding His assembly on a "rock." That "rock" was the simple confession of Peter the Apostle, that the baby of Mary and the Holy Spirit was none other than the Son of God and the anointed Messiah of Hebrew expectation. At just the place where Peter stated that, there towers a sublime outcropping of massive rock. It stands as it did when Jesus spoke His words at Caesarea Philippi two millenia past. The proof of the pudding is in the eating. More people today make the confession for the first time that "Jesus is Lord" than in any of the Christian centuries, some seventy thousand new believers daily around the world.

Jesus promised to "build" His church. That implies a process in the church universal and the church local. That process is never perfected. Every local church is a partial reflection of that greater eternal reality, the Church. No local church can triumphantly proclaim to embody that ideal.

We are crippled, lamed, half-blind, stammering, limping outposts of redeemed humans reflecting a broken image of that great ideal Church.

He called the assembly "my church." That tiny personal possessive pronoun taken seriously could solve some ponderous problems in church history. The church belongs to Him. No pastor, however tenured, owns it. No oligarchy or cabal of lay leaders owns it. Every member and every program, every meeting and every committee, every hallway and every room belongs to Him. I know very well the temptation for the pastor to consider the church "mine." It is insidious and always there. The founder and the cornerstone of the church is Jesus Christ.

He further stated that "the gates of hell shall not prevail against it." In the biblical world, the men of wisdom sat in the gates of the cities, acting as an informal civil court for local problems. Hence the "gates" refers to the deliberations, counsels, machinations, and decisions made at those gates. The gates of Hades thus denote the malevolent efforts of the unseen world of evil. Jesus assured His assembly that nothing evil that seen or unseen powers could produce would ever finally frustrate the ultimate triumph of His kingdom. When one considers the twenty centuries of despots and empires that have come and gone while His church continues, one tends to believe Him.

Am I a cynic about the church? I am very realistic about the humanity of local churches. I am equally certain of the final triumph of the kingdom of God under its Lord Jesus Christ. When that day comes, the cast of characters described in this little volume will gather with many like them under the throne of One in Whose presence all our little games will cease and all our little empires crumble. I expect W. A. and I will have a good laugh about it all and confess that the church belonged to Him—Jesus.

Epilogue

⁓

Following the resignation, I was showered with calls, correspondence, and visitors. Out of the first three hundred letters only one was negative. Our family continued for some months in friendly relationship with some church leaders. Others made no contact with us. Dick Clements helped us sell the house we had bought nearly two years before. He also took us to dinner. We were invited to the homes of several other members. After awhile and when the defamatory campaign began, these invitations subsided. I have not seen nor talked to W. A. Criswell since my resignation. He did not call, write, or visit. Neither did I.

Our home sold in November 1992. Karl and Barbara Singer of the church extended us the courtesy of a residence in their townhouse near Turtle Creek. It was an act of saving generosity. Mrs. H. L. Hunt was of help to us beyond statement in her own quiet and self-deprecatory way.

The officers of the church attempted to change substantially the severance agreement. It was handled in a demeaning and personally humiliating way. We finally reached a compromise.

For the months following the resignation, I kept several speaking engagements in churches and conferences, and maintaned my obligations on the presidential search committee of the

Foreign Mission Board. By my own initiative I spoke with an increasing infrequency.

The internal situation of the church reached a boiling point in the several months after my resignation. The Criswellites turned on the existing lay leadership of the church and against the staff I had brought with me. Criswell got out of town a good deal of the time. Roy Fish, a Southwestern Seminary professor, was called as interim pastor. The *Dallas Morning News* carried repeated stories on the internal debacles at the church.

In April 1993 I moved to Fort Worth and in May began working as a memorial estate salesman with the advanced planning office of Greenwood/Mt. Olivet Funeral Homes and Cemeteries. This began a trial separation by mutual agreement with my former wife. In November 1993, she filed for divorce by mutual agreement. In a press release we cited long-term differences in our understanding of mutual roles in marriage. We have been in a nonadversarial relationship since that time, looking after the interests of our sons. The divorce was final December 28, 1993. At that time I canceled my calendar of speaking engagements in church related settings. In 1994 I have spoken at a Baptist church in California, at a graduation of the California Graduate School of Theology, and at the adult sunday school of First Presbyterian, Fort Worth.

I remarried July 30, 1994 and continue to work as a door-to-door salesman of funerals and burial property.

O. S. Hawkins was called as pastor of First Baptist. Dr. W. A. Criswell is still the senior pastor and will achieve his desired fiftieth anniversary in October 1994.

> Dr. Joel Gregory
> Fort Worth, Texas
> August 1994